Entrepreneur. MADE EASY Series

LEADERSHIP MADE EASY

RANDALL D. PONDER

EP Entrepreneur. Press

Editorial Director: Jere Calmes
Cover Design: Beth Hansen-Winter
Composition: CWL Publishing Enterprises, Inc., Madison, WI, www.cwlpub.com

This publication is designed to provide accurate and authoritative information in
regard to the subject matter covered. It is sold with the understanding that the
publisher is not engaged in rendering legal, accounting, or other professional services. If legal advice or other expert assistance is required, the services of a competent professional person should be sought.

> —From a Declaration of Principles jointly adopted by
> a Committee of the American Bar Association and
> a Committee of Publishers and Associations

ISBN 1-932531-59-9

Library of Congress Cataloging in Publication Data
Ponder, Randall D., 1959-
   Leadership made easy / by Randall Ponder.
     p. cm. — (Made easy)
   ISBN 1-932531-59-9 (alk. paper)
   1. Leadership. I. Title. II. Entrepreneur made easy series
   HD57.7.P663 2005
   658.4'092—dc22

                              2005007910

Printed in Canada

10 09 08 07 06 05   10 9 8 7 6 5 4 3 2 1

What people are saying about *Leadership Made Easy*...

"The future and health of any organization—military or civilian—depend on effective leadership at all levels. In this book, Randall Ponder provides an imaginative and imminently digestible road map of leadership principles and techniques of leader development that will be of great value to experienced leaders and novices alike."

> General Carl E. Vuono (Ret.)
> Former Chief of Staff of the U.S. Army

"This is a practical and hands-on guide to the step-by-step thinking and acting any leader should undertake."

> Janet L. Schinderman
> Associate Dean, Columbia Business School

"Leadership at all levels will be an organization's main competitive advantage in the new millennium. *Leadership Made Easy* is recommended reading for those within the organization who want to enhance their skills to become effective leaders and major contributors to the organization's long-term success."

> Dick Reggio
> Senior Vice President, Global Learning &
> Development, Pfizer, Inc.

"Leadership can be learned! Here are 15 valuable skills that will help the world's supervisors and managers do the right things every day—things that are necessary to make their organizations a success."

> Pam Anders
> State President, American Society for
> Training and Development

"Pfizer didn't become number one in our industry by accident. We emerged at the top by clearly defining our expectations of leaders, and engaging every one of our 120,000 colleagues in the ongoing challenge of leadership. In *Leadership Made Easy* Randall Ponder captures and conveys the behaviors needed to establish a similar culture of leadership and drive individual and organizational performance to new heights."

> Hank McKinnell
> Chairman and CEO, Pfizer Inc

Contents

Dedication

This life-changing book is dedicated to every member of my family, who all at some point gave me the encouragement and love that helped motivate me to create it and revise it. I give special thanks to Linda, forever my wife and best friend; to Eric my son who I love completely and the one person I can always count on to make me laugh; and to Josette, my mother, who has been my number one supporter throughout my life.

Foreword

WHEN VISITING WITH CLIENTS ALL OVER THE WORLD, I AM continually astonished by how many employees are over-managed and underled. Instead of focusing on the basics, most managers and team leaders spend inordinate amounts of time, energy, and money following the latest management fad. If you are tired of fads—which at best provide only short-term results—you are ready for *Leadership Made Easy*.

The topic of leadership has been discussed and debated for years, and many books are available to introduce you to this vital subject. However, *Leadership Made Easy* goes beyond the basics to explore the 15 areas that all great leaders must understand and implement to be successful.

The overriding point of this leader's guide is that leadership can be learned. All one needs to do is practice the fail-safe strategies outlined by Randall Ponder. These are some of the analytical and technical skills that you must master if you want to be an effective leader. However, Randall does not stop there. He takes you beyond management and shows you step by step how to master the fundamentals needed to initiate and sustain healthy relationships with your team members, colleagues, and customers. He provides you with a guide for achieving dramatic and strategic improvements in performance, productivity, and profitability.

The everyday challenges of commercial, nonprofit, and community organizations—challenges such as global competition, change, downsizing, restructuring, and employee retention—will become increasingly acute throughout the world in the 21st century. Organizations of all sizes can realize competitive, economic, and financial advantages in the proper leadership of their colleagues. When people are properly led, there are no insurmountable challenges because their creativity, loyalty, job satisfaction, and commitment increase dramatically.

Leadership Made Easy will teach you leadership in easy-to-understand language and motivate you to apply this knowledge because of the dramatic results you will achieve. This book outlines new roles for supervisors, managers, and team members—roles they must master in today's super lean, and often mean, corporate, nonprofit, and community organizations. Mastering these new roles and responsibilities is particularly important since most traditional managers and team members, who often have little knowledge about leadership, will continue to be asked to assume more of the duties and responsibilities once solely reserved for executives.

Regardless of how long you have been a supervisor, manager, or leader, *Leadership Made Easy* will show you how to master the 15 core essentials of leading people. So what are you waiting for? Don't just read this book—devour it, and I am sure that you will thrive in this highly competitive and rapidly changing global economy.

—Wolf J. Rinke, Ph.D., C.S.P.

Wolf J. Rinke is a management consultant, executive coach, keynote speaker, and author of 13 books, including *Winning Management: Six Fail-Safe Strategies for Building High-Performance Organizations* and *Don't Oil the Squeaky Wheel and 19 Other Contrarian Ways to Improve Your Leadership Effectiveness.*

Preface

CONGRATULATIONS ON TAKING A MAJOR STEP TOWARD BECOMING A more effective leader. Though focused primarily on the business setting, this book is for those of you who have leadership responsibilities in many walks of life: work, community, social, religious, and family. It is a comprehensive and quick way for you to understand the significant issues involved in getting the right things accomplished when you are in charge of the results. You may have already studied many of the individual subjects discussed in this book and you may be quite knowledgeable in some areas. This book will provide you with the opportunity and framework to consolidate your knowledge with time-proven principles of leadership, while focusing on your use of common sense, sound judgment, and a blending of managerial and leadership skills.

The techniques and principles in this book are fundamental concepts that are presented in the context of leadership. You can put them to use immediately. Later, you can study specific areas in more detail by using other available resources that will help you gain as much expertise as you desire.

When using this book as a guide, no situation, challenge, or task will be too great for you to face. You can benefit from using this book whether you are a newly appointed supervisor, the owner of a small business, a team member, a manager in a community nonprofit organization, the head of a club, or the chief executive of a global organization.

This book will help you:

► Increase your knowledge of leadership principles and how they apply to your specific responsibilities;

► Intensify your leadership presence by helping you become more effective, proactive, and results-oriented;

► Learn specific skills and techniques to utilize change, to resolve conflict, and to increase the productivity and improve the morale of your subordinates, team members, and co-workers;

► Gain support and commitment from subordinates and team members by inspiring them to achieve results and be more self-directing, and by guiding them to seek more leadership responsibility;

► Enjoy being a leader.

—Randall D. Ponder, May 2005

Part One

Understanding Leadership

Chapter 1

Importance of a Leader

Tom works as a brilliant and productive member of a project development team. Melanie heads a 20-person marketing staff for a large publicly held corporation. Jim is in charge of a customer service department for a retail store, with a team of five dedicated employees. One thing these eight people all have in common is that they have the potential to be great leaders within their organizations.

L EADERSHIP IS THE ABILITY TO GET THE RIGHT THINGS ACCOMPLISHED at the right time with the assistance of other people. Several words in this definition will be explained as you proceed through this book. How do you get this ability? How do you determine the right things and when are they considered accomplished? Finally, who are the people who will help you and how do you get them to assist you?

Leaders are ordinary people who usually have an official position of responsibility. Organizations, subordinates, superiors, and peers depend upon leaders to do the best job that they can. Since so many people rely upon them, leaders have an obligation to do everything within their power to do their job. An exciting aspect of leadership is that anyone who chooses to can become a leader, including individuals at all levels of an organization.

Leadership is the ability to get the right things accomplished at the right time with the assistance of other people.

There has been much debate over the years as to whether people are born as leaders or if they can be developed into leaders through experiences and education. The consensus is that a willing person can learn specific skills and knowledge and emerge as a leader or a better leader than he or she is now. You can become a leader whether you are shy or extroverted, educated or not, organized or disorganized, charismatic or dull. The only requirements are a desire to become a leader and a willingness to develop the skills.

Everyday Leadership

A central point of this book is to show how much more effective you will become if you practice being a leader in your everyday life, at work, in your leisure, and at home. This does not mean that you must always seek to be the person who takes charge and plans everything. Everyday leadership means that you use simple principles and concepts to approach all leadership situations with a sense of purpose, the right attitude, and a commitment to achieve your goals with the able and committed assistance of other people. Since a leader directs or participates in the activities of people in numerous and different organizational settings, this book will often refer to teams, team members, peers, and subordinates. These terms are used interchangeably in this book based upon those people with whom you are exercising leadership.

Although people often think of leaders as being at the top rungs of an organization, this belief is not realistic, because leaders exist at all levels in an organization.

Although people often think of leaders as being at the top rungs of an organization, this belief is not realistic, because leaders exist at all levels in an organization. Most of the leaders at the pinnacle of any organization got there by learning and honing their skills at lower levels. If you have an entry-level job in a restaurant, for example, you can be a leader simply by practicing the skills required of leaders, participating more in the company's decision-making process, and assuming as much responsibility as you want. As a leader in low-hierarchical organizations, such as in small businesses or in the high-technology industry, you may work in teams with other leaders and nonleaders and find your roles changing as teams regroup from project to project.

In addition to applying to the work environment, everyday leadership helps you become more successful at home and during after-hours activities. You will find that as you practice leadership skills, your family will function more cohesively, with fewer conflicts between parents and children and among siblings. Leadership knowledge is particularly helpful in your group activities such as school associations, neighborhood meetings, sports teams, and clubs. Often in these settings, several people may feel either that they have the right answers to get the job done or that they just simply want to be the leader, whether they have the skills or not. By effectively applying leadership principles in these situations, you can assume the leadership role yourself or help others become better leaders.

Leadership vs. Management

Most people use the terms "leader" and "manager" interchangeably. A closer look, however, shows that a leader may or may not excel at management and a manager may or may not be a good leader. What are the distinctions between the two roles?

Leaders focus on areas such as identifying problems, managing changes in the internal and external work environments, structuring the organization, and motivating groups to achieve their goals. Their mission is to ensure that the organization achieves specific objectives by people who are energized and excited about their vision and direction. Leaders and their teams of motivated subordinates and co-workers implement their strategy by using specific managerial techniques, such as planning, organizing, problem solving, and communicating. Leaders feel comfortable about challenging the status-quo methods of running an organization, motivating their subordinates and departments to get moving in support of organizational objectives, and dealing with the changing business environment. Leaders must do more than identify opportunities, establish vision, and set broad goals. They must have the means to achieve their goals; otherwise their organization will stagnate. This is where the management component of leadership is important.

Managers concern themselves with getting the job done in the most efficient and effective manner. They know there are problems, identified by their leader, and they want to find solutions, so that projects and operations stay within budget and on schedule. Although concerned with the broad leadership issues identified above, managers focus more on the short-term, day-to-day, and week-to-week goals for pursuing the leader's vision without taking a lot of risk. A traditional listing of a manager's general functions includes planning, organizing, communicating, and monitoring.

A leader can put to good use many of the specific managerial skills shown above, and the manager can be more effective when thinking as a leader thinks. A wide, overlapping area exists where a leader routinely performs several managerial functions and the manager assumes leadership roles. It is exciting, therefore, to envision what the leader and the manager can accomplish if they focus on the specific skills necessary for them to do their jobs better. This set of skills will broaden their abilities by helping them become better managers if they are already leaders or to become better leaders if they are managers. The best overall situation for an organization, whether it is a business, nonprofit, or family unit, is to have a sufficient number of people who can function both as strong leaders and as strong managers. Otherwise, major organizational needs will go unfulfilled, as you will read about later in the book.

Many managers do not desire to become leaders and are more interested in simply doing their jobs well. However, by beginning to think and act like leaders, they automatically will become better managers. With the huge amount of complex change that will continue to occur in this century—such as competitive domestic and global pressures, speed of technological innovation, restructuring, and constant economic uncertainty—traditional ways of managing organizations will not work well or at all in the future. Organizations of all types need more people at every level thinking like leaders, not managers. Leaders with vision, persistence, and skill will be the primary driving forces that will enable organizations to succeed.

Organizations of all types need more people at every level thinking like leaders, not managers.

This book's goal is to help you understand that to succeed at leadership you must learn certain skills and apply them to your specific duties at work, at home, and in the community. You will perform best as a leader if you concentrate on doing certain skills well. It is not necessary to do each one perfectly, and it is reasonable to believe that you may have some reluctance or difficulty in sharpening some of these skills. Nevertheless, successful leaders are aware that, since they must attend to many areas in their organization, it is wise to gain some knowledge about those areas and apply that knowledge on the job. You can, one step at a time, master simple techniques that will help you lead others in all walks of life.

Leadership Skills

Leadership skills are classified into three categories: technical and analytical, relationship, and strategic. The technical and analytical skills, which are discussed in Chapters 4 through 9, are the primary skills traditionally thought of as the management of things. These six skills are mastering job-specific skills, solving problems and making decisions, managing priorities, managing a project, monitoring progress, and promoting training and development.

Relationship skills, discussed in Chapters 10 through 15, form an intermediate level of people skills. These skills are communication, teamwork, motivation, diversity, conflict resolution, and coaching.

Finally, strategic skills, in Chapters 16 through 18, constitute the upper level of leadership skills: the leader provides long-term focus and direction for the organization through vision, strategy, and change.

Chapter 2

Your Leadership Style

Susan is a hard-charging, let's-do-it-now type of manager. Joe is more hands-off and prefers that his team members create the solutions, coordinate briefly with him, and then implement the decisions. Who is the better leader?

AN IMPORTANT POINT IN THIS CHAPTER IS THAT EFFECTIVE LEADERS can be true to their own nature and not have to assume radically different personae when in a leadership position. A person's mannerisms and personality typically do not have to change when assuming a leadership role. This does not mean that great leaders do not make some changes in their leadership presence and style, especially when changes are needed. These changes occur primarily after self-study, evaluation sessions with superiors or subordinates, or on-the-job experience. Develop your own leadership style, therefore, based upon your own set of beliefs and personality traits, as well as what you learn from studying leadership.

Theories of Leadership

There are scores of leadership theories, models, and studies available for you to examine, if you choose. Although developed primarily in the 20th century by scholars, leadership ideas have existed at least since A.D. 100. Thanks to these great men and women, the curious have been able to analyze leaders on the basis of personality, situations, interaction with others, psychology, politics, humanism, and perception, to name a few factors. In addition to the theories, there are countless leadership surveys, tests, and aptitude indicators that are available to determine a leader's style and interests.

What can you do when faced with this complexity of leadership information? Most leaders do not study the many theories of leadership in detail. Some general knowledge is helpful, however, to know what the relevant major issues are so that you can use that knowledge in your specific situation. These issues will be explained in this chapter. Then you can choose to study in more detail those areas that are of most interest to you.

Effective leaders can be true to their own nature and not have to assume radically different personae when in a leadership position.

Leadership Orientations

To help prepare you for your leadership role, you will briefly examine five leadership orientations in this chapter. Since every leader has a distinct style made up of combinations of these orientations, it is impossible to accurately predict your style without a thorough analysis. As with most leaders, you will tend to use different styles when faced with different situations. Each orientation presents two extremes between which leaders have to determine the right balance for themselves, based upon their personality and specific leadership challenges. For example, there are effective leaders who have high orientation scores in both relationship and task; others score high in relationship and low in task. By understanding these five leadership orientations, you will be better able to understand the framework within which most leaders operate.

As with most leaders, you will tend to use different styles when faced with different situations.

- ▶ Democracy or autocracy
- ▶ Participation or direction
- ▶ Relationship or task
- ▶ Consideration or initiation
- ▶ Action or inaction

Democracy or Autocracy Orientation

These two orientations are the first classification because they encompass attributes of the other four orientations. It makes sense that leaders tend to lean naturally toward one or the other because followers will do either one of two things. They will do what they are asked to do, thus requiring the supervision of a teaching and facilitating type of democratic leader, or they will do what they are made to do, which requires a more punishing and coercing autocrat.

There is no conclusive proof as to which type of orientation is more effective at getting bottom-line results. One may be more effective in different organizations or situations than the other. A person's style of leadership, however, does affect employee job satisfaction, although the effects vary among employees. A higher degree of satisfaction in an organization will encourage loyalty, teamwork, and sharing of the leader's goals; each of these can lead to higher levels of personal and organizational productivity.

A person's style of leadership affects employee job satisfaction, although the effects vary among employees.

Democratic leaders focus on their followers because they feel the welfare of their team is of great importance. They tend to be easily approachable, relationship-oriented, and considerate of others' feelings. They prefer to lead their teammates by collaboration and empowerment. They are convinced that tasks will be better accomplished if they consider their subordinates' needs. These teammates tend to have high job satisfaction.

Autocrats primarily are concerned with tasks for which they are responsible. They believe the key is to focus less on subordinates and their needs and more on the work-related issues. In doing so, they use their position to prescribe solutions and direct others to comply. This type of leader usually has more subordinates with low levels of job satisfaction than does the democratic leader.

Participation or Direction Orientation

Leadership also can be analyzed in terms of how much contribution the leader obtains from subordinates before solving a problem or making a decision. As previously discussed, most leaders are situational and they use both styles on different occasions.

A popular leadership trend since the 1980s has been to encourage employee participation in problem solving and decision making. By obtaining and considering the suggestions of subordinates, a leader has access to more data, experience, and opinions.

Participation can occur when the leader either delegates total responsibility for tasks or allows subordinates to participate in problem-solving and decision-making processes. A more restrictive form of participation is used when a leader discusses the task with subordinates but ultimately makes the decision as to what will be done. By using a participative style of leadership, a leader does not relinquish the responsibility to get the job done, but gives subordinates the authority to help arrive at the right decision to get the job done correctly. Participation is particularly effective in less structured or rapidly changing work environments.

Leaders who have a direction orientation decide what needs to be done and communicate this to subordinates. They may or may not explain why they chose a course of action and they may use persuasion techniques to bolster their directives. These leaders autocratically assume that, since they know the right answer, seeking input from subordinates is unnecessary. They may rationalize the use of a directive style by citing organizational problems, such as low employee educational levels and competence, even though this may not be applicable. The degree to which a leader may be directive depends upon a number of factors.

For example, leaders tend to be more directive when there is high uncertainty in the situation, little time is available, a short-term increase in productivity is needed, or they exercise a high degree of positional or organizational power. Directive leadership tends to be used more than participative leadership in slow-changing situations or where less employee input is needed.

Relationship or Task Orientation

The best leaders concern themselves both with people relationships and the tasks for which they are responsible, because tasks usually are accomplished more effectively when human factors are considered. The degree of integration of task and relationship varies considerably with each leader; the exact mix partly depends upon task urgency, subordinates' work performance and ability, organizational climate, and the leader's natural inclination toward one orientation or the other.

The best leaders concern themselves both with people relationships and the tasks for which they are responsible.

Leaders who set relationships as a priority recognize the synergistic effects of attending to the human side of work. This does not mean they are less concerned with accomplishing tasks but that they know the best way to achieve high-quality success is to make sure they are consider subordinates' and team members' needs. They do this by maintaining warm, close, and friendly relations with their followers and co-workers and by openly trusting and supporting them.

A complete task orientation means that a leader has foremost in mind the job that must get done. Without seeking input from subordinates, the leaders structure the work, define the goals, allocate resources, and focus on achieving production quotas or delivery of services. People are of concern, but only because they are necessary to get the work done. This leader uses an inflexible, no-nonsense approach with subordinates.

Consideration or Initiation Orientation

Considerate leaders do what any considerate person would do, but in the context of leadership. Since they concern themselves with subordinates' interests and well-being, they are sensitive toward their feelings, needs, and goals. Before making decisions, they seek suggestions from subordinates and consider what effects these decisions will have on the team. By openly praising and privately correcting subordinates, they establish a working environment in which people trust, respect, and follow them.

Initiation refers to a leader's ability to start activities and organize work. Strong initiators prefer not to let the group completely structure its work or make all of the on-the-job decisions. They prefer not only to determine what must be done but also who does it and how it is to be done. Consequently, they focus on tasks: most of their daily initiatives occur simply to facilitate achievement of work-related goals. Since there can be overlap in these two orientations, a leader could be both highly considerate and initiating and still be effective.

Here's a good example. Susan, who was mentioned at the chapter's beginning, is a leader who is quite particular about structuring the work, but begins to consider what effect the structure will have on subordinates. People appreciate a thoughtful boss, but they also are thankful if he or she is organized, structured, and mission-oriented. Their positive reaction to an initiating leader, such as Susan, could lead to increased consideration by the leader—a winning situation for all.

Action or Inaction Orientation

Action-oriented leaders involve themselves with fulfilling work responsibilities. They take charge of these responsibilities by using the leadership and management principles discussed in this book and by realizing that subordinates perform better when their leaders are aware of work-related issues, interested in seeing goals achieved, and actively monitoring performance. Active leaders establish and communicate their subordinates' authority, responsibilities, and work parameters. Having this knowledge of what is expected of them and the encouragement to perform well, employees will gain the autonomy that most of them crave. There are distinctions between action and inaction. By asking a subordinate to complcte a task, for example, the leader is actively delegating an assignment, not avoiding taking action.

Leaders who are inactive are much less engaged in their work than active leaders. On a spectrum of reasons for such inactivity, you will find leaders who consciously shirk their responsibilities and those who do not realize that they are less active than they need to be. Inactive leaders tend to react to a daily work challenge after someone tells them about it, whereas the active leader proactively seeks out impending obstacles. In addition to thc risk that inactive leaders pose to their organization's ability to achieve goals, the leaders themselves risk being perceived as irrelevant or ineffective by their subordinates.

There is much room for leaders who have various combinations of leadership styles.

Personality, Psychology, and Leadership

The previous discussion of leadership orientations shows you there is much room for leaders who have various combinations of leadership styles. Most leaders take a situational approach and use different styles under different conditions, depending upon the urgency and nature of the task, experience and expectations of subordinates, and thc dcgrcc of trust and rapport in the work relationship. A central concept in leadership study is that to better understand the behaviors of leaders and subordinates, it is useful to understand the psychological nature of the people involved. One popular and extensively used resource is the Myers-Briggs Type Indicator. After individuals respond to questions based upon how they usually would feel or act in different situations, this survey classifies them into one of 16 types, based on four continua: extraversion-introversion, sensing-intuition, thinking-feeling, and judging-perceiving. These types will provide insight into their work preferences and decision-mak-

Use of Profile Resources

Dozens of questionnaires, tests, studies, and other resources are available to help you assess your leadership personality. Developed primarily by psychologists and management consultants, these tools quickly allow you to put yourself into various categories, predict how you prefer reacting to different leadership scenarios, and determine areas in which you can improve. Most of them are alike in that they classify leaders into similar categories that have catchy descriptions. Although there is much research available in this area, it is not necessary for you to get too involved in all this resource material. It is useful, however, to look over the commercial products that are available and integrate one or more into your leadership duties.

ing patterns. A leader can use this as a tool to gain insight into his or her sub-ordinates or team members; it can be a useful way to increase understanding.

Although these resources will give you a quick profile of yourself or your subordinates, it is important to be careful when using them and never completely rely upon them. They should be used only in conjunction with skill development tools and other resources. There are several reasons for this. First, though many companies use the tests, the experts disagree considerably as to their reliability. Unfortunately, there is no magic formula for what test is best. It is up to you to examine those that are available and make the best choice for you and your organization. Second, these resources are sometimes misunderstood. People often make major style changes based upon the results of one survey, without realizing the extent to which those results were due to bad testing conditions or the person's mood at the time of the survey. Third, some people are skeptical of tests or resentful of being arbitrarily typecast. You can avoid this reaction if you take the time to explain the process and results to them.

Qualities of a Leader

As scholars have studied leaders over the years, they have attempted numerous times to identify leadership qualities. There are certain recurring qualities that seem to surface in the best leaders. To give you an idea of what makes a great leader, here are some of the best qualities.

- ▶ Adaptable
- ▶ Ambitious
- ▶ Caring
- ▶ Confident
- ▶ Convincing
- ▶ Creative
- ▶ Curious
- ▶ Courageous
- ▶ Discerning
- ▶ Decisive
- ▶ Empathetic
- ▶ Ethical
- ▶ Fair
- ▶ Honest
- ▶ Innovative
- ▶ Persistent
- ▶ Responsible
- ▶ Self-directing

Nevertheless, these sample qualities provide great insight into leadership behavior and help provide you understand why some leaders are more effective than others. As you read this book, you will see how you can integrate these qualities into your daily leadership challenges. You will reach your leadership potential as you use these and other qualities when thinking and acting daily as a leader at work, at home, and in the community.

Leadership and Leadership Qualities

It is difficult to conclude the degree to which these 18 qualities help people become great leaders; therefore, it is important to understand three points about leadership qualities. First, there is no complete list of leadership qualities. If you attempted to list every possible quality of a leader using published studies since the early 1900s, you would have hundreds of qualities. Second, very few, if any, leaders have all the qualities on any given list. It is not necessary nor is it possible for a successful leader to completely fit a leadership mold that someone suggests is best for him or her or for his or her organization. Leaders, like their subordinates and team members, are individuals who are alike and different in many respects and can be successful without radically altering their inherent qualities. Third, a person can possess many leadership qualities and still not be a leader.

Chapter 3

A Leader's Attitude

Elisabeth thinks highly of her organization and team members, and she is so enthusiastic and solutions-oriented that everyone enjoys working with her. Chris also strongly supports his team, yet he forgets to acknowledge good performance and he immediately reacts to new project requests with doubt and worry. How can Chris adjust his attitude?

ATTITUDE USUALLY REFERS TO A FEELING OR STATE OF MIND TOWARD something. You probably agree that you have different feelings and emotions when faced with various circumstances and events. While it can be guaranteed that you will react in some way to your leadership challenges, one of the decisions that you do control is choosing how you react. Fortunately, attitude can be adjusted at will and made positive or negative or, additionally, more positive or more negative.

By habitually focusing on the positive aspects of any situation and de-emphasizing or ignoring the negative, you will reap several important rewards. First, you will begin to perceive daily challenges as opportunities that you expect to seize, not as intrusions that distract you from your work. This positive attitude provides you with a sense of calmness, resolve, and courage that will give you an edge in getting things accomplished. Second, when inevitably something does not go the way you had intended, your positive frame of mind will allow you to quickly accept it and move on to your next challenge. Third, with a positive attitude, you will become gradually less dependent upon external sources of satisfaction such as wealth or social status and more interested in developing solid relationships with others. Friends and co-workers will soon see you as fun and interesting. Finally, the overwhelming positive effects of a great attitude will neutralize any self-imposed barriers to success, such as unhappiness with your physical appearance or lack of self-confidence.

By habitually focusing on the positive aspects of any situation and de-emphasizing or ignoring the negative, you will reap several important rewards.

Importance of a Leader's Attitude

As a leader of subordinates or peers, it is crucial that you are aware of your attitude and work at improving it because your attitude has a tremendous effect on your subordinates and team members' work performances and attitudes. Since you are responsible for setting the tone of the work relationship with your subordinates and co-workers, imagine the positive impact you can have by being known as the leader with a great attitude.

Your attitude has a tremendous effect on your subordinates and team members' work performances and attitudes.

Attitude Characteristics of Leaders

Ten examples of attitude characteristics a truly great leader will display are: 1) loyalty to the organization, 2) appreciation of subordinates, 3) focus on solutions, 4) we-can-do-it approach, 5) authority with responsibility and accountability, 6) enthusiasm, 7) curiosity, 8) leadership image, 9) balance of professional and personal life, and 10) integrity.

Loyalty to the Organization

One key reason you are in a leadership position is that your organization's leaders depend upon you and your good judgment to help them achieve their goals. By being openly supportive of your organization, you will be part of the solution, not the problem. Loyal leaders, regardless of their level in an organization, are not complacent when they see threats to their organization, better ways of doing things, or opportunities to question decisions, policies, and procedures. Because of organizational loyalty and commitment, they will raise questions and seek answers to the issues that puzzle or inspire them. They respond to the call of leadership with purpose.

Appreciation of Subordinates

Great leaders recognize that they need the best efforts of their subordinates in order to succeed at their jobs. Some leaders go as far as saying that employees are their most important asset, a declaration that is true in most if not all organizations. As a leader, you will have numerous opportunities to show your subordinates just how much you value them and want to act in their best interests. You can do this by being accessible, rewarding, and fair. You also can demonstrate how much you value them by training them, listening to them, coaching them, and creating a great work environment for them. Subsequent chapters in this book will show you how you can lead your organization to greater successes and gain the commitment of your staff. No one assumes that you can do it by yourself. You need your subordinates and team members as much as they need you.

Focus on Solutions

By focusing on solving a challenge or making something work better, you will reap more and quicker success than if you concentrate on why you have a problem. This is not to say that you should ignore the causes but instead that you do not use the causes as a reason to blame, avoid taking action, or become paralyzed with fear. You and your team will think more creatively and work more proactively if you are boldly pointed toward the future, not lamenting the past.

By focusing on solving a challenge or making something work better, you will reap more and quicker success than if you concentrate on why you have a problem.

We-Can-Do-It Approach

Your positive and competitive winning attitude will go a long way in motivating your subordinates to achieve goals. It is important to realize that, since your team members or subordinates often depend upon you to provide them hope, direction, persistence, and resources to get their jobs done, you can increase the likelihood of success simply by demonstrating to them that you know anything can be done and that you are determined to do it in the best possible way. Let them know, however, that the team needs them to work hard and smart in order to succeed. Lead the way by setting and enforcing high standards of performance. Imagine the possibilities with them and minimize dwelling on limitations or possibilities of failure.

Authority with Responsibility and Accountability

Authority is the right that your superiors give you to lead your organization and fulfill certain responsibilities or expectations of performance. The chief executive of a company has the ultimate authority to fulfill all possible responsibilities, but due to numerous constraints, he or she assigns to you and other leaders many of these responsibilities and, hopefully, the authority to go along with them. However, the chief executive cannot delegate accountability because he or she alone is accountable to the organization and its shareholders. This concept applies to leaders at any organizational level and, therefore, you as a team leader or team member cannot evade accountability for your responsibilities by blaming others or using excuses. Accept credit for how much or how little you accomplish and then, if necessary, do better next time.

Enthusiasm

Most people naturally admire and respect their leaders. Why not take advantage of this and reward your subordinates and team members by being a leader who is fun to be around, enjoys leading, and has a high energy level? Not only is this attitude great for your well-being and success as a leader, it will catch on with your subordinates, who will begin copying your actions. An important part of a leader's enthusiasm is the ability to act on a great idea. This ability to take risks is not reckless but is calculating and well conceptualized.

Curiosity

Leaders envision possibilities and avoid the complacency of the status quo. A central component of this attitude is a natural curiosity of the work environment, including people, industry processes and products, and customers. Leaders question subordinates about their jobs, suggestions, and daily challenges. When difficulties occur, leaders attempt to isolate the origins and resolve them with an open-minded approach. Their intellectual curiosity is further evidenced by reading books, attending personal development seminars, and taking university classes.

Leadership Image

The image that you present to subordinates, superiors, and peers is vital to your success as a leader. The image is affected by several factors, including your ability to understand and fulfill job requirements, solve problems, get along well in relationships, react to stressful situations, and communicate. In addition to increasing your ability to lead, the right image will do wonders for your career advancement, either within your company or outside it. The

The image that you present to subordinates, superiors, and peers is vital to your success as a leader.

skills you learn in this book, therefore, will go far in boosting your image to where it should be.

Balance of Professional and Personal Life

Do you ever notice people who get completely absorbed in their work and neglect their families or personal lives? They tend to associate happiness or satisfaction with achievements on the job. Eventually they suffer from these choices because instead of attaining happiness and fulfillment, they often make themselves miserable due to increased family or health problems.

To counter this trend, it is helpful to develop an idea of what you value most in life. Researchers have shown over the years that people do not find true happiness at the workplace; it resides elsewhere, such as in family, religion, or community. Once you decide what is really important to you, then you will make better choices between work and home, and your overall contentment and attitude at both places will improve.

Integrity

A strong sense of personal integrity is one of the most frequently listed attributes of outstanding leaders. Your organization and subordinates depend upon you to get the right results while the details of how you achieve them often are left up to you. Although you could achieve a short-term gain by cutting corners, stealing, not keeping your word, or lying, you would certainly suffer some negative consequences in the long term. Other examples of possible integrity violations include accepting or giving bribes, ignoring a conflict-of-interest policy, and avoiding potentially damaging organizational problems. Because one of the most important components of your integrity is honesty, your ability to lead effectively will suffer if you are perceived to be dishonest. An act of dishonesty or a pattern of such behavior will suggest to others that you are untrustworthy.

Does this mean that successful leaders never slip up and make mistakes? No, they deal with these decisions and temptations every day. The more successful ones, however, continually develop and adhere to a set of values that evolve from what they believe is right or wrong. Consistent statements of truth, objective and impartial interpretation of facts, and honesty with others and yourself will go far in anchoring your belief system. Thereafter, if you act with unwavering integrity, it will demonstrate to everyone that you are serious about matters of integrity and that you expect them to be equally serious. In the long term, your integrity becomes a compass that will help you consistently make the right decisions in leading your team or organization.

Importance of Maintaining Your Leader's Attitude

You now know how a leader must think and act. By truly believing these powerful concepts and applying them in your daily life, you are on the way to being a successful leader. Experience tells you that your leader's attitude will be challenged several times a day by people, events, and you yourself. Your reaction to such inevitable challenges determines how quickly you will bounce back and continue on with your leadership responsibilities. The skills that you learn in this book will help you tremendously in maintaining your attitude by making you more confident in your ability to handle leadership challenges. In addition, these daily attitudinal challenges give you the opportunity to use a series of steps to periodically adjust and retain your leader's attitude.

Three simple steps to help you maintain your leader's attitude each day are:

▶ Eliminate the challenge to your attitude.

▶ Adjust your attitude.

▶ Replenish your attitude.

Eliminate the Challenge to Your Attitude

Identify what conflict is causing you to lose your positivity, such as a subordinate's performance or a meeting that did not conclude in your favor. Recognize that you must first deal with that situation by deciding what your reaction will be, then quickly react. After eliminating the challenge, your attitude will bounce back and you will reap two benefits. First, you will be able to move on to your next task and not be continually burdened by what just happened. Second, you will not get involved in plotting useless strategies to get even or win the next round of conflict.

What are some typical responses you may use? Sometimes it is your behavior at issue. If you are responsible for or involved in causing the conflict, it is helpful to bring up the issue with the person involved and explore why the situation turned out as it did. Simply by talking about what happened or explaining why you made a certain decision, you will go a long way in eliminating the conflict. If appropriate to the situation, apologize sincerely.

If someone's behavior disturbs your positive attitude, consider whether that behavior is a one-time occurrence or part of a pattern.

It is best to forget isolated actions, such as a subordinate's first tardiness in two years, or your normally supportive supervisor's decision against your proposal. If you constantly think about these events, your attitude will suffer and your subordinate and supervisor will notice the negativity— whether you believe they notice it or not. Since you are not able to change the subordinate's tardiness or the supervisor's decision, why not pleasantly accept their behavior and concentrate on things that you can influence? You will feel better and the people who work with you will perceive you positively.

What if the behavior occurs frequently? Often, you face attitude challenges that are repetitive; sometimes they are related to your daily leadership responsibilities. For example, if a subordinate consistently underperforms in his or her job, it is essential for you as a leader to improve the employee's performance. By determining how best to solve the situation and then implementing your decision, you will improve the productivity of your organization and the employee's performance as well as retain your positive attitude.

You will learn specific techniques later in this book to resolve such situations. The important point now is that by resolving a situation you will protect your positive attitude.

In another example, you may encounter consistently negative or hostile people at your work site. Decide if your involvement with these negative people is necessary. If so, be as positive as you can be when you deal with them, but minimize your contact with them. In time, your consistent positive attitude may cause them to change their behavior. However, if the negative people are unrelated to your duties, avoid them as much as possible. You will find that by withdrawing from selected negative work-related or personal relationships, you will better guard your positive attitude.

Adjust Your Attitude

You can use specific techniques to help retain your positive attitude, Some may be more effective for you than others, so choose what works best.

You can use specific techniques to help retain your positive attitude. Some may be more effective for you than others, so choose what works best.

One technique is to focus on your successes. You have numerous reasons to be happy and thankful. Why not think of them when you need an emotional lift? If one team member is having problems, be thankful for the others who are doing a great job. If your flight just got delayed, be grateful for some additional quiet time to think or read. By focusing on your successes, you will crowd out the negative thoughts, fears of failure, and other doubts.

Another technique is to improve your self-image. People notice fewer physical characteristics of others than is widely suggested by advertisements.

When you project a positive confidence to others, they notice this attitude more than any physical flaws that you might have. You can develop a great self-image by taking more pride in how you look to yourself, not others, and how you feel. You will then find that others will compliment you more frequently, thus making you feel all the more confident.

Keeping a humorous perspective is always a good technique. The adage that laughter is the best medicine is a great principle to use. When you look at the funny side of unpleasant or unexpected events, you disarm their potential negativity. By lightening your mood, you are in a better mental state to either resolve the challenge or move on to other things.

It is important to remember your purpose. Knowing why you choose to do what you do will give you the energy and focus to maintain a great attitude every day. Your goal may be to move up the corporate ladder, retire early, or provide for your family. Regardless of your reasons, you will find it easier to cope with leadership challenges because you realize that surmounting these attitude hurdles is just one step along the way toward achieving personal and professional goals.

Replenish Your Attitude

You are faced daily with threats to your attitude. Even with the techniques described above, sometimes it is helpful to pause and give yourself time to recover from work, family, and personal challenges. As a leader, this is especially crucial because you are constantly making important decisions, supervising people, being a helpful team member, and handling quickly occurring situations. It sometimes seems as if you have no time to yourself because so many people are demanding that you help them with their needs. Although you will explore stress management in more detail in Chapter 6, the key to replenishing your attitude is to realize that you must regularly practice techniques to restore it.

For daily replenishment, establish certain routines that will allow time for you to relax, think, and reinvigorate. Possibilities include closing the office door, reading from a positive book, listening to an inspirational tape, exercising, praying, confiding with a close friend, or thinking about your pets. The possibilities are endless.

Unless you work seven days a week, you probably will have one or two days that you can use at will. Do whatever you can to make yourself feel better and to recharge your batteries. Great attitude adjusters include trips, movies, or religious activities.

The key to replenishing your attitude is to realize that you must regularly practice techniques to restore it.

23

Take personal holidays several times during the year to help you revitalize your attitude, focus on your goals, and simply relax. This personal time can take many forms, such as three-day weekend trips, extended vacations, job-related conferences, or family retreats.

Have you ever thought that a person whom you had met casually had a bad attitude or that a fellow worker would be easier to work with if he had a better attitude? As an extra benefit to you, the concepts discussed in this chapter will not only improve your own attitude but help you make substantial progress in changing the attitudes of people around you: subordinates, peers, superiors, and family members. By helping them adjust their attitudes, you will become a more effective leader because they will improve their work behavior and, consequently, you will more efficiently and effectively achieve your goals. In the long term, others will view you as a great leader, simply because of your infectious positive attitude.

As subordinates and peers emulate your attitude, you will see a dramatic increase in their morale and output, team productivity, and work environment harmony.

As subordinates and peers emulate your attitude, you will see a dramatic increase in their morale and output, team productivity, and work environment harmony. Additionally, you will find that your good reputation will spread across your organization and into others. This, in turn, will help you as you develop important relationships within and outside your organization. As you change your attitude and use the other skills you learn in this book, you will be on your way to leadership success.

Part Two

Technical and Analytical Skills
(Primary-Level Leadership Skills)

Chapter 4

Job-Specific Skills

Tammy and Mark are co-workers discussing the need for developing each other's job skills. They feel they need to know more about a certain area of production management if they are to complete a project successfully. How should they proceed?

Job-specific skills include those that are specifically related to your job position and that you must acquire in order to work according to standards. Examples include using a computer, operating a machine, administering payroll, selling a product, preparing a production schedule, or interpreting a financial statement.

To help you determine exactly what is expected of you in your job, several documents are usually available from the human resources department or your organization's files. These include the job description, job analysis, and job specifications. It would help you to get copies of all three and study them thoroughly because they are the official word on what you are supposed to do in your job. Not only do they address your specific technical duties, but they could indicate additional responsibilities in the areas of relationship and strategic leadership skills.

The job description summarizes the most important aspects of the job, including tasks and specifications. The job analysis is a detailed mass of data that explores all aspects of the job, such as its required skills and responsibilities. It is developed by observing people in the job, examining all data available in the company, and studying external research. Finally, job specifications give a summary of the job analysis but provide more detail than the job description.

Importance of a Strong Skills Foundation

Before you progress to more advanced leadership skills, it is helpful to realize that the first set of building blocks relates to the nature of your job. You will succeed more quickly as a leader if you fully understand the technical aspects of your job and those of your subordinates and peers. With the leadership training available in this book, you soon will be performing and supervising these functions as a better leader. As a result, you and others with whom you work will further develop overall in skills and knowledge. The intent of this chapter is not to teach you these job-specific skills; it is to show their importance to you as a leader and to demonstrate a framework that you can use to build your skills inventory.

It is competence in these primary-level job skills that enables you and your organization to function smoothly. For example, if your intention is to become a great marketing manager, it is imperative that you know as much as you can about marketing. A corporate logistician needs to know the nitty-gritty details of transportation, such as those related to shipping, trucking, and railroads. A controller is concerned about the language of finance, including cash forecasting, capital expenditure controls, budgeting, and automation. If you are in charge of or a member of a diverse team of experts in software development, a knowledge of programming and coding will help you contribute and lead the team to success.

Though knowing the many skills of your job is crucial to your success, it is not necessary or realistic to know all the minute details of every job position in your realm of responsibility. Many of your subordinates and team members will perform their jobs much better than you could since they usually have more experience, expertise, and training in their specific skills than you have, unless you have mastered those skills. It is extremely helpful, however, to learn as much as possible about their jobs because such valuable information will enable you to make better decisions, understand your organization more fully, and monitor what occurs more precisely. This large base of knowledge will help you develop your leadership intuition, which will permit you to make quality decisions when working with limited time or facts. Additionally, your subordinates will better appreciate you and accept your leadership authority more if you demonstrate that you understand the many aspects of their jobs or at least show that you are willing to learn.

Job-Specific Skills

Most business organizations have training programs for skills development. They could be known as management training programs or apprenticeships and typically vary in terms of length, training location, and degree of supervisory control. The programs may even be part of a probationary period in which you have to meet established training standards in a variety of tasks or face dismissal from the program. Although your supervisor will coach you during this program, it is your responsibility to manage the process proactively. This includes thoroughly learning the skills within the established time frame, ensuring that your supervisor evaluates you when required, and completing the paperwork required by your training office.

Skills in Other Areas

Once you master the skills involved in your own job, it is time to make yourself more helpful to other leaders in the organization. By making the effort to branch out into unfamiliar departments in your organization and to learn new skills, procedures, and ways of doing business, you will benefit both yourself and your organization. You will broaden your skills inventory and make yourself more valuable to your department by developing an expansive picture of the organization and the industry's business issues.

The knowledge you obtain from seeing business done in other ways gives you a fresh perspective and will help you better lead your department and contribute on a team. In addition, you will meet interesting leaders throughout your organization. This can serve you well later as you develop cross-functional working relationships and a power base within the company. Finally, by learning about other areas, you will become more valuable to the company, which can help you later if other leadership positions become available. It is in your interest, therefore, to broaden your network by seeking opportunities to help a fellow leader, serve on a committee, or socialize with your counterparts in other departments. This exposure will earn you the reputation of being supportive of the organization overall.

The knowledge you obtain from seeing business done in other ways gives you a fresh perspective and will help you better lead your department and contribute on a team.

It is important to note that, in helping others, your primary goal should not be to get credit; if so, others will soon perceive you as hungry for power. Credit will naturally arrive as others realize you are a caring leader and loyal to your co-workers.

Formal Education

There is little debate as to whether a person needs a high school diploma. Most employers expect it; employers often encourage those workers who do not have a diploma to get one by offering on-site classes or time off to attend classes. You will probably agree that you prefer working with high school graduates because they possess a knowledge base that allows them to be trained more easily than those without diplomas.

What are the implications of formal education for a leader? Depending on which industry you are in, a college education may or may not be required. There are some employers that would prefer a great leader and team player with strong technical skills and no bachelor's degree to one with a degree and no skills. However, the consensus is that leaders on the way up the corporate ladder require a bachelor's degree; a master's degree would be an advantage after the candidate gets some actual work experience. Moreover, most executives concur that having a degree from a school that has high standards is valued over a degree obtained through minimal standards. Even so, there is substantial disagreement over the value of a master's degree, in particular the master's of business administration (MBA), since most employers tend to promote based upon performance, not educational credentials. Some employers would rather train the leader through their in-house training programs, which provide heavy doses of on-the-job skills training as well as development of common sense.

The mere possession of a college degree does not necessarily make you any better or more intelligent than someone who does not have one. It does, however, give you several advantages that will help you develop as a leader. First, the experience of taking 40 to 50 college courses will give you a wealth of knowledge to draw upon as you progress in your career. Not only will you learn specific skills in math, science, communications, and language, but the humanities and other elective courses will also make you a much more culturally diverse leader, which is useful in today's global environment. Additionally, this wide exposure to knowledge will develop your overall creative intelligence, which will be advantageous as you assume increasingly more challenging leadership assignments at higher levels. Second, a college degree can help you get a promotion. If two leaders are equally qualified and motivated, the one with the degree probably would advance more quickly than the high school graduate. Third, getting a college degree proves to you and others that you can start a major project and see it to its end.

There are several routes to continuing your education. If you are already in the workplace and your employer permits it, you can attend school part-time and take classes in the evening or occasionally during the day. This low-cost option takes more time to get a degree, but you will not starve in the process. If your finances permit, you could quit work and attend school full-time. In both cases, your employer may help you with the costs if you make a commitment to remain employed there.

The mere possession of a college degree does not necessarily make you any better or more intelligent than someone who does not have one. It does, however, give you several advantages that will help you develop as a leader.

Maintain and Improve Your Skills

In continuously seeking improvement in your job area, consider using two resources. First, consult with those experts within and outside your organization who have developed considerable job or institutional knowledge. Often they are quite helpful in passing along tips about the details of jobs. Second, stay up-to-date in your functional area by reading industry magazines and publications, attending professional development seminars, and networking at local professional organizations.

You and your team must develop an attitude that learning does not end when you complete a training program or obtain a college degree. The early years of the 21st century have brought great global change and upheaval; the world will continue to change at a rapidly increasing pace. As a leader, your best way to cope with this change is to build upon your knowledge base by continually seeking to update that knowledge. This will give you the foundation to improve your skills and to better address challenging situations.

Chapter 5

Problem Solving and Decision Making

Sandra and her sales staff are in disagreement as to why the sales seem low in their retail clothing store. Their commissions are lower than last year and there are fewer customers browsing the aisles. They decide to ask their manager, Mr. Fergus, for his opinion.

O F ALL SKILLS, PROBLEM SOLVING AND DECISION MAKING ARE THOSE that leaders use most often at work, at home, or in the community. Like communicating, they relate in some way to practically everything you do and they are components of all the other leadership skills that you use. Your ability to solve problems and make decisions is crucial to how effective you seem as a leader—to yourself, your subordinates, and your superiors.

Problem solving and decision making are closely related in that they are both action processes and frequently overlap. Solving a problem initially involves determining possible solutions. For example, you may be concerned about a low level of customer satisfaction. You determine that several solutions would fix the problem, such as hiring more customer service representatives or increasing the frequency of training. Then, you must use decision-making techniques to choose which of the alternatives to accept and implement.

The purpose of this chapter is to show you how you can approach any problem in a logical manner, resolve it without spending a huge amount of time, and then decide on the best way to implement the solution. The approaches are simple and effective and you can use them routinely as your sole problem-solving and decision-making tools or supplement them with the more complex procedures that you currently use. We will first examine problem solving and then address the slightly different issue of decision making.

> *Your ability to solve problems and make decisions is crucial to how effective you seem as a leader—to yourself, your subordinates, and your superiors.*

The Problem-Solving Process

It is not necessary or possible to examine every fact and analyze every possible scenario when solving problems or making decisions. Your job is to take the initiative to think through the situation, use good judgment, and act decisively. The best way to do this is to use an eight-step process for problem solving that can be used in all situations.

1. Identify symptoms.
2. Collect information.
3. Compare desired results with actual results.
4. State the problem and its effects.
5. List, analyze, and eliminate possible causes.
6. Choose probable causes.
7. Identify and examine possible courses of action.
8. Choose and implement the best course of action, then evaluate.

As you get more familiar with its use, you will find yourself mentally going through this process every time you encounter a problem. Use the problem-solving process even if you only have seconds or minutes, because a proper diagnosis of the problem now will later save you much further effort and time. If you think about your problem in terms of the structured process shown here, you will be less likely to ignore potential causes of the problem and will generate better solutions. You will arrive at solutions more quickly because you are dividing the problem into manageable pieces that you can examine more easily. To better explain the details of this problem-solving process, we will use our example of the retail clothing store.

> *Use the problem-solving process even if you only have seconds or minutes, because a proper diagnosis of the problem now will later save you much further effort and time.*

1. Identify Symptoms

Determine what is happening that indicates something could be wrong.

Sandra alerts her manager, Mr. Fergus. He notices that sales are down 15 percent from the same period last year.

2. Collect Information

Get any information that you believe could be related to the symptoms, including input from your subordinates, peers, superiors, and customers. This information can include observations, organizational performance, studies, or industry data. Tap the wisdom and knowledge of subject-matter experts within and outside your organization.

Mr. Fergus questions his sales staff and finds out that customers seem to be buying the same number of items per visit. He queries a nearby clothing store manager who says that her sales are up from last year. Finally, after speaking with a few valued customers, he hears that his personalized sales service recently has been deteriorating.

3. Compare Desired Results with Actual Results

The objective here is to clearly show what is expected in an ideal situation and what is actually happening with performance or behavior.

Mr. Fergus examines projected vs. actual sales for each of the ten salespersons and notices that four of the ten have not met their monthly goals for the past three months. One of these missed the objective only slightly each month; the others were off by 20 percent or more. In addition, because of recent negative customer comments, Mr. Fergus knows that he is not performing up to his expectations since the store's policy is total satisfaction with the shopping experience.

4. State the Problem and Its Effects

The problem is the difference between the desired results and the actual results identified in step three. Clearly and concisely state the problem and examine its effects upon you, the work environment, goal achievement, or customers. Notice that you do not actually identify the problem until this step. This allows you sufficient opportunity in steps one through three to correctly identify the problem by asking the right questions and probing for facts.

Mr. Fergus concludes that his two problems are that three of his sales staff are not consistently meeting their monthly goals, causing him not to achieve store sales projections, and that customer service is deteriorating and is alienating his loyal customers.

5. List, Analyze, and Eliminate Possible Causes

By examining possible reasons for your problem, you will begin to isolate the actual causes. Avoid eliminating possible causes prematurely, before you adequately consider them or consult with others about them. You will soon develop a list of possible causes for your problem. To determine whether a possibility is actually a cause, ask whether its absence would eliminate the problem.

Mr. Fergus considers several possibilities, but concludes there are three likely causes: the three underperforming salespersons could have a sales training problem, the three could be experiencing personal problems that are affecting their customer relationships and ability to sell, and the three's underperformance could be affecting the performance of all the sales staff, thus contributing to customer alienation.

6. Choose Probable Causes

By using methods such as logical reasoning, investigation, tests, or a group consensus, pick the most likely cause of the problem. Many problems have multiple causes, so do not be surprised if you find more than one cause.

After questioning the sales staff again in more detail, Mr. Fergus determined that seven of the ten salespersons were extremely motivated when everyone showed up for work. However, when a full crew was not available to properly serve the customers, salespeople had to come in on their day off on short notice or had to work more quickly to take up the slack and risk offending customers who were used to personalized and lengthy attention. Mr. Fergus examined work records for the past three months and found that the three underperforming salespersons were five times more likely than the others not to show up for work on any given day; those absences definitely affected their performance, which was otherwise excellent. He concluded that the underlying cause of his two problems was the three salespersons' inability to consistently work five days per week.

7. Identify and Examine Possible Courses of Action

The objective is to find solutions that could eliminate the cause of the problem. Determine some possible solutions, either by yourself or with the help of others through brainstorming and creative thinking. After listing and examining the possibilities, keep those that are acceptable and realistic to you. You may need or want to consult with staff or other leaders for their thoughts. In the interest of time, tell them what information you need and when you need it.

Mr. Fergus decided to speak with the three salespersons. He found that all three were having significant family problems that sometimes required them to stay at home on short notice. He listed four possible courses of action: a pay system revision that would focus more on commissions and less on base pay, to motivate them to show up more frequently; intense coaching focused on their inconsistent work performance, to improve their behavior; a contingency plan that better predicted absences, to give the other employees more notice when they were called in to substitute; and hiring new salespersons if the three did not change their behavior.

8. Choose and Implement the Best Course of Action, Then Evaluate

Examine the effects, costs, and practicality of each possible solution and choose the best solution. List any obstacles that may prevent you from implementing that solution and generate ideas to overcome these obstacles. Communicate the solution to others and then direct the implementation of your plan. Evaluate the results and modify the plan if necessary. The how-to-choose part of this step will be further explained below in the decision-making process and the implementation and evaluation steps will be explored more thoroughly throughout the book.

Mr. Fergus chose to implement the second and third courses of action immediately and the fourth later, if necessary.

The Nature of Decisions

As you just saw, minor decisions are made constantly in the problem-solving process. For example, as you collect data and interpret information, you have to make decisions about what data to collect and how to interpret it. Those kinds of routine decisions typically are easily learned and eventually become instinctive through experience. As you move along in the problem-solving process to steps seven and eight, you make increasingly complicated decisions, such as evaluating options and choosing the best alternative. The following sections address these decisions that have important implications to you in terms of long-term consequences, risks, unpredictability, and achieving your goals.

The Decision-Making Process

Identifying courses of action does you little good unless you weigh their pros and cons, determine which one is the best, and consider the consequences of implementing it. Such consequences could include likelihood of success or

Questions for Decision Making

The problem-solving process described above will provide you the structure to thoroughly explore and analyze problems. It is up to you to construct a decision-making process for each situation by using techniques that are most appropriate for that specific decision. You can best do this by exploring and understanding some of the major issues involved in making decisions, by asking yourself these five questions.

- ▶ What are the time constraints for making this decision?
- ▶ Who will participate in the decision making?
- ▶ Will this decision be recurring or one time?
- ▶ What are the components of this decision?
- ▶ What techniques will be used to make this decision?

Identifying courses of action does you little good unless you weigh their pros and cons, determine which one is the best, and consider the consequences of implementing it.

potential implementation problems. A logical path after determining the cause of a problem, therefore, is to think in detail about how best to eliminate the cause or causes and implement the solution successfully, despite challenges, barriers, and uncertainty. This is decision making.

What Are the Time Constraints for This Decision?

After you identify when you will make the decision, you then can outline a decision-making process based upon a realistic schedule. Assuming that you have enough time and that you start the process immediately, you will be able to choose from more resources, such as group assistance, advanced decision-making tools, and extensive research. You can use several methods to assist you in making the decison; some are simple and easy to apply to all facets of work, while others are much more complicated, time-consuming, and math-intensive. This chapter will concentrate on using simple processes of decision making that conserve time. You can then explore more advanced methods as you choose.

Who Will Participate in the Decision Making?

Since the decision-making process usually involves several individuals, coordinate your actions with theirs in order to better manage the process. This will help you eliminate duplication of effort, minimize frustration, and ensure that you make the best decision. Seek the input of those individuals whose contributions are obvious in helping you evaluate courses of action, including technical specialists in areas such as marketing, human resources, legal, customer service, or accounting. Contact those people who will be affected by your decision or who must be committed to it for you to implement it successfully; these include your superiors, subordinates, team members, and customers. You are not consulting with these individuals for their approval, necessarily, but for information, experience, and guidance to help you structure your decision-making process, pinpoint the decision's long-term implications, and identify any competing interests that may affect your decision or its implementation. In addition to the immediate benefits of involving others in your decision making, you likely will notice more long-term acceptance of your decision by the participants.

Will This Decision Be Recurring or One Time?

Decisions are either programmed or unprogrammed. Most of your decisions are programmed if they routinely occur, are mostly predictable, and can be scheduled. These include decisions such as inventory reorders or customer service inquiries. Responses to these situations are predictable and can, therefore, be standardized wherever possible by using written procedures or rules that clearly show how to make the decision. This will facilitate decisions throughout your organization and will permit you to delegate more decision-making authority to your subordinates.

Unprogrammed decisions are those that occur less frequently and can have enormous consequences for you or your organization. Examples include opening a new manufacturing plant or retail store, restructuring the organization, redesigning processes, or revising the incentives program. Because these decisions are not routine and possibly unprecedented, can involve a high degree of uncertainty, and are usually vitally important to your organization, you should have as much knowledge about them as possible to guide you through the decision-making process.

What Are the Components of This Decision?

Decisions have three elements: conditions, courses of action, and consequences. *Conditions* refer to the uncertainty and risk that always exist in your business or personal environment. Since very few of your actions will have results that are completely certain because of factors and circumstances that are usually uncontrollable, you must isolate and estimate the uncertainty and risk involved in your decision. *Courses of action* are simply potential solutions to a problem. *Consequences* are the implications resulting from each course of action.

Mr. Fergus's clothing store's sales revenue on a given day could be conditional in part upon whether all, most, some, or none of the sales staff show up for work. Before the store opens for business, the manager will evaluate the actual *conditions*, i.e., check to see how many salespeople are at work. If there are fewer or more than scheduled, then he has a staffing decision to make. He must implement one of several possible *courses of action*: call in one or more salespersons, send one or more home, or neither add nor subtract. Each of these alternatives has different *consequences* on total sales for the day. Ideally, the manager would have determined in advance some courses of action by predicting the workplace conditions, their probability of occurrence, and the consequences of each course of action.

> *Decisions have three elements: conditions, courses of action, and consequences.*

What Techniques Will Be Used to Make This Decision?

There are several techniques to help you structure decisions and guide you to your best decision. Use them individually or in combination. Discussed below are some of the most popular techniques.

> *There are several techniques to help you structure decisions and guide you to your best decision.*

Prioritization. By establishing a system for ranking possible courses of action, you can more easily choose. For example, if you need to decide who among several volunteers gets the opportunity to work overtime, you could prioritize them according to the amount of overtime worked thus far in the month. Your choice could be the person who has worked the least overtime so far. Prioritization works best for recurring decisions, such as allocation of resources or customer service procedures; it is not as good for one-time decisions.

Checklists. In simple decision making involving few alternatives, such as to accept or not accept and to buy or not buy, it can be helpful to list significant factors that affect the decision, such as cost, dependability, and servicing. You can then simply check off the factors as acceptable or not, decide the impact of any unacceptable factors, and then choose the best alternative—to accept the proposal or reject it, to buy the new computer system or not buy it. This process is helpful because, before you check off a factor, you examine the factor in detail and thoroughly understand its implications. The main drawback to this technique is that typically it does not allow you to weight the factors unless you modify the technique to fit your needs.

Brainstorming. Brainstorming encourages members of a group to let their minds wander in an environment free from criticism and judgment to find creative ways to solve problems and develop alternative courses of action. As the group leader, you designate someone to record the ideas while you facilitate the session. Because this technique will help you generate ideas and alternative solutions, it is a tool not solely for making decisions but also for helping generate options that will lead eventually to your decision.

Intuition. You develop your intuition through experience on the job, solving problems, and making decisions. This knowledge hones your intuitive skills sometimes to the point of allowing you to trust your feelings completely. As you will see during the discussion of payoff charts, intuition can provide you with some basis to start the decision-making process. Although some leaders are quite successful in primarily using their intuition for decision making, most leaders do not rely totally on their hunches without having some other, more objective techniques to provide balance.

You develop your intuition through experience on the job, solving problems, and making decisions.

Payoff Charts. When one main decision is needed, you can use a payoff chart to help structure your options in a clear, concise manner. A payoff chart consists of a simple diagram that shows each of your various courses of action and their consequences. Constructing a payoff chart forces you to think through all the details of your decision. A complete example of how to use a payoff chart is given in the next section.

Decision Trees. This popular tool is used when multiple decisions are made at different times, a situation that cannot be managed by the payoff chart. A decision tree allows you to graphically chart decisions, consequences, and conditions in an easy-to-read diagram that branches out like a tree. It is indispensable for tracking complicated decisions and their effects on subsequent decisions. It is best to consult a detailed guide that will explain the many nuances in constructing decision trees to help you integrate them into your decision making.

Advanced Techniques. There are dozens of advanced decision-making techniques. These include synectics, a problem-solving process that focuses on group creativity; morphological analysis, searching for connections and linkages among concepts; and operations research and decision theory, both of which seek the best solution using math- and statistics-intensive processes. No one technique is best, because each has limitations, is applicable in certain situations, and has ideal conditions of use. If any of these interest you, consult the many instructional texts that are available.

The Payoff Chart

Conditions, courses of action, and consequences—the three elements of decision analysis—are shown in more detail in a payoff chart. A payoff chart

Assumptions for a Staffing Decision Payoff Chart

In the example of the clothing store, Mr. Fergus expects eight salespeople to arrive for work. The actual number of arrivals results in different consequences, or net sales revenue, which is total revenue less sales salaries. Assume the following:

- ▶ Each salesperson is paid $50 per day in base salary, plus $20 if he or she has to come in on short notice or as a replacement.
- ▶ The largest possible revenue for the store is $8,000 per day when a normal staff of eight works—$1,000 per salesperson—and if fewer than eight work, then the revenue for the store is $1,000 per salesperson.
- ▶ There are 11 salespeople.

lists all practical courses of action, which are distinct and exclusive of each other. A close look at a fully detailed example of a payoff chart can help you use this technique in your own situations.

The staffing decision payoff chart (Figure 5-1) indicates which course of action (CA) is best for each condition (C) and clearly shows that when a salesperson does not show for work, it is always best to call for a replacement or sometimes two. This may appear obvious, but by constructing a simple chart, you can actually see in detail your options and the anticipated consequences of each under multiple conditions.

In this example, the manager must ensure that not too many salespersons are working on any given day or potential income will be lost. The

Condition (C)	Course of Action (CA)			
	CA 1: Do nothing	CA 2: Add 1 sales-person	CA 3: Add 2 sales-people	CA 4: Add 3 sales-people
C1: 8 salespeople arrive for work	$7,600 Best CA	$7,530	$7,460	$7,390
C2: 7 salespeople arrive for work	$6,650	$7,580 Best CA	$7,510	$7,440
C3: 6 salespeople arrive for work	$5,700	$6,630	$7,560 Best CA	$7,490
Totals	$19,950	$21,740	$22,530	$22,320

Figure 5-1. Staffing decision payoff chart

example used was a simple one. In other words, most store managers would intuitively recognize that it is a good idea to have eight salespersons working per day because this would maximize the store's revenue and that it would be a good idea to telephone for a replacement if someone does not show for work.

The payoff chart has a number of limitations. First, it can be used only when one decision is needed, not multiple decisions over a period of time. Although you could construct a chart for each phase of a multiple decision, it is more practical to use more advanced tools, such as a decision tree. Second, the payoff chart does not completely show all possible conditions for the store manager. It is possible, for example, that no worker will show up for work or that a busload of customers could arrive, which would require using all 11 salespersons. Third, the payoff chart does not account for the uncertainty inherent in any decision situation. In the example, the manager was certain how many employees were at work on any given morning because he counted them. But there may be times when the store manager cannot call for his replacement workers during the morning and must decide by the previous evening how many workers will probably show up for work.

Uncertainty like this exists in most decisions. Rarely does a leader make a decision in absolute certainty. You can address this concern through two options, by using intuition or probabilities.

Estimate Uncertainty by Using Your Intuition

A payoff chart enables you to decide quickly on a course of action, depending on whether you feel optimistic, pessimistic, or neither about what conditions will actually prevail. These feelings are important because in making a quick decision, you may be forced to rely upon them. Additionally, as you become more experienced as a leader, you will increasingly begin to trust your intuition. This can become valuable to you in assessing which conditions are most likely to occur in different situations.

*R*arely does a leader make a decision in absolute certainty. You can address this concern by using intuition or probabilities.

Return to the staffing decision payoff chart. If you are optimistic that all eight employees will arrive, you could quickly decide that CA 1 is the best option, since it has the highest payoff of the three courses of action when eight employees arrive. If you are pessimistic and believe that only six will show, simply pick the lowest or most pessimistic payoffs in each CA, which are $5,700, $6,630, $7,460, and $7,390. Then select the highest of these values, $7,460 in CA 3, as your best option. Finally, if you are neither optimistic nor pessimistic and believe that each condition is as likely to occur as the others, you could choose the CA that has the highest total for its three expected conditions or consequences. In the example, CA 3 with its $22,530 total is the best choice.

Estimate Uncertainty by Using Probabilities

It is best if most important decisions are not left completely to chance and feelings. More formal methods are available to assess the likelihood, or probability, that one condition will prevail over the others. These methods provide needed structure for the intuition, experience, and information used by the decision maker. This chapter examines only one simple method and it avoids the details of probability, which you can eventually learn as time permits. Many fine guides are available to teach you these fundamentals and help you develop the important skills of assessing the uncertainty inherent in a decision and choosing the right course of action. The purpose here, however, is to give you a method that you can put to use immediately.

The next chart (Figure 5-2) shows probabilities, or best estimates, as to the likelihood of each condition occurring. It shows that the store manager, based upon his experiences and personal knowledge of his sales force, believes that there is a 60 percent probability of all eight workers arriving, a 30 percent probability for seven workers, and a 10 percent probability for only six workers. These probabilities are more specific than the optimistic and pessimistic intuitive predictions made in the previous section. In this example, simply multiply each probability by the resulting revenues for each course of action in each condition; you will get an expected revenue (ER). This is a weighted revenue that accounts for the uncertainty by predicting the likelihood of conditions one, two, or three occurring. In this example, after totaling the individual ERs in each course of action, choose CA 3 because it has the highest expected payoff, $7,485, of all four courses of action.

The main point of this exercise is that, to be an effective decision maker, you must make a judgment about the uncertainty in your environment and then predict the likelihood of your potential conditions for making the decision. The best way to do this is to use the concepts of probabilities. Since this chapter barely scratches the surface of probability theory, read more about it when you get some spare time, because it is essential to your development as a decision maker.

Condition (C)	Proba-bility	Course of Action (CA)			
		CA 1: Do nothing	CA 2: Add 1 sales-person	CA 3: Add 2 sales-people	CA 4: Add 3 sales-people
C1: 8 salespeople arrive for work	0.6	$7,600 ER = $4,560	$7,530 ER = $4,518	$7,460 ER = $4,476	$7,390 ER = $4,434
C2: 7 salespeople arrive for work	0.3	$6,650 ER = $1,995	$7,580 ER = $2,274	$7,510 ER = $2,253	$7,440 ER = $2,232
C3: 6 salespeople arrive for work	0.1	$5,700 ER = $570	$6,630 ER = $663	$7,560 ER = $756	$7,490 ER = $749
Totals	1.0	$19,950 ER = $7,125	$21,740 ER = $7,455	$22,530 ER = $7,485	$22,320 ER = $7,415

Figure 5-2. Staffing decision payoff chart–probabilities and expected revenues (ER)

Creative and Critical Thinking

Some say that leaders get paid to solve problems and make decisions. A better statement would be that they get paid to solve problems correctly and make the right decisions. In this chapter, you have seen several methods and techniques to help you solve problems correctly and make the right decisions. This final section will put these in broad perspective by showing you how your problem-solving and decision-making abilities can improve simply by the way you think about your challenges.

Think About Your Style

Leaders get paid to solve problems correctly and make the right decisions.

People tend to think in one of two styles, adaptive or innovative. Neither of these is right nor wrong. What is right is what is natural for each person. Adaptive thinkers are characterized by goal orientation; adherence to policies, procedures, and structure; and great organizational abilities. Their brain's left hemisphere, which is the logical, analytical, and detail-oriented side, dominates. Innovative thinkers, on the other hand, tend to be more free spirited, less organized, and open to new methods of solving problems. The brain's right hemisphere, which is the emotional and creative side, dominates.

No matter what your orientation is, you can practice using the opposite orientation to strengthen those characteristics and become an overall better thinker. For example, if you are not too innovative, try using unconventional ideas in your work, such as meeting new customers, changing your daily work routine, or trying new problem-solving techniques. If you want to ground yourself more in adaptive thinking, try progressively implementing time management principles or referring more often to your own or your department's goals.

Think Thoroughly by Questioning Others

As you noticed in this chapter, problem solving and decision making involve others. As you move through the process, remember that you cannot do all the work yourself. Question your customers, subordinates, peers, and superiors about their thoughts on the problem by asking them leading questions that will pinpoint both the problem and potential solutions. You will soon find out what their concerns are and will be better able to devise winning and long-term solutions that will benefit everyone.

Think About Other Things

Giving your mind a break from the problem will invigorate your creativity. Listening to soothing music, watching fish in an aquarium, or exercising will give you a chance to look at the problem from a new perspective. Additionally, by focusing on the attributes of the music or fish, you may be able to associate what you see with potential solutions to your problem. For example, a fish in your aquarium may be swimming slowly and competing with other, quicker fish. This could prompt you to wonder whether your proposed product line will gain market share quickly enough compared with your competitor's products.

Think About Your Objective

If you periodically remind yourself why you are solving problems and making decisions—to achieve a specific objective—then you are more likely to remain on the path of critical thinking, use relevant tools and techniques, and minimize distractions.

Decide with Confidence

Sometimes you make decisions several times per minute; more complex decisions can take you days or weeks. You solve some problems completely by yourself and other problems with team members or committees.

You already use a wealth of experience and intuitive ability in solving your problems and making your decisions. By combining this knowledge with the techniques in this chapter, you will make better decisions regardless of the volume of information, the deadlines, and the uncertainty. With methods that you can readily use in your business and other challenges, you will be able to approach problems confidently and know that you can be proud of the results.

Chapter 6

Priorities Management

Robert always seems to have his day well planned. He is organized and efficient and wastes little time. What are the secrets of his success?

HOW YOU MANAGE YOUR PRIORITIES AS A LEADER IS IRREFUTABLY linked with how successful you are at achieving your objectives. This chapter will discuss how to manage priorities well, given the constraints of time and the inevitability of stress. You will soon be able to accomplish more in less time and you will gain more valuable time to spend wisely on the crucial job of leading in your organization.

Control Your Time

Time, one of the few commonalities among people, is a resource you use to put your life in order at work, home, and leisure. Although everyone has the same number of hours a week to accomplish a multitude of tasks and obligations, some people are more effective than others at managing their time. Fortunately, it is not difficult to observe successful time managers to see how they achieve their priorities. They use simple techniques and principles to help them proactively choose what they want and need to do.

How you manage your priorities as a leader is irrefutably linked with how successful you are at achieving your objectives.

Since most leaders have a considerable amount of personal contact with others, they sometimes erroneously believe that they have little control over how that time is spent. This is simply not true. The key to effective time management is gaining control of your time and then taking steps to retain control. No matter how busy you are or what your work circumstances are, you can learn how to control your time and to free up time for more important work. For example, you may not be getting important work accomplished because your subordinates or co-workers constantly interrupt you during the day. There are many solutions to this situation, such as limiting the amount of time you spend talking with any person who interrupts, asking someone else to speak with a person who interrupts, or reserving specific time periods during the day exclusively for yourself.

You can use the following time-management process not only to gain control of your time but also to maintain control by periodically repeating the process.

The key to effective time management is gaining control of your time and then taking steps to retain control.

1. Analyze your current use of time.
2. Eliminate nonessential and inappropriate tasks.
3. Delegate tasks.
4. Improve performance of essential tasks.
5. Maintain control of your time.

1. Analyze Your Current Use of Time

Your objective in this step is to track and evaluate what you do during a typical day and when you do it. You can accomplish this by using a time journal, in which you record your activities in specific three-hour time periods throughout the course of a week. It will take you several minutes each day to document your activities, but the reward is substantial, as you will see. Get a 20-page spiral notebook and organize it so that each page is devoted to a three-hour time segment for a specific day of the week. The three-hour time segments are grouped together to make it easier for you to compare them later.

▶ Pages 1–5: for time period 7–10 a.m., Monday through Friday

▶ Pages 6–10: for time period 10 a.m. to 1 p.m., Monday through Friday

▶ Pages 11–15: for time period 1–4 p.m., Monday through Friday

▶ Pages 16–20: for time period 4–7 p.m., Monday through Friday

Keep the notebook with you at all times and document accurately every few minutes what you did during the previous few minutes. Be specific and honestly note the names of people you spoke with and the topics or specific project you were working on, the time span of the task (e.g., 9:45–9:55 a.m.), and any major occurrences, such as whether you accomplished what you had intended or if you were interrupted. Do this for each of the four time periods during all five days. At the end of each three-hour time period, take a moment to add up the time you spent in major activities such as in-office visits, planning, telephone conversations, reading correspondence, and meetings.

After five days of documenting your activities, you will make some major conclusions about what you do daily. Most notable will be startling observations such as, for example, that reading mail took 45 minutes, incoming telephone calls covered two hours, or personal business occupied one hour. You probably will find several hours during a typical day that could be characterized as wasted time, waiting time, or time not spent in support of your primary functions. In addition, you will realize that there is a certain time period during the day when you seem to get more work done, think more creatively, or are more alert. This is your most productive time, which will be discussed in step four.

2. Eliminate Nonessential and Inappropriate Tasks

By taking a critical look at your time journal, you can locate tasks that you should not be doing, either because they are not essential to your personal goals or your organization's mission or because they are irrelevant to your primary leadership responsibilities and thus should be delegated. Some typical examples of nonessential tasks are compiling data that you rarely need or use, attending a meeting that does not concern your responsibilities, and reading magazines that have no relevance to your professional responsibilities. Some typical examples of inappropriate tasks are compiling necessary data that another department already regularly collects, approving routine requests that a subordinate could handle instead, and opening and reading your mail when you have a capable assistant.

Stop doing the nonessential tasks and either transfer the inappropriate ones to their rightful owners in other departments or delegate them to others.

Stop doing the nonessential tasks and either transfer the inappropriate ones to their rightful owners in other departments or delegate them to others. These actions will recoup a significant portion of your time. You can stop a nonessential task quickly if you have the authority. Otherwise, you will have to persuade your team members or superiors as to why you want the task eliminated. If you explain that the task is not pertinent to your responsibilities, this persuasion should be simple.

3. Delegate Tasks

Without question, delegation is one of the best time-tested methods of handling responsibilities. This process involves giving subordinates and others the responsibility and its accompanying authority to autonomously accomplish tasks. If you follow a few simple guidelines, delegation will dramatically increase your available time for priority tasks; train your subordinates and team to do more without your close supervision; improve others' performance, morale, and job satisfaction; and improve the overall performance, creativity, and reputation of your organization.

There are six basic guidelines to an effective delegation process.

- ▶ Decide what to delegate.
- ▶ Choose the right person.
- ▶ Communicate the task.
- ▶ Give responsibility and authority for the entire task.
- ▶ Check progress.
- ▶ Evaluate results.

Decide What to Delegate. A general principle is to delegate whenever someone else can effectively do the task for you. This allows you to concentrate on your more important leadership duties or on special tasks related to your personal strengths, skills, or enjoyments. A task that can be delegated is normally routine and of average risk and importance. These criteria are not absolute, however, because you may want to delegate an extremely difficult and risky task with the intention of developing the capabilities of a key subordinate, for example. Moreover, if you frequently delegate ordinary, unpleasant, or unrewarding tasks and keep the interesting and exciting ones for yourself, you will damage your leadership effectiveness in the long run.

A general principle is to delegate whenever someone else can effectively do the task for you.

One of your main goals should be that both you and your team members grow professionally to be the best leaders that you can possibly be. In this context, consider initially delegating important tasks associated with the primary level of leadership skills, such as implementing solutions or overseeing individual projects. As your team members prove able to accept increased responsibility, delegate more to them. Remember to stay deeply involved in the crucial relationship and strategic areas, such as dealing with the needs and concerns of your team members, structuring your organization, and implementing major changes.

Choose the Right Person. Consider several factors when choosing the person to whom you want to delegate a task. Ask yourself who is the most junior individual with work experience or interest in the task, who needs the task in terms of career development, and who has the availability to finish the assignment. By matching a person's abilities with the task's requirements, you dramatically increase the likelihood of success.

The most effective way to choose the right person is to completely understand your team members' or co-workers' personal and professional goals and motivation. Once you know a little more about who is working with you, use this knowledge to guide you toward the right choices when delegating.

Communicate the Task. Explain your concept of the task to the person, including the expected final results, pertinent details but not every detail, priorities, constraints, available resources, milestones and deadlines, expectations, and any other important guidance. To secure his or her commitment, explain why the task must be done, its history, and its importance to you and the organization. Ask the person to repeat in his or her words the details of the assignment; this will ensure that he or she receives and understands your communication and will be less likely to deviate from your intentions. Specify that since you trust this person with the assignment, you will not constantly check on his or her progress but that you expect him or her to freely approach you with any questions or irresolvable problems. Keep a record of the details of this conversation so you can later refer to it when checking progress.

Give Responsibility and Authority for the Entire Task. Tell the person that this task is completely his or her project to accomplish using the guidance that you have provided. The person must understand that you are committed to supporting his or her authority to complete the task and that you will provide the required resources and any assistance or intervention needed. When you assign the entire multifaceted task, your subordinates will gain much more experience than if they were responsible for only a component of the task.

If the person is unable to accomplish certain aspects of the task alone, he or she in turn can choose to delegate a component of the responsibilities and, in so doing, learn delegation skills. In this instance, carefully monitor the person's decisions to ensure that he or she retains sufficient control over the task.

If you decide that assigning a complete task to one person is impractical, make sure all individuals understand the importance of their responsibilities to you and the organization. As a result, you will inspire your team to commit to the assignment and see it through to its end.

Tell the person that this task is completely his or her project to accomplish using the guidance that you have provided.

Check Progress. Monitor the progress of your team members and guide their efforts by periodically meeting with them to discuss details and provide feedback. If they are having difficulties and they attempt to delegate the assignment back to you, which sometimes occurs when subordinates face challenging tasks, resist. Instead of eagerly agreeing to resolve a small problem for them, get them to resolve it by asking them leading questions such as "What do you think?" or "Is that a viable option?" This valuable coaching, encouragement, and assistance will help ensure not only that your project remains on track but also that your team members develop new skills and additional leadership experience.

Evaluate Results. Notice what caused the project to be successful or to encounter difficulties. Discuss these lessons with the subordinates involved and integrate what you learn into your next opportunity for delegation. Praise their accomplishments in front of their peers and to your supervisor.

4. Improve Performance of Essential Tasks

Now that you have freed yourself of nonessential and inappropriate tasks, look closely at the remaining ones. Determine your goals and link them to your most important tasks. Your success at performing job-related tasks and your overall success as a leader depend upon establishing short-, medium-, and long-term goals that are realistic, achievable, measurable, and time-specific.

Determine your goals and link them to your most important tasks.

Goals are one of the most powerful motivators, because with them you can overcome challenges that would have normally been insurmountable. Numerous studies have shown that the most successful people, despite obstacles or disabilities, are those who have clearly identified and committed themselves to their personal and professional goals. Take time to think about what specifically you want to accomplish on the job, at home, during your leisure, and in the community over the next few weeks, months, and years. These goals could include a job promotion, a certain level of income, a healthy relationship, or a family. Write down these goals, keep them nearby, and review them daily to help you prioritize your activities. Once you determine why you are working every day, that is, to achieve specific goals, then you will have gone far in preparing yourself to do what is necessary to achieve them.

Plan and prioritize your daily, weekly, quarterly, and annual tasks. Prioritization consists of ranking your tasks in terms of their value to you and your organization. Think of each task in terms of importance and urgency. Your objective is to spend most of your time on important, nonurgent tasks such as planning, solving long-term problems, or achieving goals. Since these high-payoff tasks are where you contribute the most to the organization, it makes sense to spend a significant amount of time on them. Throughout the day, you will encounter planned and unplanned important, urgent tasks such as personnel or customer crises. You must attend to these, but you must also minimize the disruptions they cause and the time they take away from other important priorities. Spend less time on unimportant, urgent tasks such as reading the mail or certain administrative duties because they do not significantly help you to accomplish your most important priorities, although they may make you feel as if you are getting important work done. Avoid the remaining tasks, which are unimportant, nonurgent tasks such as gossiping or computer games.

If you write your tasks on some type of planning document, you are more likely to accomplish them. These tasks reflect short-term (daily and weekly) planning, medium-term (quarterly) planning, and long-term (annual) planning. Before you leave work or before you start working, develop your daily plan by listing your required tasks in order of priority. Simply taking a few minutes to plan your activities and tasks will help you stay focused on the most important. Remember: you have the time to plan and planning is crucial to keeping focused on your important goals. Keep the plan nearby so you can easily refer to it throughout the day and coordinate it with your weekly plan, tasks that you want to accomplish during a five-day period. You follow your weekly short-term plans by accomplishing the detailed tasks included in the daily plans. You follow your quarterly plan—your goals and activities for the upcoming three months—by accomplishing the tasks in your weekly plans. Likewise, the annual plan shows your major goals for the upcoming 12 months and the following two to five years.

Use your most productive time for the most important tasks. In developing your time journal several pages ago, you identified a time period when you got more work done and seemed to be more alert. For most people, this is sometime before lunch, but it can vary. Since your energy level is highest during the period you identified, use this time wisely by working on your most important tasks.

Schedule specific time for no interruptions, specific activities, and routine events. Let daily planning liberate you to schedule what you need to schedule. First, block off time during each day when you will not allow anyone to interrupt you, either in person or by telephone. Coordinate this schedule block with your assistant or subordinates. You then can better concentrate on your high-priority tasks. Second, always schedule sufficient time

> *Your objective is to spend most of your time on important, nonurgent tasks such as planning, solving long-term problems, or achieving goals.*

53

Wasting Time

Other time wasters originate from external events such as unscheduled visitors and telephone calls, crises, and periods of waiting. Your time journal no doubt lists several of these—vivid evidence of how they creep into your daily schedule and distract you from your most important tasks. You can reclaim a significant amount of time if you simply focus on eliminating the time wasters. The best way to detect if you are wasting time and to prompt yourself quickly back to your important work is to ask yourself a simple question several times a day: "Is what I am doing right now helping me achieve today's priority tasks?"

for any planned event that requires your presence, such as meetings, ceremonies, coaching sessions, or interviews. Third, allow for time during the day when you can group routine activities, such as returning telephone calls, signing documents, or reading.

Avoid overscheduling. When tempted to schedule every hour of the day with some activity, do not forget to build in some slack time so that any crisis or unplanned event will not cause you to get behind schedule.

Eliminate time wasters. Whenever you do something that is unrelated to accomplishing your most important priorities, then you are wasting time. Examples of personal time wasters include gossiping, office clutter, and procrastination.

Here are seven tips to help you eliminate time wasters.

1. Avoid office clutter.
2. Reduce people interruptions.
3. Keep your focus.
4. Avoid procrastination.
5. Manage telephone calls.
6. Manage for crisis.
7. Avoid waiting for events or answers.

When you cannot access a document or file within two minutes or if you have missed deadlines because paperwork has gotten lost on your desk, it is time to reorganize your office.

Avoid Office Clutter. When you cannot access a document or file within two minutes or if you have missed deadlines because paperwork has gotten lost on your desk, it is time to reorganize your office. There are many books available about paperwork control, filing systems, and office layout, but here are some key points that can immediately help you.

Use documents until you no longer immediately need them, then file them in your personal filing system near your desk if you will need access to them for a specific project, in a tickler system that reminds you on a certain date of a required action, or permanently in the central files so others can find them if you are away. Never leave loose documents lying on your desk overnight. With the help of your assistant, periodically purge the files and discard documents that no longer have value to you or your organization. Keep only critical items that are legally required to be retained, one-of-a-kind documents, or key information that likely will be needed for reference.

Identify desktop items that you use infrequently and put them inside the desk or give them to someone who can use them.

Routinely screen paperwork or mail with the goal of handling it only once. If that is impractical, each handling must move the task one step closer to completion. If you are the action officer for an item, place the document in an action folder along with related documents. Act on these items according to their priority and limit the number of times you handle the paperwork. Place anything else, including mail, in folders for reading later, pass it along with comments to the proper action officer or your assistant, or discard it if it's of no use. Coordinate any deadlines with your planning system so that you do not lose track of any. After skimming magazines, don't keep them; clip any articles that are pertinent to your work and toss out the magazines.

Reduce People Interruptions. When people visit your office or work space, remember that you are in control because it is your domain. When you invite them to your office, have a clear goal and know how long it should take to achieve that goal. When you finish your agenda with them, simply stand up to indicate the visit is over. Your visitors should get the hint. If not, thank them for coming and let them know that you intend to move on to other work. You can discourage unwanted interruptions by facing your desk away from the door, closing the door, and/or instructing your assistant or co-worker to screen visitors. When unexpected visitors arrive, your three choices are to chat with a purpose, chat briefly and get back to work, or not chat at all.

If a visitor is unannounced but important and infrequent—your supervisor, a vice president, a key subordinate, or a client, for example—take the necessary time and chat with him or her, trying to keep the focus on constructive topics related to work. Even though these people are an interruption, you can insert slack time into your schedule to allow for unplanned events such as these. Take advantage of the situation and resolve important issues or get to know the visitor a little better.

Some unexpected but regular visitors may warrant a brief conversation, such as a quick update on a project. Stand up and greet them but do not invite them to sit down unless you have plenty of time. Get quickly to their

When people visit your office or work space, you are in control because it is your domain.

reason for dropping in. When finished with the conversation, indicate to the visitor that you have other work in progress.

Get into the habit of firmly, but politely telling unwanted visitors that you simply do not have time to talk. If they have business to conduct, tell them to call you at a certain time later in the day or schedule an appointment with them. Eventually, these visitors will learn to play by your rules.

Keep Your Focus. After eliminating an office time waster, immediately refocus on your priority tasks. You can gain several minutes simply by quickly getting back to what you were doing before the interruption.

Avoid Procrastination. When tempted to delay taking action on a task for whatever reason, whether it's dull, complex, or not urgent, for example, remind yourself that delay will only make your work in general much more complicated. Not only will you not finish the task but you will also constantly think about it, which will affect how well you handle other tasks. Your best solution is to commit to finishing the task, tell someone about your commitment, set a completion deadline, think about how good you will feel when you finish the task or what you will do as a self-reward for finishing it, and start work on the task immediately. Other anti-procrastination tips include delegating and breaking the task into simpler steps.

When tempted to delay taking action on a task for whatever reason, whether it's dull, complex, or not urgent, for example, remind yourself that delay will only make your work in general much more complicated.

Manage Telephone Calls. Although almost everyone seems to complain about telephone calls, phone conversations can be effective and efficient if you learn how to control them. When on the phone, be brief, to the point, and focused on work-related topics. Your assistant, if you have one, is integral in helping you screen out routine and inapplicable calls. Return routine calls during specific time periods; handle urgent ones immediately.

If you leave someone a message through an assistant or voice mail, do four things: give your name, specify the subject of the call, tell when you can and cannot be reached (to eliminate phone tag), and give your telephone number twice (for accuracy). Your voice mail message should ask callers to provide these same four pieces of information. When the recipient of a message knows the reason for the call, he or she can better prepare for returning the call. Finally, as a matter of courtesy, if you tell someone you will return his or her call, do it or have someone else return it for you.

Manage for Crisis. When an unexpected emergency occurs, it takes priority over your schedule and you delay or cancel anything you had planned to do. Your mission then is to handle the crisis so you can return to your important, nonurgent duties. The key to eliminating this time waster is to prevent crises, if possible. You can prevent some crises by analyzing the details of past crises and thoroughly planning to make similar crises less likely or at least knowing what actions to take when they happen. Keeping certain truck parts on the premises, for example, might prevent another delay of several hours if your only delivery truck broke down again. This, in turn, would save you the time you would have spent locating the parts in a crisis situation.

Avoid Waiting for Events or Answers. Waiting steals your time primarily in two ways: when you are temporarily stalled waiting for some activity to begin or when you are waiting for answers or information so that you can continue your work. In the first situation, the key is to always have something productive to do when confronted with the inevitable waiting situation; this will minimize your wasted time. Many people welcome periods of waiting because they can use that time productively to think or read without interruption. Those with long commutes often listen to professional development audio in their automobiles. To avoid wasting your time waiting for answers or information, go and dig for what you need instead of waiting for it to come to you. If someone is late in providing you with information, go to him or her and stress the importance of your getting this information as soon as possible. When you politely explain how you need this information for one of your priority tasks, he or she will likely consider it more urgent.

5. Maintain Control of Your Time

There are dozens of time management systems that you or your organization can purchase or devise. The most used systems for time management include calendars, to-do lists, master planning documents, and planners and organizers. If you have a choice in which one you can use, take the time to explore what is available and choose one you feel comfortable using as your sole organizing tool. Even though time management has evolved considerably over the years from handwritten lists to elaborate systems that keep track of your personal and professional goals and values, you may initially require only a simple system, depending upon the range and complexity of your responsibilities.

Calendars and to-do lists permit you to easily note appointments, various tasks, or long-range plans. Used alone, however, they typically do not allow you to effectively consolidate everything that you might do during the day, such as jotting down notes, tracking complicated tasks or projects that you have delegated to others, or managing frequent and recurring deadlines.

Time Management Systems

The minimum considerations for a time management system are that it be simple to use, updatable, and mobile; that it keep track of your short-, medium-, and long-term tasks and goals; that it be expandable to note telephone numbers, expenses, and other key information; and that it help you effectively control your time. Most systems will be comprehensive enough to allow you to permanently stop using scraps of paper or notes to keep track of appointments, telephone calls, or routine information. In light of this, you will probably want a system more advanced than a to-do list but possibly not one as elaborate as an electronic organizer. Some leaders may require a computer-based system if they oversee or participate in difficult projects, manage multiple customer or supplier relationships, or need frequent reminders.

A master planning document does these things by listing your significant tasks and activities over the upcoming weeks and months. It groups all these activities by priority or prioritizes them during specific days or weeks. Such a broad overview of your responsibilities will show you your activities at a glance and will make it easier to do detailed daily planning. You can list simple activities together on one sheet and devote a separate sheet to each of the more complicated projects and tasks. Most people who use master planning documents devise a format with which they are comfortable or use one of the many commercial products.

Planners and organizers are great for people who frequently travel or quickly need access to a broad range of information. They consolidate the features of the previously discussed tools and improve upon them by integrating time and goal management. With the intent of making you much more productive, some of them encourage you to explore your values and align them with your daily actions.

Traveling—however useful or even necessary for visiting customers or team members, inspecting operations, or attending conferences—is not a reason to lose control of your time. Determine first if the trip is necessary or if the work can be done through alternative means such as telephone or video conferencing. If the trip is necessary, could someone go in your place or could someone come to your location? If you need or choose to travel, consider the trip an extension of your workplace and continue using your priority and time management skills. A well-prepared travel checklist will quickly remind you or your assistant what personal and work-related items you need to take with you so that the trip will go smoothly.

Since you will be leading your organization and coordinating activities from a distance, there are four points to note. First, take special care to inform your team members in advance that you are departing so that they can properly plan for your absence and avoid inundating you with last-minute questions. Second, your superior and key co-workers must be able to contact you at any time. A good idea would be to give them a copy of your itinerary; write on it your hotel and cellular telephone number. Third, because traveling involves more uncertainty than working at the office, double-check all appointments and meetings to make sure they are still scheduled. Finally, to help keep your sanity and ability to react to on-the-road crises, allow plenty of time between appointments and flight connections. If you are a frequent traveler, consider joining airline, hotel, and rental car clubs, because they provide extra amenities and savings that can make your trip more enjoyable and productive.

As a final suggestion to maintain control of your time, consider taking a reading comprehension course. Although traditionally known as speed-reading courses, these seminars do much more: they help you achieve higher levels of productivity and performance. In addition to reading faster, you will learn how to increase your recall and comprehension of what you read. As a leader, this will help you in several ways. First, you will efficiently process the mountains of paperwork that flow across your desk and free up time to read more or to act on what you have just read. Second, you will learn proven techniques of abbreviated note taking and will soon use them during meetings, traveling, or on-site supervision. Finally, you will learn how to better comprehend difficult and lengthy material, such as technical, financial, or legal documents.

Manage Stress

Along with the enormity of your job comes unavoidable stress, which affects you differently than other challenges. It is useful, therefore, to develop your knowledge about stress so that you can recognize it and manage it. This will allow you, your subordinates, and your team members to cope more effectively with the inevitable stressful situations that occur in the workplace and, in turn, allow you to better focus on your daily priorities.

What is stress? Stress is your internal response to everything that happens to you. Higher stress levels usually manifest themselves in two ways: in your inherent circumstances, such as in your family problems, work challenges, or time constraints; and in your unique reactions to circumstances, such as in headaches, anxiety, denial, or serious physical problems. Stress intensity can range from a low level, such as when reading a document, to a high level, as when making a presentation to an audience. Temporary surges in your stress levels are not harmful and are difficult to prevent. When your system is routinely under moderate to high levels of stress, however, you will experience hormonal imbalances that could eventually lead to serious health problems.

One of your responsibilities as a leader is to proactively identify and ultimately reduce the stress in your organization. This is important for two reasons. First, by identifying stressed individuals and then committing to helping them, you will not only make them more productive, you often will identify major organizational problems and get them resolved too. Second, by becoming more aware of other people's stress, you can be more attentive to your own symptoms and then take action to help yourself. You experience the same types of stress as your team members, but since you carry the additional responsibilities of leadership, your stress levels can be higher. Your level of stress and your reaction to that stress will affect those around you; your objective is to not let it affect them negatively.

One of your responsibilities as a leader is to proactively identify and ultimately reduce the stress in your organization.

Spotting Stress

By talking with your team members and knowing what is happening in the workplace, you can spot some of the most common symptoms of stress, including an increase in employee hostility, a decrease in positive attitudes, excessive use of overtime, and an increase in family conflicts. You can remain alert to other stressful situations by observing specific employee indicators such as lethargy, illnesses, absenteeism, substance abuse, irritability, and a decrease in work performance.

There are four specific actions you can take to manage workplace stress.

Create and Maintain a Great Work Environment

As you use the leadership skills presented in this book, you will make tremendous progress in minimizing the stress in your organization. Pay close attention to all areas of your responsibilities and handle challenges as they arise, not later.

Subordinates need you to be realistic, fair, reasonable, honest, appreciative, participative, and caring. They do not need ambiguity, volatility, or indecisiveness. If they are convinced that you are concerned for their personal and professional welfare, they will cope better with workplace stress.

Encourage Open Communication

If your subordinates can easily approach you about workplace issues, such as job deadlines, career development, or any concern or dissatisfaction, they will continually relieve their stress instead of keeping it inside. Communicating periodically about stresses is a simple way for them to gain some control and power in the workplace, and it provides you with an excellent opportunity to offer them the encouragement and coaching they regularly need.

Advocate Healthy Living

Since most people do not sleep enough, exercise regularly, relax sufficiently, or eat properly, think of the opportunity you have to promote a healthy lifestyle for those who work with you. Not only will they appreciate your caring enough to think of them but they will also develop habits that will decrease their stress and help them live longer.

Stress Experts

There are experts in just about any city who can speak to your subordinates about healthy living; you also can distribute widely available literature. The advantages of these methods are that they help you avoid forcing people to cooperate and allow people to inform themselves and proceed at their own pace. Remember that your leadership actions speak louder than words, so take your own advice and pursue a healthy lifestyle.

Conduct Stress Management Training

Schedule training for your workers and expose them to these stress management concepts. Your company's healthcare agency may provide for it or a local hospital will be able to refer you to someone qualified to speak on the subject. It is ultimately the responsibility of each person to manage his or her own stress. Since stress pervades all areas of life, including family, social, and work, almost everyone will greatly benefit from formal stress management training.

Maintain Your Lead

A leader encounters a greater variety of challenges and usually has more complex responsibilities in the workday than other employees. This chapter has shown you specific techniques to prioritize these tasks in a way that will allow you to accomplish much more. The time management process will help you focus on your most important professional and personal objectives, use your time more efficiently, waste less time, and let others assume more of the work. Stress prevention will ensure that you continue to use your time efficiently and effectively, thus increasing your success as a leader.

Chapter 7

Project Management

Liz is a senior colleague in the analytics section of a marketing department in a medium-sized corporation. She was asked by her director to implement an approved, company-wide customer response system, which would be in an area overseen by another section within the marketing department. Gene is a district sales manager who volunteered to organize and implement a three-day sales meeting involving several districts within his state. What process can Liz and Gene use to get their tasks done successfully?

A PROJECT IS A UNIQUE UNDERTAKING THAT HAS A DISTINCT START AND finish, a separate budget, and an objective of producing a specific product, service, or event according to specific standards. Everyone works with projects, whether the projects are small, such as setting up a birthday party, or mammoth, such as planning an annual conference or building a manufacturing facility.

Projects differ from your usual day-to-day responsibilities because projects are one-time undertakings, not repetitive like your normal duties; require considerably more interdepartmental support, unlike the degree of departmental autonomy that normally exists; and are divided into specific sections that are sequenced and independently evaluated, unlike the unordered tasks that occur daily.

There are similarities, however, between projects and your daily operations. These include the need to use available resources to do the job and the necessity for the appropriate functional areas or subject matter experts to take responsibility and ownership of specific technical tasks under their realm of responsibility. This task ownership occurs even though the task may be part of someone else's project.

Regardless of their size, projects all share similar characteristics and processes. This chapter will present a leader's approach to project management that you can apply to all your project challenges at work, at home, or in the community. The objective is to provide an easy-to-implement process for project management, help you to organize your projects, and give you the flexibility to use your current organizational project management procedures. In time, through practice on the job or specific training, you will learn many more details, techniques, and styles of project management.

Managing projects involves utilizing your skills, the skills of team members, and established principles and methods to efficiently guide an otherwise unmanageable series of activities to their end. If you analyze your daily tasks, you can relate almost everything to a specific project. A telephone call could be part of your decision to buy a new information management system. Your brainstorming session with key colleagues could be the start of a new product launch. All projects contain similar tasks that must be performed with the cooperation of several individuals from different departments within and outside the organization. The objective of project management is simply to plan, organize, direct, and monitor this process, with the goal of producing the best end product or service that you can.

If you are in an organization that relies upon projects, it is likely you follow a prescribed methodology for managing projects, and you and your team members regularly train on the subject. Your company may even be heavily oriented toward project management as a primary method of structuring work, and you may have access to state-of-the-art computer programs to track every detail of a project. The principles you learn in this chapter still apply, however, and are important in providing you with a solid background that you can use no matter how proficient you are now, what techniques you use currently, or what size your company is.

There are several steps for successful project management; the extent of your involvement in each step will vary with each project.

> *Managing projects involves utilizing your skills, the skills of team members, and established principles and methods to efficiently guide an otherwise unmanageable series of activities to their end.*

▶ Choose the project manager.

▶ Establish objectives and requirements.

- ▶ Select the team.
- ▶ Plan the project.
- ▶ Manage the project.
- ▶ Monitor the project.
- ▶ Coordinate follow-up activities.

Choose the Project Manager

As a leader in your organization, you will often work as a project manager and be in charge of all or some aspects of a project. You will typically have this assignment in addition to your regular responsibilities. At other times, you will designate project managers and exercise supervisory responsibility over them. This section will help you to choose those people correctly.

It is important to designate project managers as soon as possible; this will enable them to be an integral part of the planning process from the early stages of the project. Due to the importance of finishing the project correctly and on time, you cannot choose project managers arbitrarily. They should have proven leadership abilities, appropriate technical skills, and sufficient cross-functional experience. If you have the luxury of choosing among several candidates, assessing three factors will help you choose the right person to manage your project: leadership ability, skills, and experience.

Assessing three factors will help you choose the right person to manage your project: leadership ability, skills, and experience.

Leadership Ability

The project manager should know how to lead a team of individuals energetically to accomplish a multifaceted project. Examine the candidates and judge if they have the variety of leadership experience necessary for your project. Since the project will require leadership skills, the candidates should have experience in using the skills that are presented in this book.

Technical Skills

It is imperative that project managers understand the technology and processes involved in the project. They do not have to be experts in the area, but they must have some depth of knowledge to effectively plan, monitor, and complete the project.

Cross-Functional Experience. The project manager will lead a team composed of individuals from various departments or functional areas within the organization. Look for someone who has worked in several areas or has

Abilities of Project Managers

The right person will be a confident and decisive leader who is particularly good at planning, implementing, delegating, problem solving, and handling multiple priorities. Since the project manager will be involved in directing the efforts of a diverse team, the person should be extremely adept in relationship skills such as communication, teamwork, conflict resolution, and coaching. Some candidates will have had experience managing similar projects; others will not, but do not automatically exclude them from consideration.

the organizational savvy to know how to approach these departments to garner support and resources.

Establish Objectives and Requirements

As the project manager, your initial work will be to clearly identify and define the major aspects of the project. By taking the time to do this correctly and thoroughly, you will save yourself time, expense, and aggravation later on. From the beginning, take detailed notes in a notebook or binder called a *project log*, which acts as a journal and clearly documents key decisions, comments, and promises made by any of the people involved in the project. It serves as institutional knowledge and will easily refresh your memory when needed or update other people if necessary.

Confer with the client so you can thoroughly grasp his or her intentions and needs. The project client is an accountable individual, not individuals or departments, who is committed to completing the project successfully and guiding you when necessary. Your client may be the person who tasked you with the project or someone that he or she designated or recommended within the organization. More likely, however, the client will be someone who has the most interest in the project or is funding the project. You may have to meet with the client two or three times to pinpoint the project's objectives and requirements. You will then have sufficient information to develop a tentative plan to discuss later in your meeting with key individuals.

Confer with the client so you can thoroughly grasp his or her intentions and needs.

Get approval to begin the project. Prepare a project proposal for the client that concisely incorporates all the information you have gathered. The key is to succinctly address all the major issues, background information, and assumptions that you and the client have made. The proposal serves as your official record of what you understand the client wants. It also will

66

Points to Cover with a Client

What are the objectives of the project? Determine what the client is looking for, how the project will serve a need or solve problems, if there are any special risks, and whether similar projects were tried previously.

▶ What is the anticipated schedule? Create a timeline with start, finish, and milestones.

▶ Who are the key people? Determine the final approval authority, other decision makers, and community liaisons.

▶ Is funding approved for the project? If not, determine when it will be approved and what the targeted cost is.

▶ What are the specifications for the end product, the standards, and the constraints? Specify details of quality, performance, reliability, applicable regulations, and any special considerations. Quantify this information whenever feasible.

serve as a key document that you and your project team will use until the completion of the project.

Assemble key individuals to define the project. Schedule a planning meeting that includes some of the following: the client, line managers who have the relevant expertise, your supervisor if requested, and any staff or peers whose input you need. Your client may prefer not to attend this meeting because he or she may not want to be involved with the details at this point. Encourage the client to attend part of the meeting if possible, because he or she will be invaluable in providing immediate clarification of any issues. Let the participants know in advance the purpose of the meeting and that you expect them to come prepared to discuss the project from their perspective and experience. This meeting will provide you with sufficient answers to update the client with any significant conclusions or challenges, arrive at better estimates, and proceed to the more detailed planning stage.

Soliciting input from all group members, analyze and discuss the project in detail. You already have the answers to some of the key questions, but the purpose of this meeting is to communicate them to the participants, validate your tentative conclusions, troubleshoot all major areas, and elicit buy-in from the participants, whose efforts will be crucial to successful project completion. During the meeting, first present the conclusions that you and your client reached. Then discuss the project in detail. Seek answers to these questions:

The purpose of the planning meeting is to communicate known answers to the participants, validate your tentative conclusions, troubleshoot all major areas, and elicit buy-in from the participants.

▶ How should the project be organized?

▶ What are the most important tasks and their major subtasks?

67

► What are the resource requirements for each category, such as people, equipment, and money?

► How will these resources be estimated, allocated, and controlled?

► Is the deadline realistic and achievable?

► What potential problems could occur?

Select the Team

You alone cannot complete the project; you will require the efforts of a cohesive group of skilled, committed, motivated, and responsible individuals. If you pay particular attention to the team's composition, responsibilities, and leadership, you will complete your project more effectively by generating superior planning and implementation tactics. This section will outline basic points about teamwork within the context of project management. Chapter 11 will further expand on the topic of teamwork.

These are the steps for creating a project team.

► List major staffing requirements.

► Identify sources of team members.

► Select specific team members.

► Create a skills inventory.

► Match skills with responsibilities.

► Assemble, inform, and organize the team.

List Major Staffing Requirements

To identify your major staffing requirements, estimate the number of people and kinds of skills that you will need to complete the project. For each position required, write a brief job description that will outline exactly what type of individual you need.

Identify Sources of Team Members

Sources include your staff, permanent staff in other departments, and part-time assistance such as temporary employees or consultants. Usually the human resources department will help you analyze employees and any part-timers or consultants who routinely assist the company. The human resources department may even centralize the process of staffing projects or give you suggestions about the etiquette involved in staffing from within the company; if so, this could simplify your task.

Seck out strong performers who have worked with you in the past. Especially note potential team members with critical skills. Avoid excluding otherwise qualified people who lack a certain skill; you later may be able to schedule training for them.

Select Specific Team Members

Once you know the type of team members you need and the departments in which they work, recruit them. Individually approach each supervisor and explain your needs and how he or she can help by supplying team members. If your organization routinely has projects or if its culture is supportive of projects, the supervisors will probably easily work with you to get the right staffing. If not, you will have to negotiate to get what you need; this will involve give-and-take from both you and the supervisors. If your efforts fail to satisfy your staffing needs, you can approach other supervisors or your senior leaders for assistance.

Sources of team members include your staff, permanent staff in other departments, and part-time assistance such as temporary employees or consultants.

Select with Care

Select your team carefully and sensitively with a firm respect for your organization's culture. Although you have the authority to staff your project, you can count on some resistance from the potential team members' supervisors, since they will not have complete use of their employees if you select them for your project.

It is always wise to interview the people you've selected before you officially make them part of your team. You want to ensure that they have a good attitude and team relationship skills and are sufficiently available for the duration of the project. The interview will permit you to explore their job experience, technical skills, and any other special skills they may have. If at the end of the interview you believe that they are the people you want working on your project, extend the offer to them.

It is always wise to interview the people you've selected before you officially make them part of your team.

Create a Skills Inventory

Once you have all the team members identified, itemize their skills by using a simple listing called a *skills inventory*. This valuable document will clearly record the team's skills and later ensure that you have both the right mix of team members and sufficient overlap among the skills in case a member becomes unavailable during the project. Though none of the team members will have exactly the same skills and expertise as the others, you certainly want each of the major skills requirements covered by two or more people, as described next.

Match Skills with Responsibilities

Prepare a *responsibilities chart* that clearly shows who has primary responsibilities for the tasks and who has supporting responsibilities. The chart officially records the project responsibilities of each team member. You will use it during the project to reassign work and to keep team members' supervisors informed of what their subordinates are doing. List all tasks vertically down the left column and the team members' names across the top. The goal is to assign the most qualified person to each task's primary position and then support each task with less-qualified people. Before you permanently assign team members to each of the tasks, use good judgment by seeking their input. This will help you identify any potential conflicts now rather than later, and it will increase the team members' long-term commitment to their project responsibilities.

Assemble, Inform, and Organize the Team

Meet with the team to introduce the members to each other and to explain the project—background and details, including objectives, work done so far, strategy, and the responsibilities chart. Then get them excited about it. They need to know how the project is important to the organization, that they are the best team for the project, and how it is crucial for them to accomplish their tasks on time, as a team, within budget, and according to project standards.

*N*ow is the time to get to work with your team to begin the planning the project in detail.

Make it clear to them that you are their leader for the project. Explain that, although they are permanently assigned to another department, you have operational control over them for the project and will provide details of their performance to their supervisor.

Prior to the Meeting

Before the first team meeting, arrange for all supervisors to personally express to their subordinates their support of the project and their desire for the subordinates to treat the project as an extension of their normal duties. It would also be a good idea for you to thank the functional supervisors for their support of your project; a solid relationship with each supervisor will help you later when you need to get tasks, decisions, and special favors handled quickly and without conflict.

Plan the Project

Your objective is to develop a project plan, which is a series of documents that explains all the project's details. It is foremost a communications plan that will let all interested parties know exactly who is on the team, where the team is headed, and how it will get there.

The purpose of project planning is to develop the details of a strategy that links the project's goals and objectives to specific implementing activities. During this process, you examine all your resources and constraints, such as personnel, supplies, time, and budgets, and organize them into a strategy by using planning tools. These tools will be described in detail later in the chapter.

You plan with your team. Since you alone cannot possibly have all the information to create an effective plan, expect to involve as many experienced people in the planning process as necessary.

There are five steps in creating a project plan.

- Design the project.
- Estimate the project.
- Schedule the project.
- Budget the project.
- Finalize and approve the plan.

The purpose of project planning is to develop the details of a strategy that links the project's goals and objectives to specific implementing activities.

Design the Project

In designing your project, you first specify the actual tasks to be performed during the project. This list of tasks is called a *work breakdown structure.* The work breakdown structure is one of your most important project tools, because it concisely shows what needs to be done and provides a framework for other project documents. For detail and accuracy, develop the work breakdown structure during several meetings with your team and, if necessary, by using questionnaires targeted to functional supervisors.

First, list all the major categories of activities of the project. You can base these categories on any one of several factors, such as stages of time, product development cycle, functional work areas, and major components of the product or service.

Next, determine all the second and third levels of activities that must be completed to achieve each first-level end product. Once you have identified all the levels, list the tasks that must be completed for each level.

The work breakdown structure is one of your most important project tools, because it concisely shows what needs to be done and provides a framework for other project documents.

Project: Office Redesign			
Level 1:	*Major Activity* Construction		*Major Activity* Temporary Office
Level 2:	*Activity* Physical Design	*Activity* Computer Wiring	*Activity* Site Location	*Activity* Relocation
Level 3:	*Tasks* Retain architect Review proposal	*Tasks* Determine needs Examine equipment Seek bids	*Tasks* Locate realtor Examine sites Sign lease	*Tasks* Hire movers Choose day Curtail work

Figure 7-1. Work breakdown structure chart (partial)

Figure 7-1 shows a partially completed chart of a work breakdown structure for an office redesign project. It identifies two of several major activities, along with their subordinate activities and tasks. Its list of specific tasks begins at level three, but there could have easily been another level or two of subactivities before the task listing began.

Continue this listing process for each major activity category until you reach a task level where you can estimate the task's completion time and resource costs and where you are certain that no major task has been left out. Usually this occurs at level four or five, but it could go lower. You and your team now identify for each of the tasks the owners (those people primarily responsible for the tasks), the people who will support these owners, the end product, and the quality standards. Throughout the process, you can divide the team into subgroups to analyze specific activities and their tasks. However, to prevent faulty conclusions, it is important to have each subgroup defend its conclusions in front of the other members of the team.

As the project manager, you should know prior to the beginning of your first team meeting what the first- and second-level activities will most likely be. You surmised this from your earlier discussions with the client and key individuals. Knowing these sublevels will give you and your team the right direction to proceed. Include sufficient detail to be able to later quantify the project's cost and duration, but avoid using too much detail at this point. To promote team discussion, it is helpful to chart your work breakdown structure on a chalkboard or flipchart.

The next step in the process is to develop the project's network. The project network shows the associations or dependencies among the tasks. The process of constructing the network is called *dependency analysis*. By sequencing the tasks on a chart, you will see exactly how each task relates to the others.

The first part of this process is to determine the interrelationships among all the tasks on your work breakdown structure chart by identifying each of them with the task preceding it. Since the work breakdown structure chart shown lists just two major activities in a large project, not all task interdependencies are given nor are the task listings complete. In reality, you will need all tasks listed in order to completely identify task interdependence. But the example shows you how the concept works.

Group tasks according to their major activity and assign them an identification number of your choice. The key point to remember is every task is accomplished in one of three ways: immediately after another task, at the same time as other tasks, or at the beginning or end of a project. Find the first task that can start the project and identify it by a dash in the fourth column in the project network chart that follows (Figure 7-2). Tasks 1.1 and 3.1 are the first ones and can begin simultaneously if you choose.

Next find the tasks that can be immediately done after tasks 1.1 and 3.1; identify them with the numbers of the tasks preceding them. For the remainder of the analysis, always ask which other tasks can be started and ongoing with each new task you analyze. These will be assigned the same predecessor task as the new task. If there are no such parallel tasks, determine what the next task is. This process continues until all the tasks are linked.

After you have determined the dependencies, define the end products for each task. The product is the result of completing the task. Unlike the task, which is listed as an action verb, the product is a noun. The final step is to estimate the time it will take to complete each task; place this number in the duration column. The next section will discuss duration estimates in more detail.

If you prefer a graphic approach for dependency analysis, there is a popular charting method you can use. A PERT (Program Evaluation and Review Technique) chart is a type of flowchart that depicts sequencing of tasks. Your objective is to list each task on sticky note cards and order them from left to right on a chalkboard or wall, starting with the lowest-level task that can naturally start the project. Then search for tasks that can be going on at the same time as this first task. If you find that some tasks have the same predecessor, then these could begin at the same time and should be placed accordingly.

Project: Office Redesign				
Task ID#	Description	End Product	Preceding Task	Duration
Construction – Physical Design				
1.1	Retain architect	Committed architect	–	2 days
1.2	Review proposal	Proposal knowledge	1.1	3 days
1.3	Seek employee input	Employee collaboration	1.2	3 days
Construction – Wiring				
2.1	Determine needs	Needs document	1.3	4 days
2.2	Examine equipment	Top equipment choices	2.1	2 days
2.3	Seek bids	Bid variety	2.2	3 days
Temporary Office – Site Location				
3.1	Locate realtor	A committed realtor	–	2 days
3.2	Examine sites	Site knowledge	3.1	4 days
3.3	Sign lease	Signed lease	3.2	2 days
Temporary Office – Relocation				
4.1	Hire movers	Moving contract	4.2	2 days
4.2	Choose move day	Company-wide move day	3.3	1 day
4.3	Curtail work	Relocatable work force	4.2	2 days

Figure 7-2. Project network chart (partial)

The PERT chart of the work breakdown structure's project network (Figure 7-3) graphically depicts the project network's sequencing of tasks.

Estimate the Project

You can make the process of estimation simple or complex, depending upon your particular project, your level of expertise, and the forecasting techniques used in your organization. Despite the potential complexity, the process is straightforward. You and your team analyze each task and decide realistically how long it will take to complete it. Write the estimates in the duration column of your project network chart. If there is disagreement on the estimate, delay a decision until the task owner can analyze it and make

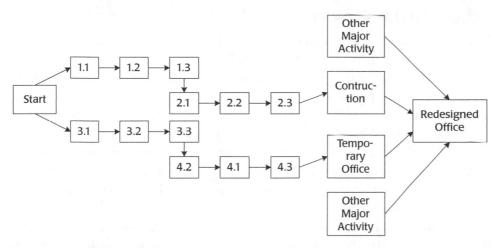

Figure 7-3. PERT chart of the work breakdown structure's project network

a suggestion to the team. Before approving a final estimate for a task, ask if it is realistic considering the task owner's experience, knowledge, and time available for the task.

Once you determine the duration of each task within the project network chart, you have enough information to compute the anticipated duration of the project or its *critical path*. This is done simply by determining which sequence of tasks, from the project's start to finish, is the longest. In the abbreviated example, the tasks along the construction activity constitute the critical path because 16 days are required for construction and only 13 for the temporary office. As the project manager, one of your major responsibilities is to frequently monitor task activity along the critical path because disruptions in accomplishing these tasks will lengthen your project's duration. If you complete the tasks sooner than expected, you will shorten your project's duration.

Your job as the project's leader is to understand all the nuances of task duration so that you can supervise a valid estimation process. You must know how to speed up completion of the project or what to do when faced with unexpected bottlenecks. It would be helpful before beginning a project to study a manual on project management or consult with an experienced project manager in your organization. You then will have access to detailed knowledge and techniques that only a comprehensive source can give you. As you practice using the many estimation techniques, they will become second nature to you.

Your job as the project's leader is to understand all the nuances of task duration so that you can supervise a valid estimation process.

Schedule the Project

Placing each task on a *timeline* gives you a broad picture of the task sequencing for the project, which will be useful in your final planning. There are many ways to schedule a project. At the very least, your scheduling document should have two axes, a vertical sequencing of the tasks and a horizontal listing of time.

Your organization may have its own scheduling format or it may use one of the many computer software programs. These tools will help you better manage your project, but you cannot completely rely upon them to monitor events because it is you who is responsible for the project, not a management tool.

The simple scheduling document shown in Figure 7-4 is patterned after the popular Gantt planning chart. Notice that each task is scheduled for completion during a specific time period. The critical path tasks, numbers 1.1 through 2.3, are listed in the priority position at the top of the table. The remaining tasks, which are on a noncritical path, are shown next. Tasks on noncritical paths have *float time*, additional time in which to accomplish them before the critical path tasks are finished. If necessary, this float time can be used to keep your project on schedule when unplanned events cause you to miss your anticipated timelines.

If your schedule shows that you cannot finish the project by the comple-

Task ID#	Days 0	1	2	3	4	5	6	7	8	9	10	11	12	13	14	15	16
1.1		▓	▓														
1.2				▓	▓												
1.3							▓	▓									
2.1										▓	▓	▓					
2.2													▓	▓			
2.3															▓	▓	▓
3.1		▓															
3.2				▓	▓	▓											
3.3								▓									
4.2										▓							
4.1											▓	▓					
4.3													▓	▓			

Figure 7-4. Gantt chart (partial)

tion date, make adjustments to the individual tasks in order to compress your timeline. Verify that all critical tasks are crucial to the project, then examine if you can redesign them so you can accomplish them more quickly.

To speed up these tasks, consider redistributing them or assigning additional resources to them. Another alternative is to review the sequencing of tasks and attempt to complete more of them at the same time rather than sequentially. Finally, you could start a task after its predecessor is only partially completed, thus reducing the total time committed to that particular path.

Budget the Project

Your next objective is to assign specific team members to each task and identify other needed resources. The net effect of this step is a firm estimate of the cost of the project. This step is commonly called *resource and cost loading* and can require several revisions before you develop a viable budget.

The key to task assignment is to balance the workload equitably within the project.

The key to task assignment is to balance the workload equitably within the project. Consider your team members in terms of factors such as expertise, availability during the project, and whether a member has a primary or supporting role for the task. Identify the percentage of time each team member will work on each task during each time period. If, after making the assignments, you determine that an imbalance exists, there are creative ways to further balance the workload and still keep your project on course, such as using overtime or temporary help to eliminate a labor shortage. After communicating the assignments to your team, ask them to determine what other resources are needed to accomplish their tasks.

Once you identify the required resources, coordinate their use with others who need them. This intraorganizational balancing may be centrally controlled within your organization, but most likely it is handled at each functional level or department. Regardless, this coordination is crucial to your project's success and you must do it before obtaining final project approvals.

Coordination is crucial to your project's success and you must do it before obtaining final project approvals.

After coordinating the resources, accurately determine all the costs related to the project. Using input from the team and the previously identified supporting departments within your organization, identify the costs associated with each individual task. Include costs related to personnel, overhead, training, research, and all other resources, such as material, equipment, and supplies. Most departments can easily identify the costs after you give them detailed information on the tasks, such as specifications and standards. Document the costs on an easily revised budget document, such as on a spreadsheet or project management software.

Finalize and Approve the Plan

By now, you have spent considerable time and effort in developing the best plan for your project. Assemble all your planning documents and examine your work objectively to determine if you have planned a feasible project. Check whether you are meeting the client's guidelines and project objectives, using the assigned resources effectively and efficiently, identifying frequent milestones to evaluate progress, and assigning responsibilities for every task.

Contingency Planning

Since you and your team members already have discussed possible disruptions to your project, now is a good time to formalize contingency plans with them. Develop these plans from an in-depth risk assessment in which you examine all areas of the project and prioritize them for their riskiness and potential for failure or disruption.

Contingency plans specify what you will do when events do not proceed exactly as planned or if resource and cost factors change. For example, critical tasks could take longer than expected, you could lose a key worker, or a major resource could be disrupted. In addition, identify what preventive measures you can take now to minimize the possibility and impact of disruptions, especially in the high-risk tasks, such as assigning a risky critical task to a top team member or estimating a critical task's duration more closely.

Once you have finalized the plan, your objective is to get final concurrence from all key individuals and to proceed with the project. Obtain written approval from departments that are supporting the project and from your supervisor, if necessary. Present the project's final outline to your client and explain the major areas of your plan, specifically noting any changes from your previous meetings. The client now decides if your plan is acceptable, given his or her knowledge of competing requirements within your organization, such as other projects, funding, and resource constraints. Once the client grants approval, notify your team and everyone else involved in the project.

Manage the Project

By completing the steps thus far in the project management cycle, you have done the most difficult part of the work, even though you have yet to start the project. You have now assembled a project team of people who understand what to do, how to do it, and when to do it.

> ## Preparatory Work Pays Off
>
> This detailed preparatory work will ultimately save you a tremendous amount of time and enable you to concentrate on completing the project in a timely manner. You will rely on your leadership skills to keep your team enthused, encouraged, and focused on the right path. Because these skills are so important, they are discussed in depth in later chapters.

Start the Project

Communication during the implementation phase is crucial because of the certainty of change, the possibility of disruptions, and the need for team and interdepartmental coordination. As the leader, it is your responsibility to create and maintain an atmosphere where everyone feels free to raise questions, seek guidance, and make suggestions.

This communication starts at the kickoff meeting, during which you will present your team with all the project's details. These details, which should not surprise the team members in light of their recent input into the planning process, will include organizational structure and responsibilities, assignments and timelines, policies and procedures, and reporting and control mechanisms. Tell them you plan to regularly update them, the functional managers, and the client, so the team members must keep you regularly updated.

Since you are the person on the team with the most knowledge and broadest overview of the project, it is imperative for you to stay involved in all aspects of the project. This will make it easier to spot trends and identify problems at the early stages, thus giving you more reaction time to solve the problems. Staying involved means daily monitoring of task progress, financial developments, and resource conditions. The best way to do this is to continually use the project's control procedures you developed during the planning process. You can count on staying busy, conferring with a multitude of people, and resolving several conflicts each day.

Communication during the implementation phase is crucial because of the certainty of change, the possibility of disruptions, and the need for team and interdepartmental coordination.

Respond to Change

Plan on encountering many changes to your project because no project is completed without some change to the original plan. These changes will start occurring within hours of obtaining the plan's final approval and will continue to the project's end. The changes typically affect two major areas, the end product and the plan. Your reaction to these changes will determine whether or not you complete your project successfully. It is your responsibility to identify and study these changes, then to respond with a viable solution that will allow you to continue on with your project management.

Now that you have noted this inevitable onslaught of modifications, a simple solution is to have a well-prepared change management plan that will easily allow you to integrate the changes into your project cycle. The ability to adapt to and implement change as a strategic leadership skill is the topic of Chapter 18; its application in project management is discussed next.

*P*lan on encountering many changes to your project because no project is completed without some change to the original plan.

Changing the End Product. These types of changes, which modify in some way your end product, originate either from the internal environment, with key individuals involved in the process, such as the client or team members, or from the external environment, such as in technology, government, or business. For example, your client may decide after approving the plan that he or she wants to make changes to the end product specifications. A team member may recommend a major change based upon information that he or she discovered while working on the project. Emerging technologies may affect how certain tasks are completed. Finally, new regulatory constraints or the competition's moves may require that you alter aspects of the end product.

Your responses to these concerns must be well reasoned, because a minor change in the end product could involve significant changes to the project plan, such as in cost, resources, and scheduling. To assist you in choosing a response, involve other people in a change management process. The person who believes that a change is necessary should submit a written request through you to a committee that has responsibility to consider, investigate, and approve the change. The committee is composed of representatives of the functional areas or departments involved in the project, the individual who has the authority to fund the change, key organizational decision makers, and you as the chairperson. The committee has the authority to decide if the change request warrants further action or not and, if so, to approve an investigation, if justified, to determine the details of the change and its impact on the project, and to approve or disapprove the change request and its funding.

As the project manager, you will lead the committee and control this process to ensure that it works efficiently and matters don't get bogged down in committee. Do this by monitoring ongoing actions, keeping committee members informed on the status of each action, and reminding the committee members that since their time and their subordinates' time is valuable, they must make change decisions intelligently and quickly. Once a change has been approved, integrate it into your project by updating your scheduling and control documents, assigning task responsibility, and keeping your team updated.

Changing the Plan. As just shown, a change to the project's end product will most certainly cause you to make some adjustments in your plan. The other type of major change does not immediately change the end product but it changes the plan that you have developed to produce that product. Whenever any aspect of your plan is altered, such as cost, schedule, or resources, the change must be managed. This type of change can originate from the internal environment of client, team members, process, resources, and the organization's hierarchical levels, or from the external environment of government, regulation, economy, competition, and society. Adding complexity to the situation, change may occur on global, national, state, or local levels. Regardless of where the change originates or what the change is, you have to expect threats to your plan and to be prepared to respond to them.

When dealing with changes to your plan, use a different approach from the end-product change management process suggested for changes in the end product. In most cases, the changes will occur whether you want them to or not. Your best reaction, therefore, is to develop policies and procedures that will allow you to smoothly integrate the changes into your plan.

First, ensure that all team members know that you want to be notified of all significant changes immediately, while less important changes can wait until a regularly scheduled time, such as a weekly meeting. It is up to you to determine what is significant and communicate this to your team. Second, clearly define those changes you want to approve personally and those that you delegate to leaders on your team; then, enforce this rule. Third, since you will probably make changes to your plan regularly, make sure that you communicate the changes to people who need this information, including team members, the client, and other departments. Finally, while realizing that change is inevitable, do not make changes without considering their impact and whether there are other options to try first.

When dealing with changes to your plan, use a different approach from the end-product change management process suggested for changes in the end product.

Monitor the Project

Monitoring a project simply means knowing how close you are to achieving the components of your plan and then using this information to take any corrective actions necessary to put the project back on course. Monitoring, sometimes referred to as controlling, involves much more than passively watching the events of your project unfold. The leadership skill of monitoring is discussed in more detail in the next chapter, but it is addressed in this chapter as it pertains to project management.

You can monitor best by involving yourself daily in the activities of your project and team members and by instituting formalized control procedures. Each day, go where there is project activity. By actually observing team members as they complete their tasks, you will see firsthand your plan in action and instinctively track your progress. As a result, you will quickly know of problems before they become crises and you will be in a better position to react to them. Not only will you more thoroughly understand the individual tasks and their relation to the overall project but you will also be able to talk with team members in their own environment. They will be more likely to speak frankly with you and raise issues that they might have avoided had you met in your office. While conferring with your team members, praise those who are doing a great job or making particularly good suggestions. This will motivate them to greater achievement and prove to them that you are an involved, approachable leader who cares not only about the project but about them as well.

In addition to your daily involvement in the project, it is essential to have formal monitoring procedures that will supplement your on-site efforts. Some procedures will be mandated to you by the client, regulatory authorities, or your organization; you can develop others. The results, which you should usually gather and examine at least weekly, will help you objectively analyze your project's status, confirm what you discovered during informal monitoring, and get the detailed information you need to prepare status reports. In a formal monitoring process, you must do the following:

▶ Collect information and identify variances.

▶ Analyze the causes and effects of the variances.

▶ Take corrective action.

▶ Communicate the action to your team and others.

Collect Information and Identify Variances

Use the planning documents you developed to analyze your progress in all areas, including cost, task accomplishment, schedule, labor, and resource use. The planning documents will indicate where your project should be and the information you collect will show you where the project is; the difference between the two is the *variance*.

Collect information from team members through personal contact, scheduled review meetings, and project-tracking documents. These documents should require only the information you need; plan on collecting them at a regularly scheduled time. To keep your team members concentrating on their project work, avoid seeking information from them when you can obtain it from your organization's functional departments, such as human resources, payroll, or accounting. Armed with this information, identify the variances from your plan.

Analyze the Causes and Effects of the Variances

Using the problem-solving method described in Chapter 5, determine the causes of the variances and their projected effect upon the project. Possible causes include higher-than-expected resource cost, low team member performance, or unrealistic estimates. Possible effects include increases in project cost, duration, or risk. If you do not anticipate that the variances will have any effect, do nothing. However, if you anticipate the variances will negatively affect the project, take corrective action.

Take Corrective Action

Modify the plan to eliminate the variance. You often will be able to make changes in the plan without significantly altering your budget or timeline, such as by shifting resources or compressing the schedule. If you determine you will need additional resources or that new deadlines must be approved in order to deliver a quality end product within the planned time frame, obtain clearance from the functional department or the client, if necessary. If you do not obtain the additional resources that will allow you to complete a quality project as planned, then you are obligated to negotiate a change in the scope of the project.

Communicate the Action to Your Team and Others

Because your decision to correct the variances will alter your plan, you must communicate any changes to team members, functional departments, and the client. Do this by issuing status reports and revised plans and by conducting regular meetings and formal presentations. You will probably update your team members more frequently than the other parties; tailor the updates to your audience by giving more detailed information to your team than to the functional departments or the client.

It is equally important to keep people who are not on the team properly updated on the project's status. You will gain more cooperation if you make a special effort to keep them updated, both informally throughout the course of the project and formally at scheduled presentations. The key to effective communication is to clearly explain how the project is doing overall in terms of schedule and cost, what has recently occurred, what corrective action will

Because your decision to correct the variances will alter your plan, you must communicate any changes to team members, functional departments, and the client.

be taken, and what you need your listeners to do. Remember to use any encounters with your team members as opportunities to seek their input about all aspects of the project. In addition to issuing status reports to your team, periodically update and issue a revised plan whenever the plan changes. Note the changes specifically in order to save everyone reading time.

Coordinate Follow-up Activities

As you reach the end of your project, coordinate the transition of the final product from your team to the client.

As you reach the end of your project, coordinate the transition of the final product from your team to the client. Typically, this involves arranging for inspections, testing, and installation, if applicable. Redistribute any excess resources to the functional departments or according to your plan. Prepare a summarized project report for the client that details your major project accomplishments, significant events that altered the plan, and any major lessons you learned that could benefit the client. Also prepare a detailed internal report that compiles the main experiences of the team during the project. Feel free to be candid about difficulties, successes, and recommendations.

Your final action will be to reward your team members for a job well done. You probably have been rewarding them throughout the project, but now is the time to make sure that they know how much you, the functional departments, and the client appreciate their efforts. At a minimum, schedule the client to personally recognize your team members and thank them for their hard work. Your team members also will appreciate a letter of thanks from you, an end-of-project party, and recognition from their functional supervisor.

Chapter 8

Monitoring

John wants to periodically evaluate the progress of his team's latest information technology upgrade project. The project is essential to an expansion plan for his company and he wants to ensure without doubt that the project remains on track. What are his options?

MONITORING IS A CONTINUAL PROCESS THAT YOU USE TO CHECK progress in all your leadership activities. It provides you with a framework to boost your goals into reality, your plans into action, your instructions to subordinates and team members into accomplishments, and your organization's objectives into success.

A crucial aspect of monitoring is a proactive effort to not only observe what is happening but also do something about it if necessary. This effort involves affecting the potential outcome of events by changing the behavior of people or other resources with which you are involved. It also relieves you of the need to wait until a project ends, a subordinate completes a task, or a crisis arrives to discover that there are significant problems that need correction.

When you monitor while doing your leadership duties, you will reap several benefits. First, you will better understand the challenges, issues, and concerns facing your team and organization. Knowing what is actually happening

A crucial aspect of monitoring is a proactive effort to not only observe what is happening but also do something about it if necessary.

in your organization, not just what you think is going to happen, will give you the knowledge and conviction to direct team members to the proper path. Second, monitoring allows you to quickly identify bottom-line trends that signal a threat to you and your organization. These dangers include unexplained declines in profits, revenue, operational performance, or customer satisfaction; unexpected variances from your plans, directives, or intentions; and people-related issues such as discontent and high turnover. Finally, if you monitor your environments consistently, including your business, economic, political, and cultural environments, you will spot more slowly evolving trends that might impact you, your team, and your organization.

Monitoring Tips

You can easily integrate monitoring into all your duties because almost everyone is aware of the concept and expects monitoring. Despite the obvious need for monitoring, some people resent it as a manipulative process used to keep track of their activities. It's typically called "controlling," a term that suggests images of dominance and power. Your challenge is to promote monitoring as a useful, necessary, and positive activity that is crucial to everyone in the organization. You do this by communicating the benefits of monitoring to your team, clearly publicizing the methods you use, and consistently using your results to make needed changes quickly and decisively.

Use of Monitoring

Monitoring is either anticipative or reactive and is implemented by either formal or informal systems.

Although monitoring is simple to understand and to do, it is helpful to examine how to use it in the context of your leadership responsibilities. Monitoring is either *anticipative* or *reactive* and is implemented by either *formal* or *informal* systems.

Anticipative and Reactive Monitoring

Leaders are responsible for both anticipating future events and anticipating the consequences of unexpected events. A well-devised monitoring system gives you feedback that will help you accurately predict outcomes by indicating whether your plan and strategy are working as envisioned, such as in the areas of costs, production quality, employee retention, or goals. Likewise, if an unexpected event occurs, such as the absence of key employees or a customer crisis, your consistent monitoring habits will have made you more knowledgeable about the potential consequences of a key absence or an unhappy customer. You then will more quickly predict the results of either of these two events and make a better decision about how to respond.

After evaluating reports, conversations, performance, or information about a past event, a leader uses this knowledge to positively influence the outcome of future events and not repeat mistakes. For example, if your monitoring shows you that your organization gets more telephone inquiries on Mondays, you plan to have more assistance available on Mondays. If customers leaving your restaurant tell you that the food was great but the service was terrible, you take action to eliminate the cause of this poor service.

Formal and Informal Procedures

Several procedures exist that enable you or other leaders to formally monitor your plans and activities. External auditing, performed by certified public accountants, is a routine procedure used to verify the organization's financial records. As a leader, you can extend this concept by using personnel from outside the organization, such as consultants, to examine and comment upon any aspect of your responsibilities. Internal, or operational, auditing is similar to external auditing but is done by you or other organizational personnel and it can address any aspect of the organization. The purpose is to check the organizational systems, operations, and procedures to verify that operational plans are being implemented.

As mentioned in Chapter 7, during the discussion of monitoring the project, a leader develops situational monitoring procedures, such as a schedule or budget, to use in assessing specific activities and projects. A leader also uses these formal procedures in numerous instances throughout the day, such as in performance management or other reporting systems. The payroll department, for example, may require you to verify the work attendance of your subordinates. Moreover, the organization may mandate monitoring procedures to be used by everyone. We will examine some of these formal methods later in the chapter.

An informal method to keep track of your responsibilities is an outstanding way to supplement your formal monitoring procedures. There is nothing magical about this process. It involves using all your leadership skills to remain involved with the activities of everyone with whom you work, including your subordinates, peers in all organizational departments, and customers. The next section presents a monitoring process that you can use and tailor to all your duties.

The Monitoring Process

Monitoring is an essential component of everything you do. You must integrate it into all your leadership activities. It will make your job easier and less frustrating, make your efforts more effective and efficient, and save you an enormous amount of time. Your monitoring often will be simple, occasional, and broad; at other times it will be detailed, intense, and focused. In addition to helping you fulfill your duties, monitoring will encourage your subordinates and team members to do their jobs well. Since they know you will check their work performance, being aware of your potential monitoring activities will give them a goal—to perform well according to the expectations that you and they agree upon.

Monitoring is an essential component of everything you do. You must integrate it into all your leadership activities.

The monitoring process in this chapter is derived from many processes that you probably see in your organization. Use it as a format in developing your own unique informal monitoring systems that you can use at work.

An effective monitoring process includes these four steps.

▶ Establish the monitoring plan.
▶ Communicate the plan.
▶ Evaluate the performance.
▶ Guide the performance.

Establish the Monitoring Plan

Develop separate plans of action to monitor each of your responsibilities, including recurring duties, one-time activities, or delegated tasks. The plans do not all have to be written, exhaustive, or unique; they simply need to persuade you that you have an effective way to check on progress for each activity. In developing your plan, define what activity to monitor, how well others must perform the activity, and how best to monitor the activity. Do this by identifying the objective, standards of performance, and monitoring procedure.

Develop separate plans of action to monitor each of your responsibilities.

The objective of each task or activity must be clearly identified, time-specific, measurable, and stated simply, so that you and your team members understand without doubt what you must do to satisfactorily complete the task. An objective gives both you and your team a target at which to aim; having no objective will result in indiscriminate aiming. For example, it is not enough to say that you want satisfied customers; you have to clearly express an objective by stating that you want to achieve 95 percent positive comments each week on customer surveys.

Standards of performance are intermediate checkpoints to keep you on the right path toward accomplishing your objective. Sometimes referred to as mini-objectives, criteria, or expectations, standards break down the objective into more manageable pieces and provide you with early warning if you are not on track. You can state the standards quantitatively or qualitatively, as long as they are clear indicators of performance. Standards can be described in many ways, such as in cost, revenue, investment, or intangible terms. As is the case with your objectives, clearly define your standards so that they are time-specific and measurable. In the previous customer service example, typical standards could include a telephone-on-hold time limit of one minute, total telephone time limit of three minutes, or zero tolerance for employee ambivalence or rudeness. Each of these standards contributes to the overall objective of 95 percent positive comments.

Devise monitoring procedures that you will use for the task; they may be strictly formal, informal, or a combination. They could include written or oral reports, meetings, presentations, spot checks of operations, or elaborate procedures. As is true with your leadership style, you cannot use just one type of monitoring procedure for all your activities because the procedure may be inapplicable or ineffective. Tailor the monitoring, therefore, to each of your major responsibilities.

Choosing Monitoring Procedures

Your choice of monitoring procedures depends upon many factors, including the importance and nature of the monitored activity, your level of knowledge and experience with the activity, and the degree of experience and expertise of participants in the activity. The procedures should be simple for others to understand and implement, easy for you to integrate into your daily duties, and effective in helping you keep track of your responsibilities. They must be flexible enough to still work effectively in the event of a major disruption to your plans. It is important, though, that you regularly review your procedures to ensure that they remain realistic. Finally, use the procedures consistently; otherwise they will not be of great use to you.

There are two key points to remember when designing your monitoring procedures.

Make ample use of personal contact between you and those involved in the activity; closely listen to, observe, and question people. You will learn many more details than you would have by only reviewing a report. You can never ask too many questions about what is happening with your subordinates or the progress of their activities.

Integrate your monitoring into your time management system so that you can consistently schedule time to monitor. Use the allotted time to review reports, inspect processes, and interact with people.

Communicate the Plan

Your subordinates and others must know what your monitoring plan is, how you will evaluate their performance, how the monitored activity relates to other people in the organization, and what the potential rewards are for success in the activity. If you do not properly communicate this information, you will dramatically decrease the likelihood of achieving the objective according to standards. You can use several means to communicate the monitoring plan, such as in team meetings, personal contact with key subordinates, or written guidance. It is essential, though, that the monitoring plan, like all other information for which you as the leader are responsible, be correctly transmitted to the lowest levels of your organization.

Your subordinates and others must know what your monitoring plan is and what the potential rewards are for success in the activity.

Evaluate the Performance

This step is similar to step three of the problem-solving process of Chapter 5: you compare the actual results with the desired results. If you have carefully and thoughtfully prepared the standards of performance, then it will be simple to measure the performance and examine the results. If there is an unfavorable difference between actual and desired results, you as the leader must take action to guide the performance to where it should be.

Guide the Performance

Using your leadership skills, take any action necessary to correct the performance and ensure that the activity gets back on track according to plan. This could involve directing your team to take certain actions to correct the problem or devising and implementing a new procedure to solve the problem. Every member of the team must understand that there is a problem and that they, working together, are going to correct the problem and keep it from recurring. Remember to praise them for any outstanding work and remind them how important they are to the success of the activity. After guiding the performance, continue the monitoring process by reevaluating performance and providing additional guidance until you have achieved your objective.

Using your leadership skills, take any action necessary to correct the performance and ensure that the activity gets back on track according to plan.

Formal Monitoring Procedures

Much information on formal monitoring procedures is available for you to study when you choose. To guide you, this section will briefly highlight some of the most popular methods, many of which you probably already use. By no means exhaustive, this list will give you at least an idea of the variety of formal monitoring procedures.

Budgets

Budgets are primarily numerical planning documents that you and your organization develop to achieve certain objectives. They traditionally have been, however, a popular form of monitoring because they permit you to easily compare plans with actual events and then to take corrective action. Types of budgets include revenue and expense, cash, or physical budgets pertaining to nonmonetary resources.

Financial Information

Financial data helps you to access the past and current financial status of your organization and selected departments, to make better decisions, and to understand financial and operational trends. Although you might not use financial information as frequently as other monitoring tools, it nevertheless will provide you with a wealth of knowledge and insight if you choose to analyze it and use it in conjunction with your other monitoring procedures. You will increasingly rely on these financial monitoring tools as you assume more of a leadership role in your organization. Pay particular attention to the financial documents that pertain to your responsibilities. Ask the originating departments if they can separate the bulk information to provide you with details on your specific areas of responsibility. It also would be helpful to study a brief introductory book on finance and accounting because it will give you greater understanding and show you how financial information relates to you and your responsibilities. Your knowledge of these areas also will help you as you converse with the senior and interdepartmental leaders in your organization.

Financial data helps you to access the past and current financial status of your organization and selected departments, to make better decisions, and to understand financial and operational trends.

Several specific items will be of interest to you. The financial statements, including the balance sheet, income statement, and cash flow statement, show the overall financial picture of the company. When you compare them with previous statements, you can spot trends that are developing in your organization. Use these statements and other data to determine financial ratios, which give you the statistics to compare your organization with similar ones in your industry, and to analyze trends. It is beyond the scope of this chapter to discuss them in detail, but understand that these interrelated ratios will help you spot potential problems and fix deficiencies before they become worse.

Quality Assurance

Quality assurance is fundamentally a process of ensuring that your organization produces its goods or services as intended. It is known by several names, including quality control, quality assurance, and total quality. There is practically universal agreement that most organizations need some form of quality program in order to anticipate and react to inferior production or service efforts. A well-devised and -implemented quality program that monitors the operations in your department or organization is a sound business tool. There are many variations of such programs, but most include relying upon statistical processes, monitoring customer satisfaction, controlling costs, and committing to continuous improvement.

*M*onitoring the performance of each of your subordinates and communicating to them about their performance are essential.

As with most programs that you implement as a leader, success with a quality program depends upon you. You must create and sustain the right attitudes throughout your organization and obtain commitments from your team and organizational leaders to attain quality.

Customer Feedback

Paying attention to what your customers think about your service or product is a proven method of effectively monitoring events in your organization. By actively seeking feedback from your customers, you get the opportunity to analyze detailed comments that could have enormous consequences on your organization's bottom line and long-term survival. After evaluating this information, you can guide your team members back to your strategy of superior customer service.

Performance Management

Monitoring the performance of each of your subordinates and communicating to them about their performance are essential components of your leadership efforts. The coaching process discussed in Chapter 15 presents these in greater detail, but several points are pertinent for this chapter. It is essential to clearly identify the major goals for each of your subordinates for the upcoming year and beyond and then to agree on specific performance objectives for each of these goals. A written plan for each person ensures that everyone is in agreement on what is to be done and it provides you with an excellent base document for tracking your subordinates' performance. Informal performance reviews with each person occur at least quarterly, more frequently if necessary. These reviews are usually supplemented by an annual formal appraisal.

If leaders accomplished everything exactly according to their wishes, there would be no need for monitoring. However, as you well know, it is rare that anything happens exactly according to plan. Monitoring complements the planning process by helping leaders to stay involved and to take responsible actions over the lifetime of an activity.

Chapter 9

Training and Development

Maria is the team leader of a maintenance team. She and a team member believe the team needs help on understanding a new state-of-the-art machine her company will soon receive. Tim is in charge of her company's training department. What are their responsibilities to each other and themselves individually to ensure successful training occurs? What should happen next?

L EADERS ARE RESPONSIBLE FOR CORRECTLY TRAINING THEIR SUBORDI-nates and others and then developing them into productive and contributing members of their team. There are usually differences, or gaps, between what your subordinates should know and what they actually know about doing their jobs. The purpose of training is to eliminate these gaps by helping your team acquire and apply knowledge and skills in order to improve their performance.

Development, a longer-term process that is related to training, has as its primary objective to prepare the individual for increasingly difficult or responsible jobs within and outside your organization. Both training and development occur foremost as a response to an organization's strategy; they are market-driven programs designed to help you achieve organizational goals and objectives.

Training and Development for All?

Leaders with subordinates who report to them will probably find training and development skills more applicable than, for example, a team member or co-worker with leadership roles and abilities but no direct reports. Still, all leaders will benefit from this skill because it is likely that each will be involved in some way, at some point, in training and development.

Well-trained workers, coupled with effective leadership, are essential to the success of an organization. You as a leader do not have to conduct all the training personally or to develop each of your subordinates personally. Usually you will have assistance from leaders or colleagues in neighboring departments, such as training or human resources. However, you must involve yourself in the process to ensure that training and development programs are designed, implemented, and evaluated with your needs in mind. Make sure the programs are conducted in a supportive learning environment and they meet your subordinates' needs as well as the objectives of your organization.

Training and development are not one-time occurrences; they start the day you hire your colleagues and continue until they leave the organization. Training and development take place throughout the day, not just during preplanned, formal training sessions, so you must integrate them into your daily activities. Although you will expend effort and resources and not experience an immediate sense of gratification, you will eventually see a huge payoff because of your commitment to training and development. The value of training and development is that it makes your life much easier because your subordinates will learn how to do their jobs better, which means you will have to spend less time assisting and coaching them as they develop their expertise.

Training and development are not one-time occurrences; they start the day you hire your colleagues and continue until they leave the organization.

A Leader's Four Training Guidelines

As you think about how training contributes to fulfilling your duties, consider how to structure training so that it is most effective. Effective training has three components: presentation of content, application to specific practice sessions, and follow-up to check performance. These components will be developed throughout this chapter. The following four guidelines will further help you make the right decisions as you lead a powerful training program.

Build Skills to Improve Performance

Many leaders traditionally have viewed training in several limited ways, such as an organizational requirement, an employee reward, or a means to deliver new knowledge. Training is most effective when used as a vehicle to achieve organizational goals by developing skills and improving performance. Training by itself will not eliminate all performance discrepancies, because they exist for several reasons, including personal difficulties of employees, the incentive system, and organizational conditions. However, when training is related to the causes of the performance discrepancies, it can be of tremendous benefit as a solution.

Training is most effective when used as a vehicle to achieve organizational goals by developing skills and improving performance.

Leaders must work closely and collaboratively with the training professionals in their organization to identify the causes of performance deficiencies, develop solutions to overcome deficiencies and increase skills, and create viable training programs. Although you have the primary responsibility to ensure that your subordinates participate in the right kinds of training, the training department can work with you to integrate that training into your departmental operations. If your training department does not yet operate in such a proactive manner, approach its leaders and create this kind of working relationship.

Tailored Training Programs

Training programs work best when tailored to a specific group of employees. Office and manufacturing workers, for example, require a different set of skills than middle-level managers. All groups require a mix of skills from three categories: business skills, such as customer service, quality assurance, or marketing; leadership and management skills, such as teamwork and conflict resolution; and individual skills, such as presentations or writing.

Advocate Continuous Learning and Practice

In your leadership role, promote training as the impetus for a continuous and widespread learning process that can occur informally and formally, in classrooms or on and off the job, and with the guidance of official instructors, leaders, or peers. After spending time learning skills or methods, employees must practice using them or they will soon lose mastery of them. Subordinates must understand that ongoing learning and practice not only leads to improving their skills in their current jobs but also will open the door to many opportunities within and outside the organization.

Align Training with the Organizational Mission

Training provides an exceptional opportunity to emphasize to your subordinates the organization's mission, goals, and objectives. By understanding how training and job skills directly relate to the organization's future, your subordinates will have a clearer sense of purpose and direction. An intense focus on strategic objectives also will help you quickly identify the skills your subordinates need to help achieve these goals.

Measure Training

Your challenge is to make your training accountable for helping you achieve your objectives and your organization's goals. Traditional indicators of productive training, such as the volume of training or number of participants, are not very useful to you as a leader. You are more concerned with measuring specific results attributable to specific training. Examples of results include an increase in individual performance and output, higher customer satisfaction, or new business generated. Create specific control methods, such as surveys or feedback sessions, to collect information that will help measure training results. These methods need not be elaborate or complex, but they should indicate how effective your training is.

A Leader's Three Training Roles

Training is a pervasive activity that affects almost everything you do as a leader. Because of the enormous benefits training can have in helping you fulfill your duties, you should understand your role in the training process. Most leaders will agree that they spend a large amount of time teaching, guiding, and informing subordinates and team members on countless issues and skills. At other times, the leaders direct and monitor the efforts of others who teach, guide, and inform. Occasionally, leaders are involved in or responsible for creating a training program. These routine activities represent the three roles you have in the training process: trainer, training manager, and training designer.

Three roles you have in the training process are trainer, training manager, and training designer.

You as the Trainer

You may often conduct training with your subordinates or act as a guest trainer for other departments. When you train others, it is a tremendous opportunity for you to refine your business, leadership, and individual skills; to lead by example through imparting your expertise to others; and to involve yourself in guiding your subordinates toward achieving individual and organizational goals. As you prepare for your role as a trainer, your two most important objectives are to develop training expertise and to understand your learners' abilities and preferences.

Your first objective is to develop training expertise. To be an effective and responsible trainer, you must learn how to properly train individuals. The most effective way is to attend a train-the-trainer course that is presented either commercially or within your organization. If this is not possible, ask someone in the training department to teach you the essentials; you then can supplement that instruction by reading a book on training and practicing the skills you learn. Though you later can become extremely proficient as a trainer by developing several specialized training skills, your initial objective must be to learn and practice the minimal skills necessary to lead a training session. These include using teaching aids properly, presenting material effectively, understanding and listening to the participants, creating a learning environment, and knowing your material.

Your second objective is to understand the learner. As a leader, you work with colleagues who have all types of personal backgrounds, educational levels, motivations, skills, and experience. Similarly, as a trainer you will be working with people who have varied learning abilities and preferences. It is possible, however, to better understand the participants and then adjust your training approaches according to two main learning factors.

People Learn in Different Ways. As discussed in Chapter 5, people usually have a dominant way of thinking. Left-brain thinkers tend to be more analytical and detail-oriented, while right-brain thinkers are more creative and open-minded. People also learn in terms of their left brain or right brain.

It is more difficult in group training sessions to satisfy the needs of all participants all the time. You can, however, vary the delivery methods, from lectures, readings, and self-paced instruction to team exercises, games, and simulations.

Left or Right

Left-brain learners enjoy learning at their own solitary pace, receiving as many details as possible, and forming their own conclusions. Right-brain learners, on the other hand, prefer to grasp the big-picture conclusion first, confer with others, and then look for the details to support the original conclusion. When you train an individual, therefore, you can tailor the delivery method to suit his or her preferred approach. This is a gross simplification, but it is a useful way to thnk about learning.

Motivation Is a Variable. Although we will examine motivation in more detail in Chapter 12, this section will address motivational issues that pertain to learning. One of your tasks as the trainer is to determine your participants' motives for learning and whether they have any barriers or impediments to learning. It may be necessary to probe because people are not all motivated by the same things.

You then will use this information to create a positive learning experience. Before or at the beginning of the training session, poll the participants individually or collectively to see what value they attach to the training. You could ask them open-ended questions such as why they are attending the training, how they see it benefiting them, or if they have any preconceived ideas about the subject matter. You probably will get a range of positive and negative responses, which can help you better understand their motives for learning.

As you continue with the training, make a special effort to overcome their fears and to reinforce their motives for learning. Most people will eventually form their own conclusions about the value of the training. However, you can influence their conclusions by explaining the benefits in light of whatever motivates them, such as promotion or recognition. In addition, you can make sure that the training is solution-oriented, that it is pertinent to realistic job conditions, and that the participants can readily apply it on the job.

You as the Training Manager

Not only will you have the opportunity to personally lead and conduct training, you also will be involved in the management aspects of training. Just like many of your other significant duties, training management includes such activities as directing, monitoring, and influencing the successful implementation of programs and events. As you will see in the next section, there are many details involved in the design of training. After a training program is designed, almost all these details will be reviewed for relevance once the training starts. You can imagine, therefore, the benefits of becoming involved in the design process from its very beginning, as you will soon see.

Just like many of your other significant duties, training management includes such activities as directing, monitoring, and influencing the successful implementation of programs and events.

You as the Training Designer

It is helpful for you to understand the design process, because as the training department develops a course that pertains to your department, it needs your experience and expertise to develop it properly. As a leader who will be affected by an upcoming training program, you should be involved in all stages of the design process because the information you provide the training

> ## Your Role in Training Management
>
> Even if you are not involved in the design or personal delivery of training, you probably will be involved during its implementation. The training department will need your leadership assistance in overseeing successful training sessions, encouraging your subordinates to attend and benefit from the training, and evaluating the impact on job performance. Training management evolves from your primary leadership duties; therefore, it is your responsibility as a training manager to make the training system work for you and not to accept excuses for ineffective training, poorly designed training, or, worse yet, a total absence of training.

department will be important in designing the best possible program for your department's performance problems. Depending upon the complexity of the training program, the design process can be abbreviated for routine programs or can be done in greater detail for challenging or critical programs.

Designing a Training Program

Designing a training program is a thorough undertaking that traditionally has been the responsibility of training or human resources departments. It is unlikely, therefore, that you will frequently be completely responsible for designing a training program unless you are a leader working primarily in a training capacity. Since most full-time training personnel participate in a formal course on the subject lasting sometimes a week or more, you can appreciate that training design involves many intricacies that cannot be addressed in a few paragraphs. However, this section can highlight the six steps involved in designing a training program.

- ▶ Determine training needs.
- ▶ Outline the plan.
- ▶ Develop the plan.
- ▶ Write objectives and design the tests.
- ▶ Develop the course.
- ▶ Evaluate the course.

Determine Training Needs

As discussed in the first paragraph of this chapter, the purpose of training is to correct performance gaps. If it is absolutely evident why you have performance problems and you know what the training needs are, then this step can be shortened. Otherwise, do a thorough training needs analysis, which is a three-step process that will give you the critical information you need to design the program.

Collect Data on the Performance Gap. You do this by observing and interviewing the people responsible for completing the tasks. After this, approach their supervisors to resolve and clarify any of the issues.

Identify the Cause of the Performance Gap. Thoroughly probe all areas related to the performance problem, including the conditions under which the problem occurs and recent organizational changes that could have prompted the problem. If the cause is related to knowledge and skills, then training is a solution. If the cause is anything else, such as workplace conditions, individual communication, or incentives, then training is not the answer; you may need to consider workplace redesign, coaching, a new incentives program, or other possible solutions.

Determine Costs and Benefits of the Training Solution. Estimate as accurately as you can how much it will cost you to design, conduct, and evaluate the necessary training. Compare this with the economic and other benefits of eliminating the performance gap. These benefits might include an increase in production, customer service, or quality, a decrease in costs, or improved job performance. If the benefits exceed the cost, then you have identified a viable training need.

> *Thoroughly probe all areas related to the performance problem. If the cause is related to knowledge and skills, then training is a solution. If the cause is anything else, then training is not the answer.*

Outline the Plan

As with any project, start identifying the crucial details. Though you will not know many planning particulars for a while longer, you can make tremendous progress by raising some major concerns with departmental leaders or your client. These include details related to participants, resources, training location, instructors, subject-matter experts, and others who can assist you. When you finish this step, you will have enough information to know what to do, who the participants are, when and where training will occur, and what constraints may exist.

Develop the Plan

Developing a plan involves thoroughly analyzing the two major components of your training program—your trainees and your course content. Use your understanding of the trainees to develop the heart of your training program, which is the task analysis.

If you think of your training participants as customers, you will realize that your product—training—will be much more successful if you know as much as you can about your participants.

In the earlier discussion of the characteristics of learners, you saw the importance of understanding your trainees as you prepare to train them; this understanding is just as vital while designing the training. If you think of your training participants as customers, you will realize that your product—training—will be much more successful if you know as much as you can about your participants. Analyze their education and skill levels, job experience and expertise, demographics, and motivation to learn. You then can target the training to the characteristics and needs of your participants, such as by offering multiple training sessions or using innovative methods of training.

Next you will develop a task analysis. In a process much like developing the work breakdown structure in Chapter 7, your objective is to organize the training into manageable parts. You do this with the cooperation of the people who know the job duties best, the people who do the jobs. For example, if your training program concerns the job of maintenance technician, first determine the major duties of a technician, such as maintaining equipment and ordering parts.

Separate each of these duties into tasks, or major pieces of work, that a technician must perform to fulfill that duty. Next, divide each task into subtasks. Then, list all the detailed steps for each subtask. If you follow the format just shown, you are certain to get the level of detail that you need to complete the task analysis. Here is an abbreviated example for the maintenance technician.

Job: Maintenance Technician

Duties: maintain equipment and order parts.

Tasks for maintaining equipment: read manuals, disassemble machine, perform maintenance, diagnose problems, reassemble machine.

Subtasks for disassembling machine: stop machine, prepare safety mechanisms, remove outer casing, remove fan belt.

Steps for stopping the machine: notify team members two minutes in advance, press "off" switch, unplug electrical cord using gloves.

This may seem like unnecessary work for developing course content, but it is extremely useful for several reasons. In addition to determining the exact makeup of the duties that will be the focus of the instruction, you and your team members may discover areas of disagreement, such as the subtasks for a particular task. This is a healthy process that ensures that the training you develop will be as pertinent and error-free as it can be. First, it can help you create needed procedures that may not have previously existed for certain duties. Second, the task analysis can be used as a course outline that your trainers will greatly appreciate. Finally, the task analysis will also help you write objectives and design tests, which is your focus in the next step in designing a training program.

Write Objectives and Design the Tests

Once you have completed the task analysis for each task in the designated training, use it to compose an objective for every task; objectives are not needed for the subtasks and steps. Then develop review and criterion tests to ensure that the participant has mastered the tasks.

A task objective clearly states what the training participant must do. It consists of three parts: task statement, conditions, and standards. The *task statement* is a restatement of the task itself. The *conditions* indicate the circumstances, such as resources and location, under which the task will be performed. *Standards* show how well, as in time or accuracy, you want the participant to perform the task. Here is a sample objective for the maintenance technician.

Once you have completed the task analysis for each task, use the analysis to compose objectives for the tasks.

> **Objective:** Given all necessary maintenance tools and equipment on location at the job site, the employee will disassemble the machine. All steps must be completed within 30 minutes according to the performance checklist.

Review tests serve as checkpoints that indicate the participant's progress during the training session. For every subtask, design a simple review test to ensure that the participant can do the subtask during a practice session. A review test is given after participants learn one subtask and before learning the next subtask. Review tests can be either performance tests, which are simulations done under realistic conditions, or nonperformance tests, such as written quizzes that measure the knowledge gained during training.

> **Nonperformance review test:** List the steps for stopping the machine.
>
> **Performance review test:** Demonstrate how to prepare the safety mechanism.

A criterion test is a comprehensive final test that shows if the participant can achieve the task's objective. If the participant succeeds, then your training has been successful.

Later on, after the participant has completed the training course, make sure you follow up the training to ensure that he or she can perform the task on the job. If the results of training are not periodically inspected and enforced, the training benefits may be lost.

Criterion test: Given all necessary maintenance tools and equipment on location at the job site, the employee will disassemble the machine according to the necessary steps. The trainer will complete a performance checklist during the test. All steps must be completed in order and within 30 minutes according to the performance checklist.

Develop the Course

There are three general methods, used individually or in combination, to conduct training: by the trainer in a classroom setting or on the job, by a participant or group of participants, or by training material, such as manuals or job aids.

At this point, you are ready to assemble your course content and decide how you will present the course, how participants will apply the training, and what resources you will use to conduct the training.

Choose your methods of presentation. There are three general methods, used individually or in combination, to conduct training: by the trainer in a classroom setting or on the job, by a participant or group of participants, or by training material, such as manuals or job aids.

Methods of Presentation

Within these categories, there are several methods that have their specific advantages and disadvantages based upon your particular type of training needs and audience. The first guideline is to select the method that most quickly gets you and your participants to the application phase, the practice phase where participants should spend most of their training time. Second, vary the methods based on your knowledge of the participants and their learning styles. Include methods that allow you to intersperse realistic and exciting activities, participant interaction, individual reflection, reading, listening, and seeing. Methods used frequently include lectures, seminars, job aids, and reading.

Application is the opportunity you give the participants to practice the skills they have just learned.

Consider various methods of application. Application is the opportunity you give the participants to practice the skills they have just learned. As a leader, you want your co-workers to not only gain the knowledge but also put it to use during the training session and on the job; otherwise, training is useless. As with training methods, there are many applications from which to choose. Remember to consider the different learning styles when choosing. Popular methods include practical exercises, demonstrations, quizzes, simulations, workshops, and role-playing.

Some training methods combine the presentation and application phases. These progressive techniques can be invaluable in developing a dynamic training atmosphere and promoting successful learning. Typical combination methods include computer-based training, self-paced training, on-the-job training, and workshops.

Assemble your training materials. One of the last steps you take as a training designer is to consolidate your information into a set of training materials. Each individual in the training will need information. The participant needs a set of course materials that includes all the information pertaining to the training, including training objectives, schedule of events, and evaluation forms. Develop sharp-looking and effective handouts that participants can easily write on and use during training. Distribute any reading material well in advance so that the participants can adequately prepare. The trainer likewise needs everything that the participant needs, only further in advance. In addition, you should prepare a lesson plan, which acts as a job aid for the trainer. It contains most of the information related to the training consolidated in one folder. With the lesson plan, include copies of all handouts, references, information on participants, audiovisual materials, resource listings, and any other pertinent information that the trainer needs to teach effectively.

Evaluate the Course

Before any official training begins, test your program by training selected individuals. The purpose is to make sure that the training program will work well. Look especially for logical sequencing, clear links between the objectives and what is actually taught, and dynamic presentation. Go through every aspect of the training. Take good notes, notice everything, and ask these first participants to evaluate the course. Make any needed revisions to the program and test it again with another person. If time and resources permit, test again with a group of participants similar to the groups you will actually be training.

Before any official training begins, test your program by training selected individuals.

As the course designer, you also want to know immediately after the training ends if the course was well presented, organized, and relevant. The best way to determine this is to use course evaluations. Well-designed evaluations, which can be up to several pages in length, ask for written comments on all aspects of the training including the instructor's presentation, training facilities, and subject matter. Evaluation responses from the participants, trainers, and the supervisors will tell you if the training was effective. The primary information you want is whether your course did what it was intended to do, which is to improve the performance of the participants on the job. You can determine this by surveying the participants and supervisors before training begins and again several weeks after the instruction. Always ask for any suggestions for changing or improving the training.

Development of Your Subordinates

A development program prepares your subordinates to assume positions of greater responsibility by helping them acquire knowledge and skills applicable to many job positions. It also exposes them to numerous opportunities for career advancement. While development may seem to contradict your leadership goal of keeping your subordinates happy and stable in their current job positions, there are several reasons to prepare your subordinates for new challenges through a development program.

A development program prepares your subordinates to assume positions of greater responsibility by helping them acquire them knowledge and skills applicable to many job positions.

Development gives them the opportunity to move forward with their careers and avoid remaining in a rut. If you challenge employees to make the most of their skills and provide them with the support, hope, and means to get ahead, they will be much more satisfied, productive, and loyal to you and your organization. Your investment in their advancement becomes obvious to them and they will appreciate your organization and see it as a partner that invests in their professional career needs. The employees will understand that, although you may not be able to guarantee lifetime employment, you are offering the best that you can, considering the constantly changing economic environment. When you make a pledge to their development, they will reciprocate with loyalty and commitment. Loyal and highly trained workers, who constitute the organization's vital institutional memory, are crucial to the organization's long-term survival. This is especially important during periods of turmoil and upheaval, as in restructuring, downsizing, or intense competition.

A development program helps you maintain a system to internally fill job vacancies whenever workers depart. By knowing the career interests, competencies, and goals of your subordinates, you can more easily align the organization's needs with the needs of its most important resource, its employees. It is a great morale booster for your subordinates to know that the internal promotion and advancement system is viable. In addition, it is usually less expensive in the long run to promote from within the organization.

Even if subordinates eventually leave your department or organization, they will leave more content if they have participated in a development program. They will more likely convey positive feelings about you and the organization in their next positions or while networking among peers. Your organization, as result, will build a reputation of caring about the welfare of its employees and it will continually attract superior applicants. Moreover, it is unlikely that you would prefer to retain team members who are truly

The Development Paradox

Despite its many advantages, a development program involves an issue that frightens many leaders. The company's reward system may not encourage leaders to develop and promote their subordinates. The reward system often acts as a disincentive when the leader is evaluated solely on metrics such as departmental productivity, training costs, or payroll costs. Yet paradoxically, each of these areas is negatively affected later on when you have to recruit and train someone to replace a fully trained worker who is departing due to lack of developmental opportunities. The ways to overcome this disadvantage will be discussed later.

unhappy with their positions and future in your company; sometimes it is to your advantage to let them go, if they so desire, and to replace them.

Types of Development Programs

Once you are convinced that a development program is a great way to improve your company's most valuable resource, its employees, you will have to choose which program to offer. Three types of development programs will be discussed: career planning, mentoring, and leadership development.

Career Planning Program

This program should address all aspects of a person's potential career within the organization. Even with the employment uncertainty that exists in most organizations, it is imperative that you clearly communicate to each employee the skills and knowledge that he or she needs in order to advance within the organization. A career planning program should serve three purposes: to help employees assess and promote their careers while working at the organization, provide opportunities for employees to assume responsibility for their own career growth, and build up the organization's reserve of qualified employees to meet future needs.

To achieve these objectives, the human resources department will work closely with you and other leaders to develop detailed self-assessment documents that will determine the competencies, skill weaknesses, and goals of the employees. These tools will include skill, ability, and knowledge appraisals; interest and aptitude inventories; goal assessment worksheets; and company action plans. Although the human resources department has

Three types of development programs will be discussed: career planning, mentoring, and leadership development.

107

staff responsibility for the program, leaders at all levels are responsible for implementing the program with their subordinates.

Mentoring Program

A mentor is a leader who advises and encourages a protégé on a variety of issues, including planning a career, dealing with organizational politics and power, and improving performance. Mentoring programs traditionally have been used to benefit an organization's leaders, but they certainly can be applied more inclusively throughout the organization. A well-designed mentoring program should be available to all employees on a volunteer basis, implemented from the top leader through their immediate leaders and promoted throughout the organization. You can act as a mentor to your subordinates or another volunteer can assume the role.

Leadership Development Program

A leadership development program is specifically designed to help leaders become more effective. It is a challenging and long-term plan that is linked to your organizational vision and strategy. It supplements traditional sources of leadership training and education, which are on-the-job experience and supervisory guidance. These programs provide needed structure for the often haphazard way in which leaders learn how to lead. It is a process of development that can give you as a leader the opportunity to explore leadership issues, develop and cultivate your skills, resolve challenges, and learn from the expertise of proven leaders.

This developmental process provides a system for top leaders to identify promising future leaders in the organization. You and your fellow leaders are entrusted with the responsibility of continuing and expanding the successes of the organization. A vital part of your response to this challenge is to find and nurture the next generation of leaders. As the pressures and challenges of competition, innovation, global trade, and society continue to increase, there will be a tremendous need to develop strong leaders who can lead teams and work within these external pressures. Leadership development, therefore, is every leader's job and is done in conjunction with your daily duties.

Leadership development programs are shaped differently for each organization. They can be designed internally, created with outside help, or purchased as packages from commercial training organizations and consultants. Regardless of its source, a leadership development program must have spe-

A mentor is a leader who advises and encourages a protégé on a variety of issues, including planning a career, dealing with organizational politics and power, and improving performance.

A leadership development program must have specific objectives that are linked to your organization's business goals and strategy.

108

cific objectives that are linked to your organization's business goals and strategy. You can derive these objectives from a thorough needs analysis that examines what your leaders currently do in their job positions, what leaders need to do to ensure your organization's growth and success, and what leaders need for their own professional growth. Do not automatically assume that general areas of leadership instruction will suffice for your organization. If you do so, leaders will be under pressure to transfer this generalized knowledge to their very specific job circumstances. This places an unnecessary burden on them. It is better to first conduct an analysis that will help you correctly pinpoint your needs and then to develop the specific content of the development program.

Leadership Development Resources

Many details involved in designing a leadership development program are similar to the details of designing any training program. However, you must be careful so as not to conflict with or overload the crucial day-to-day responsibilities of your leaders. Depending upon your organization's needs, you can design your program to include one or more of the following resources.

Job Rotation

Job rotation allows individuals to work in a succession of positions in the organization, including supervisory and nonsupervisory, assistantships, internships, or trainee positions. The practical experience and challenge of seeing how work is done in other functional areas or at different sites provide leaders with the broad knowledge and skills to move forward in their careers. An organization that commits to a program of job rotation will soon develop depth in its leadership ranks, be more able to move leaders to other departments when needs occur, and ultimately be able to handle growth and competition better. To make job rotation a useful learning experience, it is important that the individual provide a needed and useful service to the host department and that he or she gain experience in leading people and making decisions. The leaders of all hosting departments must remember to explain the purpose of the job rotation program to their teams. This is so the team members can understand why the rotation is helpful to the organization, the department, and the participant and how their cooperation is needed to help the program succeed.

Internal Education and Training

You will find there are numerous resources for on-site leadership education and training. These include seminars, lectures, simulations, or discussions facilitated by organizational leaders; workshops and training led by consultants or seminar companies; committee assignments, special projects, and formal presentations; and guided reading programs. Your leaders will make significant progress if they relate the reasons for their leadership education to specific on-the-job applications. In-house education can provide this applicability if it is designed well and if it is tailored to the level of leaders involved, such as first-level, middle, and top. You can present and evaluate most leadership skills training on site. The skills presented in this book are examples of those that you can include in your program. Reading programs, consisting of books related to all aspects of leadership or specific technical skills, reinforce the principle that leaders are ultimately responsible for their own career development.

External Education and Training

Many colleges and universities, professional associations, and seminar companies are willing to educate your leaders. Depending upon your budget, you may be able to partially or completely fund attendance at programs that offer a wide variety of subjects that range from one day to several weeks.

Questions About External Education

Although it is tempting to assume that these programs can be the answer to some of your leadership development challenges, ask yourself several questions before committing to external education. Will the programs significantly help you reach your development goals? Will the programs improve the leadership performance of the participants? Is the training specific and realistic enough to apply to your organization or is there too much theory? What are the quality and the professionalism of the instruction?

Social Activities

Do not underestimate the effect of informal activities that are intended to bring people together. Whether a barbecue, a dinner, or a sports event, these shared experiences provide superb opportunities for leaders at all levels to discuss work-related challenges, career opportunities, and family life. Many leaders fondly remember how personal encounters at these events significantly altered their lives.

Prerequisites for Development Programs

Like any significant organizational undertaking, the process of planning and implementing your development program takes time, effort, and collaboration. Whether you are responsible for creating the program or for providing staff support to its proponents, you can help ensure its success by attention to four prerequisites: top leadership support, ready access, fair access, and a reward system.

You can help ensure a development program's success by having top leadership support, ready access, fair access, and a reward system.

Obtain Top Leadership Buy-in

It is essential that the senior organizational leaders provide comments during the creation process, approve the programs, announce them to the organization, and enthusiastically support them. To get the programs off to a good start and to understand what their subordinates will be involved in, the top leaders and their immediate subordinate leaders can set a good example by being the first to participate in the programs.

Provide Adequate Resources

Make sure your participants are given complete information on the programs' details, adequate time to participate in development, and easy access to seminars, training workshops, and self-help material. Purchase a variety of career development books and manuals to keep available in your departmental or organizational libraries.

Administer the Programs Equitably

Since there is potential for individuals to erroneously perceive that development programs favor one person or group over another, you must carefully plan and administer the programs to minimize inequities and resentment. Areas to watch include the selection process, slotting for choice assignments, effect on organizational operations, and allocation of training expenses.

Require and Reward Development

Encourage your leaders and subordinates to participate in development programs and to develop their subordinates and reward them as well. To ensure that this occurs, you can take several actions. First, you can require your leaders to develop their subordinates as part of their official duties. They must know that you believe in this process and, therefore, they should believe. Second, when leaders are successful at developing their subordi-

111

nates, reward them with recognition, special status, merit pay if available, and protection from the departmental costs related to the development process. Finally, if your company has no official development program, organize your own, because you are ultimately responsible for nurturing your team.

As you have seen in this final chapter for the primary-level leadership skills, training and development provide specific opportunities for realizing the potential of your organization, your team, and yourself. Since these programs are of such importance to your success, promote training and development vigorously by encouraging others to see their benefits as well. No one leadership skill can be the key to your success, but training and development will help others get better and feel better at what they do and provide for the long-term success of your organization.

Part Three

Relationship Skills
(Intermediate-Level Leadership Skills)

Chapter 10

Communication

Three top officers of a medium-sized corporation are having challenges communicating among themselves and with their immediate staff. They also notice that many of their directives and pronouncements are never disseminated throughout the company; as a result, most employees do not know important and routine information. How can they improve their personal and organizational communication?

COMMUNICATION IS THE MOST IMPORTANT OF ALL YOUR LEADERSHIP skills. It is also the first skill learned by human beings. Communication is the bridge that leaders use to successfully transfer their knowledge, plans, and guidance to people who will help them fulfill their duties. Similarly, it is also the means by which leaders receive information from within and outside the organization.

While most leadership skills work in connection with and in support of other skills during the day, communication is the one skill that you use the most. Whether you are working with a subordinate, a peer, a supervisor, or a customer, virtually all your leadership duties involve the help and contributions of others. Clear communication is pivotal in eliciting their cooperation, retaining their support for future collaboration, and building long-term relationships that will help you, them, and your organization thrive.

115

Communication is the most important of all your leadership skills.

Quality communication is not the complete solution to your leadership challenges, but it is a crucial factor that permeates all areas of your leadership duties. Communicating clearly involves much more than telling someone what is on your mind. It involves determining the message you want to send, choosing how you will send it, sending it accurately, and then making sure the other person receives and understands the message as you intended it. Because you are in a position of leadership, you cannot send messages to your subordinates and others arbitrarily. People see you as a credible messenger; they expect you to prepare and present a reasoned and unambiguous exchange of communication. If you do anything less, you will lose effectiveness and esteem in the eyes of your subordinates.

The Communication Process

Fortunately, there is a three-step process to help you you communicate. You could conceivably communicate hundreds of times a day; this simple process can easily guide you through any communication situation. You also can teach this process to subordinates to improve the communication you receive from them. In the communication process, you must do three things:

Examining the purpose, recipient, and content of your message will give you the insight to prepare the most effective message for delivery.

- ▶ Determine your message.
- ▶ Choose the method of delivery and send your message.
- ▶ Monitor the receipt and understanding of your message.

Determine Your Message

Examining the purpose, recipient, and content of your message will give you the insight to prepare the most effective message for delivery.

Purpose

Knowing why you need to send a message will put you in the proper frame of mind to construct the right message. There are several general purposes that your message could possibly have, such as to request information or action or to convey specific or general information. Take a moment to think about why you want to communicate to your recipient. Determining the specific purpose enables you to focus on your communications objective and develop a concise, clear, and accurate message.

Recipient

Think about who will be getting the message and visualize yourself delivering the message to that recipient. A heightened awareness of the recipient will help you formulate a message that reflects his or her knowledge of the subject matter, your rapport and work experience with that person, and why he or she needs the message. If the recipient is someone you do not know personally, such as a customer or a top organizational official, envision his or her concerns and what he or she may be expecting in your message.

Content

Somewhere in your mind, you know exactly the details of the message you want to send. Your mind, which is a vast databank of thoughts, perceptions, and experiences, lets you process these and other numerous details quickly and subconsciously. When it is time to encode your communications message, you must sort through this collection of information so you can accurately compose your message. In particular, remember to focus on the important and essential information and to eliminate the irrelevant and inessential, which can confuse the recipient or, even worse, cause your message to get lost.

Choose the Method of Delivery and Send Your Message

After you determine your message, the next step is to choose the best method of delivery and to deliver it. As in step one, it is helpful once again to consider the purpose of the message and its recipient. This will quickly allow you to narrow your selection by eliminating some of the available delivery methods and tentatively selecting some. Although there are numerous ways to deliver a message, they fall into the two general classifications of spoken and written. Later in the chapter you will discover techniques for improving your delivery methods. First, however, you will examine these two types of delivery. As is true with most skills they use, leaders vary their communications methods depending upon the situation.

Speaking is the most personalized method by which you or someone you designate delivers your message to the recipient. If you deliver it personally, you can ensure that you quickly deliver it the way you intended; there's no possibility that someone else will mistakenly leaving out crucial information.

Speak or Write the Message?

Use your good judgment and select the more appropriate method based upon your specific situation. Often, you will use both speaking and writing to communicate a message. This combines the advantages of each type of delivery and helps ensure that you communicate your message effectively and clearly.

You also get the opportunity firsthand and immediately to answer questions or clear up any confusion that the recipient may have. If you designate a subordinate or someone else to deliver your message, it does not automatically mean that the above advantages turn into disadvantages. You just have to carefully prepare the messenger with as many details as you can so he or she can deliver the message correctly. The spoken delivery method can be used individually with one or a few people, in front of a group, or through devices such as a telephone or video camera.

Writing is particularly useful when disseminating routine, permanent, nonsensitive, technical, or previously discussed information. It can be in numerous forms, such as a letter, a computer file or electronic mail, a news release, or an organizational publication. Written delivery lacks an important advantage of spoken delivery in that it is more difficult to gauge the recipient's reaction to the message. This may not be important when informing your subordinates about an upcoming meeting, but it could be critical when announcing new customer service policies.

Monitor the Receipt and Understanding of Your Message

Leaders can send the clearest message by the most secure method of delivery, but if people don't receive it or understand it, the message is useless.

Have you ever tried to make a telephone call but could get through, because the line was busy or the answering party hung up because of a bad connection? Have you ever expected to receive a letter in the mail but it never arrived, arrived late, arrived at someone else's address, or arrived torn up? Incidents like these happen every day when you communicate with people in your organization. Leaders can send the clearest message by the most secure method of delivery, but if people don't receive it or understand it, the message is useless. For example, you can imagine the calamity that would occur if your new memo on emergency fire procedures was never distributed throughout the organization or if your customer service representatives did not know about the new product launch yesterday.

Why Do Messages Not Get Received?

It is extremely useful for a leader to know why the recipient did not receive or understand the message. Not only must you correct the specific difficulty, but it could be a symptom of a deeper or personal organizational problem for you to remedy. If, for example, a recipient is unwilling to receive a message, it may suggest low morale or disinterest. If you had asked someone to get the word out about a policy change, your messenger may have failed to do so because he or she did not know how to communicate properly; this would indicate a need for specific training. The messenger also could have failed because he or she forgot to clarify some assumption with you. If you determine that your delivery method was the cause of the problem, you can easily choose a better method or improve your writing and speaking skills, as you shall see later in the chapter.

As discussed in Chapter 8, monitoring is one of many solutions to your leadership challenges. It also is a means to ensure effective communication. You must consistently check to see if your guidance, directives, and other forms of communication are received, understood, and retained. Whether you intend the message for a subordinate, a superior, a peer, or a customer, it is possible that, despite your best efforts, someone may not receive or understand your message. This occurs for various reasons: the recipient may not be willing or able to receive the message, there may be a problem with the method of delivery, or some type of communications noise interferes with the reception or understanding of the message.

Noise, which is any type of distortion, distraction, or interference with the communications process, is the broad category most often listed as the reason for ineffective receipt or understanding of communication. Here are some examples of noise:

You should constantly search for noise in your environment so that you can minimize or eliminate it and improve communication.

- ▶ People not listening attentively to the message because they are busy thinking about other duties or problems
- ▶ People making premature judgments and conclusions about the message before it is completely sent
- ▶ Organizational issues and problems that preclude or cloud effective communications
- ▶ Physical conditions that prevent the message from being understood
- ▶ Barriers to communication, such as psychological, social, semantic, or physical

You should constantly search for noise in your environment so that you can minimize or eliminate it and improve communication.

Ten Methods for Improving Leadership Communication

You can become a dramatically more effective leader simply by improving your communications style. Here are ten methods especially applicable for leaders.

Improve Face-to-Face Communications

One-on-one and small group situations are where most communication takes place. Try to increase the quality and quantity of your one-on-one and small group encounters because they are a most effective means of delivering your message. Here are other specific suggestions to consider.

Be Approachable. If your subordinates and others perceive you as openly warm and accessible, they will come to you when they need you and not avoid bringing up their concerns. Even though you and others may be remarkably different in backgrounds, ages, or communication styles, these are not reasons for you to be aloof and distant. Approachability also implies that you are not initially judgmental whenever someone talks with you but are open to others' ideas and suggestions.

One way to develop this approachability and rapport is to be aware of the person's style of speaking and adjust yours to more closely resemble his or hers. This allows the person to feel relaxed and more likely to engage in effective communication. For example, if someone's conversational grammar, speed, and tone are completely different from yours, speak more simply, slowly, and softly as they do. If they are reluctant to talk, ask open questions that will give them the opportunity to express themselves, not simply answer with short, one-word responses. If they are using a particular gesture, you likewise can periodically use it to gain their closeness and understanding.

Be Understanding and Sincere. When speaking with anyone, try to truly understand the motivations for that person's beliefs, express empathy as you speak, and get a grasp of his or her true feelings. If you show a genuine concern for a person's needs and interests, he or she will reciprocate by better communicating and empathizing with your needs and interests. You will not diminish your position of leadership by developing sincere and understanding communications with others; you will enhance your position by effectively getting to what is truly important—good communication.

Avoid Mixed Signals. Sending mixed signals confuses people. For example, if you tell your subordinates to contact you anytime and anyplace, be receptive to them when they need to speak with you. If you have a particular style of communicating, be consistent in using it so your subordinates do not get confused. If you normally prefer to talk casually with someone before getting to the important information, avoid suddenly eliminating your chitchat and becoming someone who wants to get to the point quickly.

Repeat Messages. Make it a habit to repeat your important messages from time to time to ensure that they were received and understood. This does not mean using the same exact words all the time; restate the messages in different ways to probe for comprehension. For example, you could inquire about a detail in a request you previously made to a subordinate; his or her response and your ensuing discussion will likely indicate whether the person fully understood your request. If you have difficulty communicating with a specific subordinate, make sure that the instructions are simple and easy to understand. By repeating an instruction immediately after first giving it, you will help ensure that he or she comprehends it.

Make it a habit to repeat your important messages from time to time to ensure that they were received and understood.

Listen to Others

Because communication is a two-way process between a sender and receiver, you as a leader should spend a significant amount of time actively listening to what people are telling you. Think of the adage, "We have two ears and one mouth, so we should listen twice as much as we speak." That is certainly a target at which a leader should aim, because you can learn from everyone. Effective listening is much more than nodding your head while letting others talk. It is an active process in which your objective is to fully understand what the person is telling you by listening to it from his or her perspective, not yours; considering his or her feelings and interests, not just yours; and not interrupting. It involves being patient, blocking out distractions, and pinpointing what the person is telling you.

Speak Well

You will spend most of your communication time speaking to people in all types of roles and positions. It makes sense that if you speak clearly and precisely, they will understand you better. If your message is garbled, grammatically incorrect, incoherent, or awkward, you will not only send your

Benefits of Listening

Because it is impossible for a leader to know exactly what someone is thinking—despite the natural human tendency to assume that you know—why not let the person tell you? You have read of numerous situations throughout this book when leaders must get assistance from others to define causes of problems before deciding the solutions, such as in projects and training, for example. When you take the time to listen to others, they will become more motivated. They will enjoy working with an authentic leader who appreciates what they have to say and is not listening to them passively in order to manipulatively extract information and use it for his or her own purposes. They will see you as someone truly interested in their opinions, suggestions, and ideas, not because you *have* to listen but because you *want* to listen. This will pay you huge dividends through better communication that leads to better solutions, early identification and elimination of potential problems, and people who are more committed and loyal to you and your organization.

message badly but also send a negative impression of yourself that may counteract the positive leadership image you have been projecting. No matter how great your idea is, if you cannot communicate it effectively, it does you little good—and may even damage your success as a leader. Learn correct speaking techniques by allowing someone to coach you, by taking a self-study course, or by enrolling in a professionally taught program.

Present Well

Delivering a presentation is a common method of sending your message to one or more individuals. You know how critical it is to learn to speak well; this skill is vital in making presentations. However, you can go further and learn how to properly deliver a presentation so that it is most effective in conveying your message. Read a quick self-study booklet on the topic or attend a professional course; they are often offered in conjunction with speech courses. Augment this learning process by making practice presentations in front of someone who can knowledgeably evaluate you. This person can make frank comments on areas such as your organization, delivery, clarity, persuasive ability, and use of visual aids.

Some leaders can speak more easily and present better than others. This comes through practice. Anytime you have an occasion to speak even a few words in front of people, take advantage of it. Regardless of whether you view presentations as anxiety-filled chores or wonderful opportunities, commit to learning how to do them well since they are an inherent part of your duties.

Presentation Tips

Here are some final points to consider when making your presentation, whether the audience is one or one hundred.

- ▶ Know your topic and audience extremely well.
- ▶ Practice several times by yourself and rehearse once or twice in front of someone who can critique you.
- ▶ Plan the use of visual aids carefully, use only what is necessary, and triple-check all visual aids and equipment before the presentation.
- ▶ Be enthusiastic.
- ▶ Stay in control of the presentation.
- ▶ Speak naturally and be yourself.

Write Clearly

By improving your writing ability, you will be more able to clearly organize and convey information, eliminate ambiguity, anticipate the concerns of the readers, and decrease the time it takes to read your communications. Your readers will better understand what you are attempting to communicate and will be better able to comply with your intent. Learning to write correctly is not difficult, but writing well takes more effort and commitment. You can improve your writing one step at a time, thanks to the dozens of self-help books and training materials that can easily lead you through the many nuances and rules of grammar. Numerous confidence-building courses focus specifically on improving your vocabulary or your spelling.

By improving your writing ability, you will be more able to clearly organize and convey information and eliminate ambiguity.

Until you start this training, here are a few specific tips to help you improve your writing immediately.

- ▶ Pinpoint the purpose and main points of your document before beginning to write it.
- ▶ Think about your readers' need for your information or message, how knowledgeable they are about the subject, and what action you want them to take after reading your document.
- ▶ Use simple language, minimize jargon, and keep the document as brief as possible.
- ▶ Revise your document two or more times before sending it.
- ▶ Ask your assistant or a peer to review it for clarity, conciseness, and relevance as well as for grammar, punctuation, and spelling.

Use Leadership Words and Phrases

Avoid words or phrases that suggest incompetence, lack of common sense, or a reliance on excuses, such as the following:

- ▶ They never called me back.
- ▶ I don't know.
- ▶ That's impossible; we can't do that.
- ▶ That's not my job.
- ▶ I ran out of time.
- ▶ We're in trouble.
- ▶ I can't understand why this is happening.
- ▶ What we need is good luck.

Instead, use positive and make-it-happen language. If you use phrases such as the above or variations of them, you communicate the impression that you are willing to accept mediocrity instead of solutions. Remember: you are the leader, not an obstacle to progress; therefore, your words must reflect your responsibility to move your subordinates and the organization forward, beyond the status quo.

Be Conscious of Nonverbal Communication

Nonverbal communication consists of gestures, facial reactions, posture changes, or eye contact. These actions are easily observed by those around you. Whenever your nonverbal communication contradicts what you are communicating verbally, people notice. They rely strongly upon these nonverbal messages and make correct and incorrect judgments about you, such as that you are lying, holding back information, uninterested, or nervous. Even when you are not speaking at all, people often can surmise what you are thinking by observing your natural nonverbal communication, such as tapping a pen, which indicates nervousness, or blankly staring into space, which suggests boredom. Subordinates look to their leaders for guidance, support, enthusiasm, and curiosity; nonverbal language tells them what you're thinking and feeling, so be conscious of the silent messages you're sending.

Whenever your nonverbal communication contradicts what you are communicating verbally, people notice.

You can use nonverbal communication to your advantage in your leadership duties. By practicing using nonverbal communication correctly, you enhance your ability to communicate well. This will lead others to interpret your body language more accurately and help them better understand your meaning. Videotape one of your presentations to see yourself in action; you

Nonverbal Tips

Make an effort to send positive nonverbal messages as often as you can and minimize any negative messages, unless, of course, you intentionally want to send a negative signal to someone. When speaking with someone, fully engage the person in the conversation by looking him or her in the eye and not looking all over the room, making ample use of appropriate facial expressions when reacting to what the person is saying, and asking questions to indicate that you are paying attention. To be truly present as a leader, be alert, maintain great posture, and energetically stay involved with what is happening at the moment.

will notice positive and negative gestures and mannerisms of which you may have been unaware.

Increase Team Communication

You and your subordinates should regularly come together and communicate as a team. This could occur in team meetings, informal chats, or scheduled informational discussions. The purpose of these sessions is to give every member of the team the opportunity to raise concerns, ask questions, receive knowledge and guidance, and vent frustrations. You should routinely meet with them individually, but a group setting gives you the opportunity to show leadership by proudly standing in front of your team and taking charge of a session. As a source of information, you are the common link among your team members. Because some people are reluctant to raise issues as individuals, they welcome the occasion to see issues raised by more vocal people and to observe firsthand your responses to their concerns. Finally, instead of depending on only one communication method, such as a meeting, it is wise to develop multiple channels of communication with your team, such as newsletters, bulletin boards, or e-mail. This will help ensure that your team members clearly get your messages.

Improve Organizational Communication

By using the communications process consistently, you will make your personal communications much more effective and efficient. The details of designing an organizational communications program are beyond the scope of this chapter, but the subject is important nevertheless. It is critical for an organization to have a dependable internal communications program in effect. A specific individual usually coordinates this in large companies, while in some organizations it is a collective function of leaders at all levels.

You and your subordinates should regularly come together and communicate as a team in team meetings, informal chats, or scheduled informational discussions.

125

Organizational communication is a challenging, complex process to control due to the volume of information and the multiple channels of communication in an organization. It serves to promote a high degree of communication, morale, and understanding throughout the company. Good organizational communication ensures that the members are well informed in a balanced and straightforward way about all significant issues affecting the organization, such as business challenges, policy changes, and operational and strategic issues. Organizational communication also touches on other significant issues, such as organizational design, workplace improvements, customer service, and use of information technology. Organizations attempt to face these challenges through formal networks of communication, such as reporting channels, specific functional departments, and communication networks including voice mail, computer, and other technology systems.

Despite the challenges at the organizational level, always search for opportunities to improve communications outside your immediate realm of responsibility. As a leader, you have an obligation to identify and correct any perceived communication problems that affect your department or subordinates. Do this by actively communicating with other departments to dig out any information that you need but is not given to you. While getting this information, you can make helpful suggestions for improvements to the responsible official. For example, you could recommend ways to communicate information by creating an organization-wide newsletter or you could make suggest specific topics for a publication to cover. If you feel that interdepartmental communication is stifled because employees in each department are unfamiliar with employees in the other departments, suggest a shared function like a potluck lunch or weekend social activity.

Understand Informal Communication Networks

In addition to formal networks of communication, there's the grapevine—the informal communications network that both complements and detracts from the formal networks. Accept the fact that it is impossible to eliminate, hard to control, but easy to use. When you know how the grapevine operates in your organization, you can use it when seeking or disseminating information. If you want to determine what is happening in your organization, such as how people feel about policies or what really concerns them, chat casually with your subordinates and others. Of course, you should be chatting with them routinely, but the point is that a vast amount of information in your organization is available if you simply talk informally with people. Try to see the grapevine as an alternative means of communication for you to use, not as a threat that challenges your leadership authority. As a leader, correct and dispel any erroneous information that you discover in the grapevine. This response, coupled with an open and credible communications program, will ensure that you and your team communicate correctly.

Communication, the first of the relationship skills, is vital yet simple to learn. As you have seen in this chapter, it requires persistence, determination, and commitment. Leaders must continually remind themselves that within the sphere of communication lie the solutions to many of your interpersonal and organizational challenges. Make proper communication one of your highest daily priorities.

If you want to determine what is happening in your organization, such as how people feel about policies or what really concerns them, chat casually with your subordinates and others.

Chapter 11

Teamwork

Valerie is set to form a project team that will work together for three months. She knows she has to get the right people for the team and this concerns her. What should she consider so that the team is well formed and achieves its objectives superbly? Jennifer is planning a monthly team meeting of colleagues from several divisions within her company. Though she has been in this type of meeting before, this will be her first time as meeting leader. How can she prepare for this opportunity?

A TEAM IS A GROUP OF PEOPLE WHO COLLABORATIVELY ACHIEVE SPEcific goals. A team has numerous configurations, such as small groups working in close contact with each other, isolated groups working in different countries, a marketing department within a company, or the entire company itself. In some organizations, there are teams within teams. They have always existed in some form, going by names such as groups, crews, units, or squads.

Great teamwork—which suggests efficient, coordinated, collaborative, and successful operations—is a major goal of having a team because teamwork generates so many benefits for you, your subordinates, and your organization. Not only is teamwork the outcome of your efforts at closely organizing and coaching your team but it also is an enthusiastic attitude and set of skills that you use to lead your team to success. Your objective is to improve teamwork attitudes and skills throughout your organization.

The use of teams and teamwork skills has become increasingly relevant to leaders and team members simply because it is an effective and smart way of doing things. Leaders cannot resort to barking their orders to subordinates and telling everyone exactly what they should do. Not only is it an inefficient method of achieving objectives but it is also ineffective.

Great teams cannot exist without great teamwork. If you are to thrive as a leader and take your organization to new levels of growth and achievement, you must seek innovative solutions to your increasingly complex challenges. It probably comes as no surprise to you that leaders do not individually have the right answers to all their challenges. They must pursue these solutions and implement them with the collective help of other people who have a variety of knowledge, skills, and interdisciplinary experience.

Teamwork means focusing less on what you can individually accomplish as a leader and more on how you can empower others to accomplish important things as a team. The idea of teamwork may scare some leaders who falsely believe they must surrender power to a group. In teamwork, you are sharing power with others to achieve greater levels of success. Leaders who have teamwork attitudes and skills recognize that they will be more successful by letting all members of the team contribute as much as they can.

Great teamwork allows the leaders to concentrate on the larger issues involved in leading the organization rather than on each individual issue. Even if you do not officially organize or recognize your group of subordinates as a team, you still can use the teamwork skills in this chapter and the teamwork attitude to guide them to success. Teamwork skills simply give you another perspective from which to approach your leadership duties.

Your objective is to improve teamwork attitudes and skills throughout your organization.

Teamwork means focusing less on what you can individually accomplish as a leader and more on how you can empower others to accomplish important things as a team.

Promote Teamwork

There are many reasons to promote teamwork in your organization. Teams help you do your job more easily because team members have less need for direct supervision since they become more autonomous. The camaraderie and group effort involved in team operations permit your subordinates to feel more satisfied with their work, resulting in fewer disciplinary problems, absences, and customer complaints. This sharing of ideas and talents can lead to better collective results. This is particularly true in fast-changing environments or situations involving technical issues.

Teamwork translates directly into bottom-line improvements in work processes, productivity, innovation, and safety. Even if you do not organize all your work into teams, the concepts are still applicable in a traditional work structure and can help you achieve your goals if you use them consistently. For example, teamwork can help you revise policies, solve a long-standing internal problem, or develop new products and services.

Teams Are Not Always Necessary

Despite the many excellent reasons for using teamwork and teams, remember that organizing solely by formal teams is not the only solution to your leadership challenges, nor is it always the best solution. There may be several reasons for this, as described next.

First, if your people do not share a common goal that they can achieve better working collectively through a system of mutual interdependence, then formal teams are not the answer. Second, teams may not be necessary to improve your organizational performance. Some other action, such as improvements in communications or training, may serve your needs better. Third, if the organization's top leaders or your potential team members are not excited about or supportive of organizing by teams, they will need some convincing before you decide to implement the concept. Fourth, if the organization or department is undergoing or anticipating any major changes in key personnel, turnover, strategic mission changes, or relocation, for example, it may be best to delay implementing formal teams until there is more organizational stability.

Be aware that some issues may surface that could cause resistance to your building a smoothly running team. Such issues could be fear of change, loss of control, or financial costs. While creating a team, there will be times when you and your team members are not producing any tangible revenue, cost reduction, or other results, even though each of you is still getting paid and undergoing team training. This temporary decrease in productivity, usually accompanied by an increase in training costs, is difficult to avoid but will be insignificant once you capture the benefits of teamwork.

Besides the economic costs, a leader at any level in an organization might perceive teamwork as a threat, because it involves sharing power—not controlling it. This perception, fortunately, is not as pervasive as it once was, due to the widespread recognition and publicity of the success of teamwork. Once the top leaders believe in teamwork principles and commit to following them throughout the organization, the rest of the leaders will follow and allay their fears about the upcoming changes.

Overcoming Doubt

You can overcome these objections and others. Realize that a team structure is a major commitment by everyone because it involves changes in attitudes, work processes, and interpersonal relationships. For effective teamwork, the organization's operating systems and informal climate must be well developed and positive, particularly in the areas of employee morale, diversity, communications, training, and innovation. Then as you proceed to develop teams, pay close attention to how you plan, organize, and optimize your team.

Once the top leaders believe in teamwork principles and commit to following them throughout the organization, the rest of the leaders will follow and allay their fears about the upcoming changes.

Finally, leaders or individual team members may have difficulty in accepting or understanding teamwork. They may have preconceptions that they will not be able to work well in a group environment because they prefer to work alone, that they will receive too much responsibility in a team setting, or that they will have to learn too many additional skills. Some may doubt that the organization is really committed to teamwork, especially if leaders have shown in the past that they are not interested in rewarding fairly, eliminating organizational politics, or encouraging employees to assume greater responsibilities.

Plan Your Team

One of your leadership objectives is to organize the right teams and get them performing quickly and well. Before you organize your team, spend time deciding what you want to accomplish and what your vision is for the team. This involves considering your team's goals, its organization, and your role as a leader and team member.

Goals

Develop a clear idea of what you want to accomplish at the team level. At this point in the process, the goals are broad because later you and your team will develop them more fully, both at team and individual levels. Make your team goals realistic, important and significant to the success of your organization, achievable, challenging to your team, time-specific, and measurable.

The primary reason to identify the team-level goals is to provide an unequivocal direction for your team.

Organization

To achieve its goals, a team must be well organized. The organization of a team is based on its general purpose. If the team changes its purpose, either

131

Importance of Team Goals

The primary reason to identify the team-level goals is to provide an unequivocal direction for your team. It will help your team members to know precisely what goals they must achieve. Then they will attach importance and urgency to them, get excited about achieving them, focus more on activities that clearly support achievement of the goals, and develop personal goals that fully support the team's goals. Your team's goals will be the rallying point that you will invariably depend upon to refocus your team members when needed.

temporarily or permanently, you can always reorganize it to better accommodate its new purpose. Three general ways to organize teams are around the purposes of problem solving, implementation, and innovation. You can organize according to one purpose or a combination.

A *problem-solving* team is responsible for finding solutions to one-of-a-kind problems. It is best used when a functional department is unable for any reason to effectively solve a problem. The team is typically disbanded once you resolve the problem. A good example of a problem-solving team is a project team, which was discussed in Chapter 7. Other problem-solving teams are known as task forces or by unique names such as Team Alpha.

A problem-solving team is process-oriented and is interested in logically arriving at a solution after, not before, debating and objectively examining the relevant facts and essential points. Due to the great amount of interaction among people on a problem-solving team, it functions best when the members can easily rely upon each other, when they have confidence in each other's abilities to contribute to an effective problem-solving work relationship, and when all are committed to the team's goals.

An *implementation* team is not concerned with finding solutions; it already has one—a plan that describes all the details of what everyone must do. An implementation team is committed to efficiently and accurately carrying out a clearly defined plan that has measurable standards and explicit operational procedures. This team functions best when it makes good use of the specialized skills of its members, unambiguous job duties, and can-do attitudes to implement its plan flawlessly.

An *innovation* team is responsible for seeking new and creative ways to do things, such as improving processes, designing new products or services, or simply making suggestions. It has the freedom and the authority to seek out new possibilities and explore a variety of options. This team thrives when it is insulated from the systemic annoyances and constraints of the organization and when it is allowed to be informal and independent.

Leader's Role

Before you organize a team, it is helpful to understand the varying roles that you will soon play. Although your roles change throughout the life cycle of a team, you are still the leader who is responsible for achieving your team's goals. All the leadership skills you learn are needed in your team environment. Regardless of the role that you are playing, always demonstrate by your words and actions that you are unrelentingly committed to the team and its goals.

By using the teamwork process, you can inspire and empower your team members to assume increasingly more responsibility, authority, and autonomy. Initially, you are the leader in charge, responsible for determining the direction for the team, closely supervising its formation, guiding the bonding of its members, and commencing the start-up of the work. Then as your team gets organized, you will use your relationship skills in the roles of conflict resolver, negotiator, and facilitator. You increasingly will rely upon participative leadership, in which team members exercise their leadership abilities and take responsibility for certain aspects of the work.

Leader to Coach

Once your team is organized and begins performing, your role becomes that of a coach who encourages and oversees the team collectively and each of its members individually. At this point, your goal is to let the team members assume and maintain as much control over themselves as possible, while you monitor performance, maintain open lines of communication, and reward achievements.

Depending upon how successful the team is at directing its work, you may further distance yourself into the role of advisor, in which you are available primarily when the team requests your assistance.

Organize Your Team

As an effective leader you will want to follow a detailed outline when organizing your team. Given the fast pace of activities during team formation and start-up, you and your team members must be organized, focused, and mission-oriented.

The purpose of this nine-part outline is to guide you through the key actions needed to get your team up and running—quickly and correctly.

- ▶ Select the team members.
- ▶ Determine your team goals.
- ▶ Teach the team attitude.
- ▶ Discuss team processes and details.
- ▶ Review the goals and develop a mission statement.
- ▶ Develop a plan.
- ▶ Determine and assign team roles and responsibilities.
- ▶ Obtain commitments.
- ▶ Build team trust, belonging, and spirit.

Select the Team Members

The basic requirement is that all your team members be qualified; they also must know how to do their jobs well and how to work with others in a team environment.

There are selection principles to consider that are helpful in all types of team situations. The basic requirement is that all your team members be qualified. They must know how to do their jobs well and how to work with others in a team environment. What you want on your team are individuals who possess a variety of skills so that your team can thrive during challenging situations.

The current work location of your potential team members affects how you create your team. For example, if you are choosing solely from your own department of 10 people, you clearly have a limited selection. If, however, you have a department of 200 or if you can choose from other departments within the organization, you have more selection.

There are two keys to guide you to the best-qualified team. First, choose a mix of team-oriented people with the most important technical skills that you require. These are competent people who are extremely knowledgeable and experienced in tasks and processes that will be crucial. Second, look for people with the personal characteristics and values that you believe are necessary to work on your team. Most team leaders obviously seek motivated, enthusiastic, ethical, hard-working, intelligent, and goal-oriented individuals.

Different Teams–Different Skills

If you are creating an innovation team, you may want a mix of more creative, independent thinkers and dreamers who can guide themselves if necessary, rather than the task-focused, by-the-book, and competitive people you will need on an implementation team. Similarly, a problem-solving team may need someone extremely knowledgeable and people-oriented or someone exceptionally skilled in a particular process. Identify your most important skill requirements for your team and start the selection process as described in Chapter 7.

On the basis of your particular requirements, though, you may need someone who can help you lead the team during your absences or someone with particularly excellent communications skills.

Determine Your Team Goals

Meet with your team members and let them know what you consider to be their broad goals. Discuss the purpose of these goals and how they relate to organizational goals. Let the team members know that within an hour or so it will be their responsibility to collectively refine these broad goals into specific, prioritized, and realistic objectives. It is the collective belief in these objectives that will provide your team members the long-term determination that will turn them into a committed and cohesive team.

Teach the Team Attitude

Each of your team members must develop a team attitude: they must believe that a team can outperform individuals and that their team is going to win. Although most of them will naturally develop a positive team attitude over time, you can speed up the process by telling them what makes a great team attitude and by reinforcing this way of thinking repeatedly over time.

Each of your team members must develop a team attitude: they must believe that a team can outperform individuals and that their team is going to win.

Next is a sample pep talk you can give your team members to teach the team attitude. Adapt it by using your own words to convey these essential concepts.

The goals you have as a team member are linked to the goals of the team. Your individual performance, therefore, affects the performance of the team. On a team, you do not have to give up your ideas, opinions, individuality, personal ambition, or positive criticisms, because we welcome them as contributions that can help the team achieve our goals. However, you must give the team's goals highest priority on the job and always give your best effort to the team. Once our team reaches consensus, we expect you to support the decision and implement it. Achievement of the team's goals, your success as a team member, and the pursuit of excellence are the most important concerns for our team.

Do not let petty disagreements, self-serving behavior, personality conflicts, organizational politics, or any other irrelevant issues assume more importance than our goals; otherwise, you will lose focus and concentration. This attitude negatively affects your fellow team members and, therefore, causes the team to lose focus. There is no problem or challenge that cannot be worked out if you are reasonable, open-minded, and respectful of others.

You are part of a team and we want you to be a committed team member who supports the work of your fellow teammates, who recognizes the need for each of the others to achieve our goals, and who unselfishly does your job well. Since we stress cooperation rather than competition, we believe in encouraging each other with positive regard and feedback. For the team to succeed, you must commit to being self-starting, motivated, hard-working, and responsible.

In return, as your leader I will see to it that you all have opportunities to grow as a team and as individuals. You will participate in training and development activities that will help you grow professionally and personally as well.

Since the team needs your contributions and expertise, I will seek and use your contributions as best and as often as I can. I believe in participating and involving myself on our team, and I want you to participate and involve yourself as well.

I fully expect that many of you will assume leadership roles in several aspects of our work. For those who want increasing leadership responsibilities, I will assist you. As team members, you will have the autonomy and the authority to carry out your responsibilities. I will treat you fairly and appreciate you. Finally, as your team leader, I will do everything possible to help you achieve the team goals, as well as your professional and personal success.

Discuss Team Processes and Details

Discuss all rules, policies, and procedures that will affect your team. Your team must establish procedures for dealing with communication, problem solving and decision making, conflict resolution, meetings, and training. Determine how much decision-making and implementation authority team members have as individuals or as subteams as well as what decisions are reserved for the team and team leaders. Let everyone know that all policies will be applied fairly and consistently.

After determining the goals, set realistic but challenging standards that will inspire your determined team to work hard and eventually succeed.

Review the Goals and Develop a Mission Statement

You and your team should freely discuss the team's goals that you described earlier. Your purpose is to give everyone the opportunity to raise questions, make comments, and offer suggestions on how best to achieve your goals. Analyze any relevant topic that affects your goals. In particular, examine why your organization needs the team to achieve these goals and why this team is the one to do this important work.

After determining the goals, set realistic but challenging standards that will inspire your determined team to work hard and eventually succeed. These standards will be the gauge of how well your team achieves the team and individual goals. Consider what your clients or customers need from you and what level of quality they demand. Take into account any external issues such as regulation, resource availability, and the competition. As a team, compose and agree upon a mission statement that succinctly lists and prioritizes your major goals.

Develop a Plan

Your team's goals may be extremely technical or could involve working with complicated measurements, processes, or quality standards. Alternatively, the goals may be comparatively simple, such as troubleshooting a customer service issue or simply providing quality human resources support to your organization. Regardless of the scope or complexity, you should spend sufficient quality time as a team discussing the details, using the problem-solving process, and developing a realistic plan of action to take you from where you are now to where you want to go, given all your resources and constraints.

If your team's goals involve areas that are unfamiliar to you, do some preparation for your planning meeting so you are aware of the particular issues involved. This will help you to guide your team in the right direction. For example, many professional societies have publications that give tips on how to structure a particular problem or list the steps involved in completing certain tasks. As you well know, there are hundreds of books on every aspect of organizational functions that can give you ideas and recommendations on any situation you may have. Use this widely available expertise along with the wisdom of your team members to develop a plan.

Determine and Assign Team Roles and Responsibilities

You and your team must clearly and fairly identify the responsibilities and roles of each team member if the team is to do its best. Superior team performance depends upon the superior performances of each of its members. If feasible, let the team members themselves determine individual roles and responsibilities. Spend adequate time to ensure they do this correctly and thoroughly, because the team members will own these responsibilities and the necessary authority after the assignment. Involving your team members with all the detailed planning at this stage will pay you huge dividends later as they develop into a cohesive, collaborative, and self-directing team.

You also want to ensure that all the team responsibilities are covered, that team members understand how their roles relate to each other, and that they know how their specific responsibilities contribute to achievement of the team's goals. In addition, explain how subpar performance can affect the team adversely and that you will, therefore, monitor the performance of all individuals and hold them accountable for their responsibilities. Determine specifically how you will evaluate individual and team performance and how each person will know when he or she and the team are performing successfully. All the individual goals should be linked to high standards of performance. Set the tone now for the pursuit of excellence and your team members will pursue it until they achieve success.

Obtain Commitments

One of your primary goals as the team leader will be to keep every member of your team committed.

Obtain explicit commitments from each team member to work hard to achieve team goals, pursue excellence, support his or her teammates, participate in improving the team, and maintain a great team attitude. Take the time to speak individually with each member and then all of them assembled as a team. One of your primary goals as the team leader will be to keep every member of your team committed. Keeping them all inspired and enthusiastic about being on their special team will be crucial later in ensuring your team's successful performance.

Build Team Trust, Belonging, and Spirit

Your team will function most effectively if its members are secure enough in their relationships to openly speak to each other as peers. It is particularly important during the first days of the team's existence that you take charge of the team and let the members get to know you and the schedule of upcoming events. This starts the process that leads to a trusting team. Team members need each other; if they are to fully concentrate on achieving the goals, each member must develop a high degree of trust for the others. This trust arrives quickly after team members share new experiences on the job and demonstrate that they can be counted upon to act with integrity.

Conversely, this requires that you be aware of factors that will diminish the trust levels in your organization, such as cliques, gossip, lack of follow-through on promises, hesitancies to delegate authority, and unfairness in any form. Loss of trust among team members is one of the most difficult problems to remedy. The loss can be minimized somewhat by removing the offending member from the team. Although this approach is one of last resort, it may be necessary because if lack of trust spreads, your team may not sufficiently recover.

Focus Is on the Team

As your team members identify with each other and the team grows, look for that spirited attitude that suggests that the focal point is the team, not any one person. Selfishness disappears, replaced by a total commitment to and respect for the team. By spending hours with each other working on important activities, team members will grow emotionally attached to each other and will encourage one another to pursue excellence in everything they do. It is the collective result of these individual performances that drives a team toward success. If they perform well once, they expect to perform even better next time. This relentless drive and inspiration to do everything first class is a pervasive attitude that will develop over time if you, the leader, set high standards for your team and hold the members accountable for the commitments they make.

Optimize Your Team

Now that you have established your team, there are ways for you to capitalize on your many efforts thus far.

- ▶ Monitor the flow of information and resources.
- ▶ Promote communication and collaboration.
- ▶ Coach individual and team performance.
- ▶ Train your team.
- ▶ Reward your team.

Monitor the Flow of Information and Resources

Teamwork exists in an environment that depends on information and resources. Your team members must have quick access to the quality organizational and external information that they need. Constantly check to see that they are getting reliable information so that they can make the best possible decisions. Maintain a logbook to keep an official record of the decisions and recommendations made by team members. This will serve as institutional knowledge and help you follow up on the ideas submitted by your team. In addition, you as the leader also must ensure that the team is logistically supported by the organizational staff and any other external agency involved. The team members count on you and other team leaders to help handle external relations so that they can focus on their daily work.

Promote Communication and Collaboration

As discussed in Chapter 10, communication is vital to any organization. It is particularly crucial for a well-functioning and collaborative team in which members spend so much time together and depend upon each other. Your team members must feel free to openly discuss issues and ask questions because this is how teams create and sustain a vibrant, collaborative, and trusting environment. Open lines of communication between you and the team members and among the team members result in high team morale, pride, willingness to take reasonable chances, and adaptability to changes. The unequivocal sharing of information allows team members to understand each other better and know how they feel about issues. Doesn't it make sense that all team members, if they know that each is supporting the others, will do their best for the good of the team? Can you imagine the possible successes for your team if every team member had this high level of confidence in the others?

Your team members must feel free to openly discuss issues and ask questions because this is how teams create and sustain a vibrant, collaborative, and trusting environment.

Despite the inevitable conflict that will arise in a team environment, your team members should understand that they can positively resolve all disagreements. Regularly hold informal discussions and social activities so that team members can communicate and bond. Team training activities can increase the trust levels among members, especially if conducted soon after you organize the team.

Coach Individual and Team Performance

Use monitoring procedures to keep track of how your team members and team are performing. If you frequently measure progress against challenging but achievable standards and then communicate this progress to your team members promptly and accurately, they will all know exactly where the team stands in terms of its goals and how their individual performances are helping the team. When giving feedback to your team members, remember to focus on details, facts, and team member performance. If you detect team performance problems, let your team members know and have them develop options that will improve the performance. The team then chooses the best

You and Your Team

Your team members appreciate your interest in what they do, and you will find that your relationship with each of them will grow stronger over time. In addition, by personally coaching your team members, you will diffuse any problems and concerns that they have.

course of action and implements it. Follow up to ensure that your team members are responding to your coaching; if not, repeat this coaching process.

If you find that a team member is not working collaboratively or has other performance problems, it is essential to change his or her behavior through coaching. Tell that person specifically how his or her attitude and performance are hindering the team, and find out why the person is not performing up to the agreed-upon standards. If he or she does not improve, you should remove the person from the team because he or she will cause more damage than good—particularly when other team members become discouraged by the fact the disruptive person is not being penalized for counterproductive behavior, yet the team is bearing the penalty.

If you find that a team member is not working collaboratively or has other performance problems, it is essential to change his or her behavior through coaching.

Train Your Team

Despite your having the opportunity to select well-trained, motivated people for your team, once the team begins working you will notice additional needs for training. This does not mean that you made bad selections or that your leadership is ineffective. The reality is that team members need periodic training to maintain or improve the skills needed while participating on the team.

Specific training to include during team development is in the areas of individual jobs, problem solving, and team skills. Job training addresses those skills required of the individuals to do their jobs or the jobs of the team members they support. Problem-solving training is important because this skill is inherently necessary in most of the duties of a team, especially autonomous or self-directed work teams. It is crucial, therefore, to train team members to think logically and methodically so that they can participate equally in team decisions. This will help keep your team members enthusiastically involved in the team's activities and help avert the tendency toward ineffective consensus group thinking.

If any team members are inexperienced in working on a team, you should conduct specific training so that they can learn about teamwork concepts and practice team skills, such as communication and conflict resolution. Team training does more than just correct problems; it provides the means to empower your team so it eventually can carry out all its functions without the constant guidance of a leader. In addition, team training is specifically needed when the team is underperforming or some members have developed severe group hostility, low productivity, or low morale.

Team training is a good opportunity for you and your team members to develop cohesion.

Team training is an ongoing activity that will best help your team members if they have specific performance deficiencies. As discussed in Chapter 9, determine training needs by gathering preliminary data and surveying your team members. The key point is that in team training all members should be involved in assessing the training needs, developing training options, agreeing to the plan, and participating in the training. More experienced team members should help you lead these sessions.

Team training is a good opportunity for you and your team members to develop cohesion. The activities that you choose to help train your team can be of great benefit in achieving your training objectives if you plan the activities with your team in mind. As well as being relevant, the activities should be interesting and tailored to the character and personality of your team. The training should emphasize increasing expertise in specific skills that will enable the team members to later develop practical solutions to support both team and organizational goals. Before the actual training, emphasize your role as a facilitator who wants to guide them through the training that they themselves have selected and planned. Suggest that they all be open-minded, relaxed, and enthusiastic about spending this time together.

Reward Your Team

Demonstrate that you appreciate your team members by rewarding them externally and internally. The reward system will be discussed more in the next chapter, on motivation, but there are some specific points that you can note now. Because you are truly interested in team performance, you should base your external rewards on the accomplishments of the team, not the individuals. These external awards are many, such as the traditional bonuses, certificates, and public recognition. Find the rewards that most motivate your team and integrate them into your reward system.

Internal Rewards

More importantly, by being an involved, caring, and committed leader, you will enable your team members to create for themselves internal rewards, which some people value much more than most anything that can be awarded to them. Feelings of pride, belonging, self-esteem, and purpose will motivate people to great performance. It also will sustain them when their team faces difficult challenges.

Effective Meetings

To fulfill your leadership duties effectively, you must rally team members around specific goals and then guide them to outstanding performance. Meetings are an excellent way to do this. Meetings can be quick or lengthy, scheduled or impromptu, and conducted with many or few people. To a leader, meetings are more than a method to promote communications, solve problems, or manage priorities. A meeting, in the broadest context, is a means for you to efficiently exercise your leadership responsibilities by working closely with others in a team setting. It is often the primary way that you as a leader collectively communicate with your team members, resolve conflicts, solicit opinions, and guide the group's efforts.

Meetings are an excellent way to rally team members around specific goals and then guide them to outstanding performance.

You most likely can recall times when you or others stated that meetings are ineffective ways of conducting work, a waste of time, and simply forums for opinionated participants to dominate the discussion. You may even have wished that meetings be banned forever. It can be helpful, therefore, to identify reasons why meetings are ineffective.

Nonproductive Meetings

Sometimes meetings may not be the right response to a problem. First, do not use meetings solely for distributing or relaying information. Instead of asking ten people to give up two hours of their time, for a total cost of 20 work hours, write a memo or send information by mail. Second, meetings are often not the best means of checking progress on individual assignments if they waste the time of participants who must listen to routine updates that do not concern them. You may occasionally want teammates to hear what is occurring with each other, as it can promote communication and team building. Make an effort, however, to get individual updates from team members at their job sites, in your office, or on the telephone. Third, avoid having a meeting involving all members if a smaller group can meet and resolve the issues more effectively. Finally, do not use a meeting for seeking opinions and comments on important new ideas if the participants have not had time to adequately form their opinions or to review relevant information. Instead, notify them in advance about the ideas and send them information to read before the meeting.

Too often meetings are convened to discuss insignificant issues. Regularly scheduled meetings, such as the weekly staff meeting, can be useful if there are significant issues to discuss or resolve. They also permit the

143

participants to schedule more effectively by being able to plan to attend. It is best for you as a leader, however, to routinely assess the topics a day or two before each meeting. If you find that there is a need for the meeting, then keep it scheduled. If not, cancel it; the team members will greatly appreciate your considerate and decisive action.

Meeting facilitators sometime fail to establish or maintain control of meetings. If participants sense that the meeting lacks structure and control or that the leader allows outspoken individuals to dominate the discussion, then some participants will lose interest, daydream, and not contribute during the meeting.

Despite the bad experiences that you or others may have had, effective meetings are essential to the success of the organization and to the individuals who need to get business accomplished with the assistance of other people. Although much work can be done by using the telephone, videoconferences, and e-mail, the face-to-face communication involved in periodic meetings is crucial. Here are six suggestions for making your meetings useful and effective, whether you are leading them or participating in them.

Use an Agenda

If you determine that you really need a meeting, publish and distribute in advance a detailed agenda—and then follow it during the meeting.

If you determine that you really need the meeting, publish and distribute in advance a detailed agenda—and then follow it during the meeting. Not only does an agenda remind the participants about the upcoming meeting but it also gives them some advance knowledge of the topics so that they can prepare for the meeting and contribute more effectively. If you are planning an extended meeting of several hours, circulate a proposed agenda so that key participants can provide their comments or suggested topics. The agenda also gives you additional authority during the meeting to discuss the topics—and only those topics—and to remain on schedule.

Stay on Course

Encourage participation by seeking comments from every participant, tactfully preventing any from dominating the discussion with their own concerns, and limiting digression. If you are leading the meeting, it is wise to avoid participating directly in evaluating suggestions so as to encourage others to participate more freely. However, do speak up to get the meeting moving along, clarify issues, or make an outstanding suggestion. Evaluate your progress during the meeting to see if you are on course with your agenda schedule and making progress toward achieving the meeting's objectives.

Facilitate the meeting by asking leading and clarifying questions or by making statements that do the following:

- Encourage participation—"How do you feel about that idea, Alyssa?"

- Rephrase comments—"So, Max, you want brainstorming sessions, like Colette does?"

- Reward participants—"Good idea, Linda."

- Limit digression—"Let's see, since that important topic is not on our agenda and our time is limited, we should schedule it for the next time. How does that sound, Eric?"

- Preserve civility—"Come on, folks, let's keep the noise down while Alan is speaking."

- Maintain order—"Just a moment, Ross; let's finish hearing from Warren."

- Cause action—"Lindsey, can you and Kelley ask the vendor about that issue?"

- Summarize discussion—"Are we in agreement that finance issues are our priority?"

End the Meeting Positively and Assertively

Before adjourning, thank everyone for their valued participation and ask each person to make a brief summarizing comment of actions he or she will take or what he or she feels is important. Indicate on the agenda that you plan to solicit their comments so they will not be surprised during the meeting. This will give the participants one last opportunity to offer any reluctant or strong opinions or what they feel is the most important result of the meeting. Close the meeting by mentioning any key point that was omitted from the individual summaries and ending with a positive statement about how you appreciate the high level of their involvement. Remember to retain your meeting notes so that you can refer to them later. If beneficial to you or the participants, prepare a summary of the meeting to distribute to participants.

Watch the Details

Pay attention to all the details, such as sending out timely notification, starting on time, inviting only those who are needed, scheduling breaks, and choosing the meeting room. Meetings are more effective when the tempera-

145

ture is comfortable, there are no noisy distractions, and the room is clean. Every few meetings, ask someone to evaluate how well the meeting has flowed. Although as the leader you may believe the meetings are going well, it is helpful to have a participant confirm or refute your impressions of the meeting.

Actively Participate

If you are not leading the meeting, be an active, involved, and informed contributor. If you have something relevant to say, say it with conviction. If you have a question, ask it, because someone else is probably thinking about the same question. The meeting's leader needs your positive suggestions and valued experience. Your presence is not beneficial if you read unrelated material, distract the speakers by chatting loudly with others, offer negative or irrelevant comments, or doze.

Establish Goals

When you are solely a participant in the meeting and not its leader, identify before the meeting specific ways in which the meeting can serve your objectives, then actively participate to ensure that your needs are considered and your goals are achieved. You may have little choice in whether to attend a meeting, but if it is scheduled, you can use it to achieve goals related to your work, to resolve longstanding problems, to determine the views of other participants, or to gain cooperation from others. Remember to think of solutions, not problems. Having such a positive focus in the meeting will give you the impetus to use the meeting to help you do your job.

Remember that, by definition, a leader is one who gets the right things accomplished at the right time with the assistance of other people. These other people are your team members, whether they are people you supervise, peers or fellow volunteers, organizational staff members, clients, or family members. So you are not always the leader, but in every case you are working with others to achieve a common objective. Leadership through teamwork implies that you can harness the skills and talents of other people to create an environment where success becomes contagious.

Chapter 12

Motivation

Andy, an executive in a company, believes his team of directly reporting co-workers need more motivation. He knows he has a nice group of achievers, but not too many overachievers who are constantly trying to establish high goals. What can he do? Is it his responsibility to motivate them?

MOTIVATION DESCRIBES THE REASONS PEOPLE ACT THE WAY they do. Motivation is an intensely personal and emotional state wherein an individual feels compelled to act for any number of reasons or needs. It is because of these reasons and needs that people do superior work, fail to complete an assignment, offer to work overtime without pay, or quit an organization in disgust. So when you pinpoint why your subordinates do what they do, you are closer to establishing their motivation.

You cannot change others' motivations or create new ones by yourself; individuals have to do it internally themselves. Your primary goal is to understand the general needs of your subordinates as well as their specific needs in terms of their tasks and responsibilities. The better you can meet those needs, the more likely you are to have motivated subordinates who will succeed.

Your Role in Motivation

As a leader, don't settle for subordinates or team members who are motivated to do their job adequately. You want them to be as motivated and energized as possible, because that is how you implement your strategy, negotiate the certainty of change, and achieve great successes. A committed and enthusiastic team will overcome obstacles of all types to achieve its goals. Though it is a part of your job, you are not primarily responsible for motivating your subordinates to this successful job performance—it is ultimately their job to motivate themselves. You are responsible, however, for creating and maintaining an environment where subordinates have the opportunity to achieve a high degree of motivation, willingly strive to achieve their goals, and intensely want to do the best job they can. These are the purposes for increasing your motivation skills.

It would be erroneous to think of motivation as a leadership skill that is isolated from your other leadership responsibilities.

After you take to heart and use what has been discussed so far in this book, you will probably have enthusiastic subordinates who are motivated to do their jobs well. This is because when leaders assume ownership of their responsibilities and lead in a caring and knowledgeable way, their subordinates will already have a basic level of motivation from which to do what is right.

It would be erroneous to think of motivation as a leadership skill that is isolated from your other leadership responsibilities. The motivation of a subordinate is affected by all the variables that exist every day: needs, emotions, job conditions and performance, interactions with people, as well as all the organizational issues such as morale and structure. Nevertheless, as a leader you can affect people's motivations through determined efforts to use all your leadership skills well: for example, solve problems well, train well, communicate well, and maintain a team well. This chapter will help you integrate these and the other skills you have learned into a practical, commonsense approach to motivation. You will continue to build upon your motivation skills as you learn more during the remaining chapters of the book.

Principles Underlying Motivation

A leader influences individual behavior so that organizational goals can be achieved through the coordinated efforts of many people. Individual job performance is primarily a function of three factors: the employee's abilities, the support he or she gets from the organization to carry out the job tasks, and the employee's motivation to do that job. The first component, abilities, was addressed in Chapter 9, on the importance of training and developing a skilled group of subordinates. The second component, which is a premise throughout this book, is the effective use of leadership skills and how they can make enormous contributions to the success of your subordinates. The third component of job performance, motivation, consists of many personal factors.

Although motivation originates within the individual, you can significantly affect it if you understand six principles. You can use these principles to solidify your knowledge of motivation and help you determine the right actions to take. Later in the chapter are five steps to help you create and maintain an environment of high motivation.

These are the six principles underlying motivation that leaders must understand.

▶ People prefer positive rewards over punishment.

▶ Misused rewards cause people to act improperly.

▶ Meaningful contributions inspire people.

▶ People will pursue a worthy and achievable goal.

▶ People must believe and value your promises of reward.

▶ People want their leaders to act like leaders.

People Prefer Positive Rewards over Punishment

It is almost always better to reinforce your guidance and directives with the promise of a reward than with the threat of punishment. Punishment is often thought of in harsh terms, though it does not have to be harsh in terms of the work environment; the term accurately reflects a consequence that could range from mild to harsh. Both the lure of rewards and the certainty of punishment act as incentives, things that cause a person to take action. Since this is true, do not be startled to learn that people act foremost for their own interests, not for yours or the organization's. This does not mean that your subordinates are second-rate because they are selfish—this is just a fact of human nature.

The rewards that you offer, which vary in importance for each individual, must be of primary benefit and value to your subordinates' current personal and professional priorities, not the organization's priorities. For instance, if you want someone to work hard on a project just because the organization will reap more profits, that will not necessarily increase your subordinate's motivation. To ensure a motivational opportunity, you must

It is almost always better to reinforce your guidance and directives with the promise of a reward than with the threat of punishment.

somehow relate the project to an individual reward that will act as a positive incentive to the person, such as a share of the company's profits, an increase in the value of the company stock (if they own any), personal recognition, or time off from work.

Be clear about punishment. You may need it as a negative incentive to ensure that some subordinates take the actions you want them to take. It is not, however, an effective means for maintaining high motivation. Do not punish subordinates because they are taking action and attempting to do the work but failing on the first try. Motivation by fear is not something you want to do. If you must punish, do so because they took action but are consistently performing poorly, showing a bad attitude, or behaving in undesirable ways. Do not be afraid of punishment; you need it as part of your overall system of motivation. Like rewards, punishment has levels of intensity from which to choose, ranging from a mild conversation indicating your displeasure to progressively serious actions such as written reprimands and termination.

It is crucial that you do not overuse punishment by resorting to it for every undesirable occurrence in the workplace. That approach may only inspire more negative behavior or bitterness. Most of your subordinates do not require negative incentives to perform well; nevertheless, they must know the consequences for performance discrepancies and believe that you will firmly enforce the same fair standards for everyone. For example, if they know they will lose their jobs if they consistently are late for work, they will motivate themselves to show up on time. It is better in this example, though, for you to routinely de-emphasize the punishment aspects of showing up late and emphasize the rewards for showing up on time.

Misused Rewards Cause People to Act Improperly

Positive rewards will encourage people to do their best because it is in their self-interest to do so. When leaders misuse rewards, however, these incentives become disincentives that deter people from acting properly. For example, a company establishes employee bonuses as a reward system. However, if a leader threatens to revoke the bonus system if his or her subordinates do not perform better, it discourages them and negatively affects the trust that had been established. Other misuses include the overuse of praise or assigning credit for a job well done to the wrong person. Subordinates view their good relations with their leader as an incentive, and they expect the leader to consistently act maturely and responsibly. When leaders ignore their responsibilities or contradict good leadership practices, many subordinates will lose their hope, enthusiasm, and motivation to do well.

Meaningful Contributions Inspire People

When people believe what they are doing is important, they will feel good about their work and approach it with enthusiasm and determination. They will believe that the organization, their boss, and their co-workers are depending on them to do the job to the best of their ability because it is crucial to everyone's success. Since their work is important, they will motivate themselves to do it well because they feel important. If they do not believe their work involves significant responsibility or contributions, they will more likely take shortcuts in quality or not behave as team players.

When meaningful and challenging work is combined with the opportunity to participate in workplace decision making, your subordinates have powerful incentives to maintain a high level of motivation.

People Will Pursue a Worthy and Achievable Goal

When subordinates believe strongly that they can achieve a goal that is worthwhile, they are more likely to pursue the goal with gusto and achieve it. This shows you how pivotal you are as a leader when you guide your subordinates to expect to achieve fair and challenging goals. The more convincing and inspiring you are, the more they will believe in the worthiness of the goal and contribute to achieving it. This, in turn, promotes a valuable commitment to you and your organization. As discussed throughout this book, you must ensure that the subordinates understand what they must do and why they must do it. One effective way to do this is to clearly communicate with each subordinate during goal-setting and coaching sessions.

People Must Believe and Value Your Promises of Reward

A firm bond of trust between you and your subordinates is key to keeping them motivated. If they know that you will do what you promise, then they will not doubt you. This trust will cause your subordinates to form positive conclusions about what to expect under your leadership. In addition to believing your promise of reward, subordinates must value and desire the reward you offer. If they don't, the lure of the reward will not stimulate them to expend the effort to attain it.

When meaningful and challenging work is combined with the opportunity to participate in workplace decision making, your subordinates have powerful incentives to maintain a high level of motivation.

151

People Want Their Leaders to Act Like Leaders

Most people do not like uncertainty, indecision, disorganization, or lack of direction in a leader. They feel unmotivated to do great things when they believe that no one is in charge, that the leader does not care about their needs or appreciate them, or that the leader does not care about their comments to help achieve organizational goals. Your subordinates and team members count on you not only to provide clear direction and purpose but also to not retreat when you are confronted with tough decisions or difficulties.

It is imperative, therefore, that you understand the important connection between your subordinates' motivation and the exercise of your leadership responsibilities. All your leadership skills are vital components of a highly motivating and well-functioning work environment. Few expect you to do everything correctly, but they expect you to do your best since you are the leader. It is reassuring and comforting to them that you understand your mission. They want you to determine the right things to do and lead the way; then they will follow you.

It is imperative that you understand the important connection between your subordinates' motivation and the exercise of your leadership responsibilities.

Motivational Goals for Leaders

Now that you understand the basic principles of motivation, you can use these five goals to create and maintain an environment of high motivation.

▶ Know what motivates your subordinates.

▶ Be a sensitive leader.

▶ Reward properly, immediately, and equitably.

▶ Reward desired behavior and punish undesirable behavior.

▶ Eliminate demotivators.

Know What Motivates Your Subordinates

Since people are motivated by different things, find out what motivates each of your subordinates or team members and use this information to sustain a high state of motivation. If you communicate well with your employees, you naturally will find out their hopes and dreams, along with their needs and core values. You may uncover talents and abilities that were suppressed but can now be used for the benefit of both your subordinates and the organization. Motivations are shaped not only by personal and professional experiences, age, and tenure in the work force, but also by expectations of what will happen as they perform their jobs under your leadership. Once you

Informal Rewards

Not all people are motivated by the usual formal rewards, such as automatic pay increases, fringe benefits, and expense accounts. Some are motivated more by the informal rewards that exist or that you as a leader can initiate. For example, some subordinates enjoy a sense of control over their jobs that they have not had before. For others it may be nurturing, peer support that helps them achieve their goals. These informal rewards and benefits can be extrinsic, which are given by others, such as recognition or fair treatment. At other times the rewards are intrinsic, meaning they are primarily internal, such as feelings of self-esteem and of satisfaction in a job well done.

determine what motivates your subordinates, modify your formal and informal reward systems so you can effectively reward your subordinates based on what they value.

Staying in touch with your subordinates' motivations will allow you to react quickly when you notice that their needs have changed or become satisfied, so you can find new motivators. What motivates an individual this month may not motivate him or her next month. By keeping up with what motivates your subordinates, you will always be able to align their needs with the organization's needs. You do this by helping subordinates see exactly how they can satisfy their needs by being a productive part of your organization—a win-win situation for them and you.

When you know more about your subordinates, you will understand them better. Know details about each subordinate's family, such as the names of the spouse and children, challenges that the family faces, and what the family does for recreation. These are indeed personal details, but great leaders know these things about their subordinates, and your subordinates probably want you to know them; if they do not, they will tell you so. Remember these details by jotting them down in a notebook; refer to them periodically so that you can use them in conversations with your subordinates.

Staying in touch with your subordinates' motivations will allow you to react quickly when you notice that their needs have changed or become satisfied, so you can find new motivators.

Be a Sensitive Leader

Your subordinates are, above all, individuals. They each are sensitive to different degrees and will require, therefore, varying amounts of attention. For example, people react differently to criticism or lack of praise. Some need periodic comments from you on how well they are doing their jobs or they will believe you are ignoring them. Some subordinates are insulted if you start discussing work without saying "Good morning" or if you forget to say

"Please" when asking for assistance. Many high achievers feel slighted if you spend more of your coaching time with the underachievers than with them.

Being pleasant to your subordinates will help them maintain a high state of motivation if the pleasantries are used in conjunction with good motivational skills; being pleasant will not accomplish much by itself. If you are perceptive, empathetic, and sympathetic to others' sensitivities, your subordinates will see you as less of a threat and more of an ally. If you value and respect your relationship with your team members and do not take it for granted, you will help them attain high levels of motivation.

Reward Properly, Immediately, and Equitably

Proper rewards include a mix of external and internal awards large enough to motivate all your subordinates to great achievements.

There are many ways to structure a reward-and-recognition program. For a leader's purposes, such a program includes any formal or informal means of recognizing an employee who has performed well on the job. Several books are available on this topic; some even list hundreds of rewards you can give those at work. The key points to remember are to reward properly, immediately, and equitably.

Proper rewards include a mix of external and internal awards large enough to motivate all your subordinates to great achievements. Besides using monetary rewards such as bonuses, incentive pay, or cash awards, it is important to include other kinds of rewards. These might include public recognition, time off from work, or gifts. Vary the rewards by using some that relate to the job, such as professional seminars or training, and some that do not, such as a weekend trip or lunch. Probably the most appreciated reward that you could give someone is simple praise or thanks that comes from the heart.

The types of rewards you give are based on what you want to achieve, what works best for your organization's culture, what is financially and operationally feasible, and what suggestions you solicit from your subordinates. As discussed in the previous chapter, if your subordinates are organized as a team, the rewards should be primarily based on the team's accomplishments. If your organization depends heavily on individual contributions, reward individuals. To keep everyone oriented to your strategic objectives, you can link long-term rewards to long-term performance such as growth, not short-term earnings or sales.

Reward as soon as possible after the achievement so as to encourage a repetition of the behavior. For example, if you recognize someone as employee of the year, you should obviously do so annually as soon as the competition ends.

With more frequent activities, such as monthly sales contests or periodic projects, tie the reward into the culmination of each activity. To keep the winner motivated, others enthusiastic about the next award, and everyone's performance level high, give the reward as soon as possible after the achievement becomes known. Informal rewards can be more spontaneous, such as when you praise a subordinate for outstanding work or a great idea.

One excellent motivator is to set a goal for yourself to praise all your subordinates or team members in some way several times a day. If you think about it, most people do good things throughout the day. Wouldn't it be great for you to let those around you know that you appreciate them? Your subordinates want to know when they are doing a great job; one way of ensuring that they know is to tell them. You do not need to offer gushing praise every time. Simple statements such as "You've done a great job," "I am proud of you," or "I appreciate what you've done" will be impressive enough.

The rewards system should be devised and operated equitably. This is because people will compare their experiences with the rewards system with the experiences that other people have with it. Naturally, they will become unhappy if they perceive inequities or if rewards are not available to everyone uniformly. Areas of concern include reward systems that are too complicated, that are not appropriate for your particular industry, that do not reflect differences in geographical areas, or that do not reward the desired performance above low performance.

Although you may not have primary responsibility for the organization's formal reward system, you can provide your influential comments to the people who do. As you detect inequities or inconsistencies in the reward system that affect the motivation of your subordinates, take solutions to the responsible officials. You need to resolve these issues because if you do not reward your team properly, you will see an increase in undesirable performance behavior.

Reward Desired Behavior and Punish Undesirable Behavior

It seems obvious, but remember to follow through on your promises of reward and threats of punishment. Your subordinates will get your message a lot quicker when your actions support your words. When subordinates perform satisfactorily, reinforce this behavior by rewarding them in some way.

It is important to punish in some way an undesirable behavior and deter repetition by clearly letting people know when their behavior is wrong. If

> ## Rewarding the Right Way
>
> To strengthen their motivation and encourage them to achieve super performances, it is crucial to have some sort of merit system in which your subordinates will receive more reward when they perform better than the standard. The key is to reward the desired individual or team behavior that you want. If you want close and collaborative team behavior, do not overly reward individual performance within the team. If you need creativity, then provide incentives for your team to make creative suggestions.

you do not punish them, you are by default rewarding their negative behavior and giving them the message that their undesirable behavior is allowed. It is more likely, therefore, that they will repeat this behavior.

Eliminate Demotivators

Most anything in the work environment can potentially affect the level of a person's motivation. One part of your job is to continually identify and eliminate demotivators that cause dissatisfaction. Demotivators could include policies and procedures that are stifling, controlling, or nonsensical; a benefits-and-rewards system that is too formal; the career management system; or even the work environment itself. If you see a problem, do not ignore it but seek instead to find its solution.

Simply removing demotivators will not necessarily create motivation, but it can lead to a more positive work environment that will help eliminate negativity among your team members. This can eventually lead to higher levels of satisfaction in your organization.

When your subordinates and team members evolve to the point where they are excited and enthused about being contributing, responsible members of a winning organization, you indeed have a motivated team. Your leadership efforts will have created an abundance of internal rewards as important as any external reward.

Chapter 13

Diversity

Capital Corporation has a diversity program in place and its top officers believe there is equity and fairness throughout the company. It has been several years since the program was instituted and John, a manager, is wondering whether changes should be made. What can he do now to see if the company's program can be improved? What leadership qualities should he personally exhibit to promote diversity in his department?

DIVERSITY MEANS HAVING DIFFERENCES. YOU MAY NO DOUBT HAVE strong diversity beliefs, such as the best age or gender for a certain type of profession or that you prefer to work with someone from a similar background and heritage. It would be naive to expect you to disregard years of socialization about the variety of issues related to diversity. This chapter is not a minicourse on diversity awareness; it is intended to show you how you can be a better leader simply by considering the impact of diversity upon your responsibilities, then taking steps to capitalize upon the diversity you have in the workplace. As with all your leadership skills, you can use these diversity ideas and skills in any organization where you have a leadership role, such as at work, in your community, or in your family.

Your diversity goals as a leader are twofold.

▶ Personally exhibit, and lead your subordinates to exhibit, understanding, acceptance, respect, and tolerance in your behavior and attitude toward diverse groups.

▶ Use diversity as a valuable catalyst to increase the performance and motivation of all your subordinates so that they can achieve their full potential.

Diversity, as it pertains to your leadership role, refers to the differences among the people in your organization in eight major areas:

▶ Gender

▶ Age

▶ Race

▶ Ethnicity

▶ Physical appearance

▶ Physical abilities

▶ Background

▶ Lifestyle

Diversity Is Widespread

The last four categories are vast, and conceivably could contain within them scores of further classifications, such as educated and less educated, factory workers and office workers, or sports participants and sports spectators. Because most people could claim membership in several groups, it is realistic to think of diversity as a basic characteristic of your work force, not as a separate challenge that you must handle differently, less intensely, or more delicately than your other leadership duties.

There is some debate as to whether certain diversity classifications are more important than others. Some scholars attach more importance to gender and race than lifestyle choices and background because the first set constitutes a more permanent and significant part of daily living. This line of reasoning concludes that lifestyle choices, background, and abilities are less important because they are supposedly more fluid and easily changed.

There are several reasons why it is foolhardy for leaders to try to assign relative importance to diversity categories. First, leaders cannot accurately make those types of subjective decisions when it is the individual, not other people, who determines the value of such differences and must decide, for example, whether to think of himself or herself more as an Asian-American or as a young single parent. Of course, the legal system forces you to make these distinctions in certain categories, such as race and gender, but that does not mean that all people value their racial differences more than their educational differences, for example. Second, because there are so many conceivable classifications of diversity, it would be highly impractical and ineffective for leaders to assign a relative importance for each category. Third, if team members perceive their leaders as favoring one classification of diversity over another, they could have resentment toward the leaders that may fester and create new workplace problems.

Leaders should not think of diversity classifications in terms of a hierarchy of importance but rather should value all diversity equally.

Leaders should not think of diversity classifications in terms of a hierarchy of importance but rather should value all diversity equally. An effective leader will use these differences to create a better work environment for subordinates and more success for the organization.

The Relevance of Diversity

You or your fellow leaders may wonder why there is a need to learn diversity skills or even consider the topic, especially since handling diversity has not been seen historically as a vital leadership skill. There are several significant reasons why a leader must go beyond simple indifference to diversity.

Realize That Demographics Are Changing Dramatically

The demographics of the work force—your most important resource—will continue to change dramatically. Your subordinates, peers, customers, and supervisors will increasingly be people who do not longer fit conveniently into what was once considered the traditional majority: married Caucasian males with three children. Although you may have already noticed this demographic shift, expect it to be more pronounced in the years ahead.

Changing demographics will dramatically affect you as you try to attract and retain the best employees for your organization.

This change will dramatically affect you as you try to attract and retain the best employees for your organization. If you consult organizations that predict U.S. work force demographic trends, most foresee even greater diversity in the work force. These diversity forecasts are similar to the expected general population trends, which undoubtedly affect your responses to customer service, marketing, and community interaction.

Potential Employees and Diversity

Because competition for the smaller pool of younger, diverse employees will increase, entry-level workers will most likely examine very closely how a potential employer handles diversity issues. Those organizations that effectively make the most of their diversity will be viewed as progressive and attuned to the needs of the labor force, while those organizations that do not will be seen as inferior places to work. This inevitably will create challenges for the recruitment and retention efforts of organizations.

Do Not Ignore Change

Diversity, just as with most challenges you face as a leader, is a part of your environment that is here to stay. Although you may be able to change customer opinions about your product, improve the quality in a manufacturing facility, or successfully ignore naysayers when launching a new service, you cannot significantly change the diversity in your environment. Ignoring it will only cause you to miss opportunities for yourself and your team and increase the level of dissatisfaction in your work force. As a leader, you must respond.

Consider the Benefits of Diversity

The concept of a diverse work force parallels the discussion in Chapter 11 in that there are huge advantages of having team members who possess a wide range of knowledge, skills, and experience. By actively seeking and using the varied ideas, opinions, and talents available, you will leverage your work force. Diversity then becomes an advantage and a competitive edge. As a result, you will better understand the needs of your domestic and international customers, the potential applications of your existing or new products and services, and the right approaches to targeting diverse customers in the entire marketplace.

By actively seeking and using the varied ideas, opinions, and talents available, you will leverage your work force.

Remember that one aspect of your responsibilities as a leader is to bring everyone together as a team to get the right things done. As you hone the leadership skills presented in this book, you will make tremendous progress toward building and maintaining a high-performing team. If you incorporate the issues of diversity into your leadership activities, you will make more progress because these issues represent a vital dimension to your success.

When your team members and others know that you are not just tolerant but completely accepting of their diversity, your job will be much easier because they will respect you as an empathetic, concerned leader. Your team members are all individuals with unique personalities, needs, heritages, and backgrounds. They will respond better to your leadership if they know that you value them personally, not just for what they can do for you and the organization. This does not mean that you tolerate unacceptable performance from subordinates because you fear they may label you as racist, sexist, or intolerant. This does not mean that you have to relearn all your leadership skills so that you can treat or lead members of diverse groups differently than other members of your team. What it means is that you consider your leadership responsibilities in the context of the diversity within your organization. It also requires that you exercise your duties fairly, comply with legal requirements, and treat everyone with dignity and respect.

Acknowledge, Understand, and Respond to Diversity

Many leaders assume that it is safest to treat everyone the same and avoid the issues of diversity. Although this approach may have been successful in the past for some leaders, it does not work well as a general leadership tactic—and certainly not in a diverse environment. As is true of any leadership challenge, avoidance is usually not the best solution because it will eventually cause further disruption. Ignoring diversity and doing nothing, therefore, will lead to critical performance problems, such as increased interpersonal conflicts, overt discrimination, tension, low morale, and high turnover, and thus to increased financial costs for the organization.

You can avoid or minimize this possibility by addressing the issues of diversity proactively. It is important for you and your subordinates to recognize and acknowledge the differences among the people in your organization. An environment where communication about diversity is open, not closeted, will foster widespread respect for diversity among your subordinates. This will lead to a team of subordinates who will commit to your diversity efforts and your desire for organizational success.

Diversity Basics for Leaders

It is beyond the scope of this chapter to fully explain differences among diverse groups, unique discrimination histories, or particular cultural nuances. You can research this information in as much detail as you want. Yet it is important for you as a leader to understand some diversity basics so you can immediately begin developing a solid plan of action to address diversity within your team or organization. There are five important points regarding diversity with which leaders concern themselves.

It is important for you as a leader to understand some diversity basics so you can immediately begin developing a solid plan of action to address diversity within your team or organization.

161

Diversity Shapes People's Perceptions

Even though your team members may work together on the same tasks, this does not mean that they perceive their work in the same way. Their background and differing characteristics shape their views on everything, such as how to do work, how much they enjoy the work, and whether they are willing to improve work processes. These characteristics and backgrounds also affect the ability of some to concentrate on the job and relate with others. This leads to stereotypes that often interfere with the ability to form objective opinions about co-workers and customers. As you lead your team, remember that each person is a complex individual with specific needs and perceptions.

Quotas, Affirmative Action, and Diversity Programs Differ

Because there is widespread confusion as to the meanings of certain terms, understand their differences so you can eliminate the confusion among your team members and fellow leaders whenever possible.

Quotas are inflexible and fixed allocations of opportunities based upon a diversity classification such as race or gender. Examples are job positions and training opportunities.

Affirmative action is a program that attempts to correct diversity imbalances in workplace positions. It may or may not include quotas, but the objective is still the search for *qualified* people from diverse backgrounds.

A *diversity program* approaches differences among people from an entirely different perspective. It emphasizes naturally proactive, long-term, and fundamental organizational changes so that there is eventually no need for quotas or affirmative action. In a well-designed diversity program, everyone is seen as an individual with unique contributions to offer and people are judged on the quality of those contributions, not on subjective or irrelevant conclusions based on a diversity classification.

Assimilation Is Outdated

For years, leaders have assumed that it is better to encourage assimilation, which makes individuals in the organization adapt to each other's behaviors, express less individuality, and become similar or homogenous. Leaders typically have done this by treating everyone the same and ignoring differences. In return, people were expected to conform and follow the example of successful role models and leaders within the organization.

The main idea behind assimilation is that it is better to treat all employees equally in the same manner than to treat members of any group differently. In recent years, assimilation has been legally supported by affirmative action programs. Assimilation also serves to maintain the organization's original norms and culture. The mainstream employees, who are members of the traditional groups, usually welcome assimilation because it is not a threat to them. Assimilation often continues indefinitely within an organization because policies and systems perpetuate it.

An overemphasis on assimilation encourages people who are different from the dominating group to blend in and suppress their individuality. This eventually deprives the organization of the creativity and contributions of people with a lot to offer. It results in underutilization of people and unnecessary anxiety, division, and resentment in the workplace.

Some conformity is necessary for the survival of the organization, such as in following safety rules, learning to use certain types of equipment, or obeying organizational directives. The key is for leaders to recognize where assimilation has gone too far and then make a committed effort to correct it.

One response has been the development of support networks for members of diverse groups, as a natural reaction to the stifling effects of assimilation. These networks encourage communication, networking, and camaraderie among the members and provide a means for them to seek the emotional support and mentoring that are often unavailable in an organization that encourages conformity. However, these networks often are not in support of the organizational culture and some members of the dominant group perceive them as suspicious or hotspots of conflict. The irony is that if the culture encouraged everyone in the organization to participate and contribute despite their differences, there would be much less need for these networks.

If you choose, as a leader you can slow down assimilation considerably with a widespread, committed effort. Emphasize the strengths of all your sub-

An overemphasis on assimilation encourages people who are different from the dominating group to blend in and suppress their individuality, depriving the organization of their creativity and contributions.

Organizational Effects

Behavior that encourages homogeneity and assimilation, occurring for years in many organizations, affects the long-term success of the organization. For example, if dominant groups in your organization establish policies and procedures in a vacuum without the assistance of others, the resulting solutions probably are not the best and may not meet the needs of your employees who differ from the dominant norms or your customers. Since organizational culture often frowns upon people challenging decisions, change—however much it may be needed—is seldom ever made.

ordinates and encourage them to be more successful. By recognizing the benefits of diversity, you can redirect your efforts to capitalize on the varied talents and expertise of your subordinates, instead of forcing them to conform. You will see an upsurge in cultural awareness because of more interaction and less isolation among the diverse groups. This, in turn, will promote cooperation, trust, and understanding. Eventually you will have more fulfilled individuals who will build a harmonious and successful organization.

Prejudice and Stereotyping Are Destructive

Almost everyone has prejudices and uses stereotypes occasionally. Prejudices are prejudgments or conclusions that people make before they know or accept the facts. In the organizational setting, prejudice refers to the overstated and sometimes intense personal beliefs and bias that irrationally perpetuate the dominance of certain groups over others. Examples are the beliefs that older workers are less vigorous than the younger ones or that men are better workers than women. Stereotypes are highly oversimplified generalizations made about certain groups of people. An example of a stereotype would be that younger workers feel no loyalty to the organization or that they like to stay up all night dancing and drinking.

There is much danger to your organization and team if prejudices and stereotypes are allowed.

There is much danger to your organization and team if prejudices and stereotypes are allowed. These attitudes are destructive forces in the workplace, hampering your efforts to promote diversity on a large scale. In addition, they will disrupt your leadership activities that involve relationship building, such as teamwork, innovation, and effective communication.

Since these beliefs and generalizations seem to be formed from early socialization and reinforced continually in life, you cannot force everyone to eliminate their prejudices and stereotypes from their minds. You can, however, slowly make progress in limiting the impact of these beliefs by taking several actions. First, coach your subordinates so they avoid making generalizations and focus instead on the facts before they make conclusions. This will help them develop solid alternatives to the off-the-cuff remarks that may be stereotypical. Also, whenever you hear someone make comments that express prejudices or are based on stereotypes, let him or her know immediately that such comments are inappropriate in your organization. People will learn over time to suppress remarks that interfere with working relationships.

Make sure that you as a leader never speak or act in terms of prejudices or stereotypes, as certainly there will be people who will follow your lead or, worse yet, lose respect for you. Read up on common stereotypes so that you can immediately spot them in your company policies and procedures. You then can teach your team members how to better recognize prejudices and stereotyping among themselves, realize its negative impact, and change their behavior.

Finally, the close interaction and teamwork you develop among your subordinates will help you eliminate these detrimental attitudes and statements. It may take a while, but you can reduce the problems of prejudices and stereotypes over time.

Communication Is a Vital Component of Diversity

The way people communicate adds to or detracts from an environment of diversity. The most important point to remember about the impact of communication on diversity is that anything you or your subordinates communicate, either verbally or nonverbally, may offend someone—whether you intended to or not. By taking just a few actions, however, you can dramatically increase the quality of your communications so they have a more positive effect upon your diversity efforts.

Just as harmful, though, are subtly inappropriate comments and expressions. Many people may not notice them at first, but inappropriate expressions negatively affect the work environment. Following are some suggestions for avoiding unsuitable uses of language. These suggestions can be helpful to you as well as to anyone whose behavior you can influence.

Eliminate any silly or joking comment to anyone—friends and superiors included—when it relates to diversity classifications, despite how humorous you think it may be.

Refer to people in your organization by their names and avoid describing them in terms of how they differ from the majority, such as "our Chinese payroll supervisor," "that black man," or "our wheelchair-bound employee." Never characterize others in a mean-spirited or degrading way, such as "sissy man," "manly woman," or "our shell-shocked military veterans."

Stay current on lists of terms that are considered offensive or unsuitable, such as "minorities," "blue-collar workers," "Negroes," "gals," or "handi-

The way people communicate adds to or detracts from an environment of diversity.

Language Can Harm

There are many well-known examples of racist or sexist language, ethnic slurs, or lifestyle comments. Although their use has decreased tremendously in recent years because of greater awareness and new legal constraints, they still appear covertly. As a leader you are responsible for promoting an environment where such behaviors are not tolerated.

capped." Use instead more positive references, such as "Asian-Americans," "first-line supervisors," "people of color" or "African-Americans," "women," and "physically challenged."

When speaking with an individual or to groups, use various examples and comparisons that reflect all types of diversity, such as international and minority leaders, successful women, and ethnic role models. Avoid relying on overly used analogies from sources with which some people may be less familiar, such as sports or the military.

People of all diversities have different communication styles. It is important to realize this as you send or receive messages so that you do not misinterpret information, offend others, or have unrealistic expectations. Styles differ in numerous ways, but here are five significant, easily observable factors:

People of all diversities have different communication styles.

▶ use of formality, rationality, and logic in conversations

▶ tendency to dominate or submit during conversations

▶ degree of assertiveness in conflict resolution

▶ characteristics of speech

▶ personal openness, physical contact, and space boundaries during conversations

Since anyone can exhibit a combination of these factors, it is important to understand that no one will be exactly like you and that differences in styles of communication are all right. The key is to recognize that there are differences and adjust to them whenever you encounter them. You then will be less likely to draw inaccurate conclusions about people based on their style of conversation. As you become more aware of communication styles, you will learn to base your opinions of people on facts and performance results, not upon faulty assumptions or stereotypes.

When you encounter someone who has a different communication style, you do not have to drastically change your style. It would be helpful, though, to occasionally mirror the other person's style to make both of you more comfortable. In addition, by being more aware of your own style of communication, you can recognize how others might misunderstand your communications. You then can better attune yourself to the perceptions of others during conversation to make sure that you are sending your messages properly and others are understanding them correctly.

Diversity as a Long-Term Process

The phrase most often used for handling the issues of diversity is *managing diversity*. That term implies that there is a certain process involved, and many proponents insist diversity management is more a process than a program. This is generally true if the organization's top leaders commit to promoting diversity. All too often, though, people fear diversity because it represents change, uncertainty, or too much of a commitment. Leaders may prefer short-term programs, such as affirmative action or valuing differences, because they produce more immediate results and pacify some people. Consequently, diversity management never reaches its potential as a solution to the needs of the organization or of individuals.

A better phrase might be *maximizing diversity*. It connotes achieving the most from what diversity offers for both the organization and individuals, rather than simply managing a process. Maximizing diversity still involves management processes and selected programs, but the design and implementation is approached from the bold, equitable, and win-win perspective of a leader—not from the narrow perspective of traditional programs. This process of maximizing diversity can be so complementary to your leadership efforts that it gradually replaces the traditional short-term diversity programs.

Actions to Maximize Diversity

There are specific steps you can take to introduce diversity concepts and practices into your organization. You do not have to take them all at once, but they can be part of a comprehensive program to maximize diversity. When the process involves several functional departments or when someone else is leading an official diversity effort in your organization, consult with other leaders so you can devise a program correctly and collaboratively.

Here are eight leadership actions you can take to maximize diversity.

> *There are specific steps you can take to introduce diversity concepts and practices into your organization.*

▶ Approach diversity as a resource, not a problem.

▶ Use your leadership skills.

▶ Get the facts on diversity.

▶ Assess conditions in your organization.

▶ Determine specific and measurable goals.

▶ Involve diverse groups in developing your plan.

167

- ▶ Communicate and get commitment.
- ▶ Align your organization with diversity.

Approach Diversity as a Resource, Not a Problem

Diversity is not a sacred or taboo subject; it is a fact of life that should concern you as much as competition, inflation, or customer service.

Diversity is not a sacred or taboo subject; it is a fact of life that should concern you as much as competition, inflation, or customer service. You must truly believe that your organization's diversity is a resource as valuable as a brand name, geographical location, or any other competitive advantage that you can imagine.

You now must do everything in your power to exploit this advantage in all your responsibilities. Whenever you solve problems, brainstorm, or deal with your team, remember to consider diversity as a strategic resource that is part of the solution. Teach the benefits of this diversity philosophy to your fellow leaders and subordinates so that everyone will understand and accept this attitudinal approach.

Use Your Leadership Skills

You can make great strides in maximizing your organization's diversity simply by focusing daily on doing the best job that you can as a leader and encouraging other leaders in your organization to do so as well. One primary reason that organizations do not maximize diversity is that leaders do not clearly see or act upon the opportunities that diversity provides. You and your fellow leaders will not overlook these opportunities if you do the following:

- ▶ Communicate well with your subordinates and fully understand their concerns.
- ▶ Create and maintain an environment where teamwork, fairness, mutual respect, personal and organizational excellence, and goal achievement are the standards.
- ▶ Stay closely involved in empowering, coaching, and developing your subordinates.
- ▶ Monitor and share information about what goes on in your organization and where it is headed strategically.
- ▶ Communicate your vision fully and gain commitment from your subordinates to support it.

Remember that leadership skills—not trendy gimmicks—will help you overcome any of your leadership challenges, including those pertaining to diversity. It is your responsibility to use your skills to make the most of what diversity has to offer you and your organization.

Get the Facts on Diversity

It would be a superb investment of your time if you perused diversity material that is available commercially or in your library. This knowledge, which is crucial to developing your diversity skills, will give you specific ideas to help maximize diversity. In addition, you will get valuable insights about the diverse groups within your organization. If you knew just a little more about a religion that has followers in your organization or a country that has contributed skilled workers to your department, you would probably be more empathetic of your team members' customs and beliefs. Most importantly, this knowledge and concern could lead to better communication between you and them, improve their performance on the job, and generate innovation along the way.

Assess Conditions in Your Organization

Before you create diversity improvements, assess the status of diversity within your department or organization. This will give you an accurate basis for planning improvements and for gauging your progress in maximizing diversity.

The initial step is to determine what specific information you need. Address the areas of policies and procedures, skill levels, attitudes, perceptions, interactions of diverse groups, and obstacles to diversity. Such information will orient you to the right approaches as well as provide a true assessment of the current environment, which can tip you off to other challenges to address. Seek perspectives from as many people and job levels as possible. In addition to surveying workers, analyze any existing data that may be of use, including personnel data and employment statistics on recruitment, terminations, the rewards system, race, gender, and age.

Several diversity questionnaires are available commercially that you can use as guides in designing your own questionnaire. During the assessment, be on the watch for people who are truly interested in diversity and who may later be resources for your program.

Determine Specific and Measurable Goals

Diversity awareness training as a sole solution to diversity challenges has received mixed reviews in the workplace. It does not accomplish as much as a more comprehensive approach to diversity. Most awareness training lacks specific follow-up requirements, rendering the training ineffective. After listening to a seminar, viewing a film, or participating in a discussion, people often go their separate ways with no requirement to implement what they have learned. You and your team need to have knowledge of diversity issues; education is a necessary part of implementing organizational change. It is also necessary, however, for individuals to apply that knowledge in specific ways. It is unrealistic to hope that information alone will result in changes in attitudes.

Examples of specific goals may be to increase the gender or ethnic diversity in a particular department, to develop diverse leadership for your future staffing needs, or to better serve diverse international markets. All training, however, must be linked to specific goals that support your overall diversity improvements and specific business objectives.

Involve Diverse Groups in Developing Your Plan

While developing and implementing your diversity improvements, include representatives from all of your teams or departments, including those from several organizational levels.

While developing and implementing your diversity improvements, include representatives from all of your teams or departments, including those from several organizational levels. Explain that you need their advice and cultural knowledge to make the best decisions. They will give you valuable insight into what they perceive to be relevant diversity issues, such as barriers to achievement in the organization, current relations among diverse groups, culture clashes, and policies and procedures that promote assimilation.

Communicate and Get Commitment

As with any of your plans and programs, communicate your diversity objectives to everyone in your department or organization. Diversity is one of those topics that scare some people. Many will feel anxious if they perceive themselves as targeted for criticism or blamed for injustices. Consequently, it makes sense to explain to everyone the actions that you are taking. At the same time, seek their commitment to diversity. While not everyone will completely agree with your reasoning, ask for and expect their support in making changes.

Align Your Organization with Diversity

A commitment to diversity as an organization-wide value must permeate all levels if the organization is to truly reach its potential. This is an evolutionary effort that must be piloted by the top leaders in the organization. To take complete advantage of the enormous benefits of diversity, your organizational objectives must be aligned with your company's diverse culture, not in conflict with it. Maximizing diversity in an organization is a long-term goal of three years or more that will evolve from the many short-term changes described in this chapter; departmental improvements can be achieved sooner.

By now, it should be of no surprise to you that traditional workplace policies, procedures, and systems will not effectively support the needs of a diverse work force. You will need to redesign and continually monitor all your systems so that you can elicit the best performance and behavior from your team. The following are just three examples of actions that you can take after you gain input from your subordinates about their diversity concerns.

Revise the Benefits Program. Ensure that your subordinates value the benefits that you offer. You could modify the benefits program to reflect the diversity of your employees force and include innovations such as flexible work hours, self-selected holidays, child care, or elder care.

Diversify Social Events. Instead of exclusively entertaining clients or team members at sports events, which are viewed by some people as male-oriented events, also use restaurants, museums, exhibits, or the theater.

Monitor Human Resource Programs for Trends. By continually evaluating the selection, training and development, promotion, and rewards programs, you will better maximize and recognize the talents of your colleagues. The diversity statistics from these areas will tell you much about the success of your inclusion efforts. In addition, you will more quickly identify and correct diversity barriers that are impeding your efforts at departmental or organizational change.

Leaders at all levels have a responsibility to respond correctly to the diversity opportunities in their organization. This does not mean you can decree that everyone in your organization will coexist in a harmonious state in which all diverse needs are satisfied, every policy reflects the unique concerns of everyone, and no one is ever offended again. Such goals are unrealistic, and it is not necessary to aim for such perfection. Focus on those things that you can change to help your team and your organization grow. By looking for ways to use diversity to everyone's benefit, you are acting responsibly as a leader.

Chapter 14

Conflict Resolution

George considers himself an excellent team member who gets along well with others and always supports their requests. He is frustrated, though, that he often does not get the resources he needs to support his projects. What can he do to improve his ability to get what he needs while decreasing the likelihood of raising conflict with others? Frank is assertive and makes his wishes known at work, though he believes he is not that skilled at negotiating successful solutions to everyday challenges; he seems to give more than he gets. What can he do?

Y OU SEE EVERY DAY HOW CONFLICT EXISTS ALL AROUND YOU AND IN all types of leadership situations. It is practically impossible for leaders to avoid conflict—and undesirable as well, since conflict often leads to the changes that you and your organization need. Thus it makes sense to learn all that you can about handling it, particularly given the effect that conflict has on your own success or failure.

As you learned in the previous chapter, human differences are certain and many. Differences in culture, perspective, skill and knowledge levels, goals, and communication styles, for example, affect the varying levels of agreement and disagreement among people. Conflict is synonymous with disagreement, whether slight or intense. In the workplace, people can conceivably disagree over anything, such as policies, decisions, ideas, strategy, the brand of coffee to use, or how much they like co-workers. Disagreements are not necessarily bad, because they can lead to better decisions, innovation, and bonding among people.

Despite the inevitability of conflict, the way people respond to these differences is their choice. People can choose one of three responses during conflict situations. They can:

▶ Compromise amicably to turn disagreements into agreements.

▶ Continue to privately disagree but fully support the final agreed-upon decision.

▶ Continue to disruptively or publicly disagree.

> *It is practically impossible for leaders to avoid conflict—and conflict often leads to the changes that you and your organization need.*

Conflict Resolution for Leaders

Your objective as a leader is to resolve conflicts in one of the first two ways. This chapter will guide you by suggesting simple techniques applicable to any leadership situation at work, in the home, or in the community. First it will provide the foundation for conflict resolution by showing you four specific steps to a satisfying resolution. Then it will strengthen this foundation by introducing the skill of negotiating, which you can use to help resolve many other types of conflict that you encounter as a leader.

Steps for Successful Conflict Resolution

Follow these four steps for successful conflict resolution.

▶ Separate misunderstandings from conflicts.

▶ Create a positive environment for conflict resolution.

▶ Focus on people's interests, not their positions.

▶ Communicate clearly.

Separate Misunderstandings from Conflicts

Many of the situations perceived as disagreements are not really disagreements but misunderstandings. Misunderstandings can be easily remedied. Before you assume that you have a conflict, find out what the other person believes about the situation. You may find he or she is misinformed or does not have all the facts about the situation and may be willing to change his or her position.

173

Conversely, you may find that it is you who misunderstands the situation. In either event, if both of you can come to a quick agreement based upon a clarification of the facts and assumptions, you have resolved the misunderstanding. If you cannot agree and there remains a conflict, go to the next step.

Create a Positive Environment for Conflict Resolution

You can create a positive environment in two ways.

First, separate the problem from the person. Stay problem-oriented by retaining a clear and vigorous focus on the problem and not conveying an adversarial attitude that the person is the problem. If you communicate to the other person in the conflict that both of you are part of a team that must solve a problem collectively, then you will more effectively frame your attitudes and respond to the upcoming challenge. You still are concerned about the person's needs, feelings, or emotional condition, but by objectively concentrating on the problem and not personally attacking the other person, you can find ways to solve the problem without antagonism. This will, in turn, reduce the tension between the two of you.

Second, portray an attitude of win-win. Win-win means finding a solution in which both you and the other person win and no one feels like a loser. Win-win means that both or all parties walk away from a conflict feeling good, not frustrated or angry, about having successfully satisfied their needs in an environment of cooperation. If you help people achieve what they want to achieve, you also will benefit by better performance and increased loyalty to you and the organization. You convey a win-win attitude when you let people know that you are looking for a mutually beneficial solution, one that is unifying and highly acceptable to both of you.

To create a positive environment for conflict resolution, separate the problem from the person and portray an attitude of win-win.

Focus on the Problem, Not Person

As an example, if you want to convey to a subordinate that he or she is not performing well, avoid hostile opening phrases such as "You are not doing a great job." Instead, focus on the problem by saying, "Your job position requires that all customers be treated with respect." You then can discuss the criteria for effective job performance from a less confrontational approach and be more successful at defusing the conflict and improving behavior. When examining the problem, remember to spend time looking at it from your subordinate's perspective. Understanding his or her point of view and accepting his or her feelings are not going to make you a weak leader or negotiator; instead, understanding and accepting help you resolve the conflict more quickly, efficiently, and permanently.

A win-win attitude is so crucial to a leader that everything discussed throughout the remainder of this chapter centers upon finding and applying win-win solutions.

Focus on People's Interests, Not Their Positions

In a conflict situation, you want to resolve it not just with any agreement at hand but with a durable and fair arrangement with which everyone is reasonably content. To do so, it is best to focus not on people's positions, which are their stated demands, but on their interests, which are their real needs.

A position is what people state they want, such as more salary, more vacation days, or fewer hours at work. Individuals view their position as the best possible solution to their needs. This may or may not be the case, because they may be embellishing their position to strengthen an argument or they may not be clearly defining their needs or examining their alternatives.

Interests, on the other hand, are the true reasons behind the position. If you both focus only on your own stated positions, you become emotionally and sometimes irreversibly attached to them and will find it difficult to compromise. But if you focus on your interests and not as adversaries, you will develop many more creative solutions that are fair and rewarding to you both.

For example, a subordinate may want a higher salary and more vacation time. In probing further, you discover that his true interest is a desire to spend more time with his family—hence the request for increased vacation time—and a desire to place his child in a more expensive day care center that is closer to work and home—hence the request for a raise in salary. Once you know your subordinate's true interests, you can compare them with your interests and see how far apart the two of you are on the issue. Your interests in this situation may be that you want the subordinate to do his job

It is best to focus not on people's positions, which are their stated demands, but on their interests, which are their real needs.

The Value of Interests

Deeply held and valued interests are ultimately what concern most people, not arbitrary, quickly formed positions that result in temporary solutions that may or may not help them satisfy their interests. If satisfaction of everyone's underlying interests is your objective, everyone will be much happier when all can agree upon practical, innovative, and realistic solutions. In many cases, you have to question people thoroughly to determine their interests, because they intentionally and unintentionally mask them from you and from themselves. Once you find out why they want something, you will best be able to mutually decide how they can obtain it. Then they will believe that you can help them meet their needs and the conflict will soon be resolved.

well without disrupting anyone else's work. Once you and your subordinate confer, you both can discuss the problem in detail and collaborate on solutions that will allow you both to achieve your interests. Possible solutions could be for the subordinate to arrive earlier and leave earlier on certain days or to telecommute one day a week or for you to study the feasibility of an on-site day care center for the organization.

Communicate Clearly

Good communication builds the trust that helps to resolve conflicts, while ineffective communication will hinder agreements and increase complications.

In addition to the communication principles discussed in Chapter 10, there are some additional suggestions that are particularly well suited for conflict resolution. The main point to remember is that good communication builds the trust that helps to resolve conflicts, while ineffective communication will hinder agreements and increase complications.

Keep a Positive, Agreeable, and Relaxed Attitude

Although you as the leader may be in a higher position of authority than a peer or a team member, it is not helpful to misuse this relationship when resolving a conflict with him or her. This principle also applies to any other conflict situation you may have, such as with a client or in a contract negotiation. Since emotions will probably be intense in a conflict situation, it is always best not to be swept up into an atmosphere of anger, fear, or resentment. Avoid this by recognizing that both of you will be somewhat emotional but that emotions can be kept in check by understanding them and acknowledging them openly.

As you begin your discussion, always open with a positive statement, such as referring to the interests you both have in common. Maintain this positive approach throughout the discussion. By keeping a respectful, empathetic, and caring attitude toward the other person, you will be seen as someone who is interested in resolving the problem. Avoid using "you" statements; instead use less accusatory "I" statements. This transfers the focus away from the other person and toward yourself, allowing you to express your needs and interests while subtly encouraging the other person to express his or hers.

Never resort to making negative accusations, becoming disagreeable, or losing your temper. Although you may feel better temporarily, it will not help you to resolve the conflict. If you convey to the person that you are committed to resolving the problem while trying to understand his or her feelings and needs, the person will be more open to win-win thinking.

Stay on Course

So you both can stay focused on specific issues, at the beginning of the discussion determine and agree upon what the problem is. If either one of you begins to stray from the topic, refer back to the stated problem to get the discussion back on course.

Once you identify the issues involved in the conflict, avoid lamenting about the what has happened in the past; focus instead on solutions for the future, which is something you have control over.

Be an Active Listener

People want their views heard, so remember to demonstrate visibly that you are actively listening, as described in Chapter 10. You will go far by allowing others to speak without interrupting them, acknowledging what they say, questioning them when needed, and repeating exactly the key points to prevent misunderstanding. Whenever anything is unclear or omitted, ask for clarification. There is nothing wrong with occasionally nodding agreement with what the other person is saying. This is assuring because it conveys respect and acknowledges him or her as a person, even though you may disagree with some of what he or she says. Eye contact is particularly important during discussions because it conveys honesty and trust to the other person.

Listening will enable you to examine the other person's perceptions about the conflict. These perceptions are important to you because they will help you better understand the person so you can help develop viable solutions for his or her needs and interests. By allowing the person to talk freely, you gain information you may not have obtained had you talked instead. You also will gain insight by analyzing what is not said and the areas that are avoided.

People want their views heard, so remember to demonstrate visibly that you are actively listening.

Negotiation and Conflict Resolution

Most of the ordinary and routine conflict that you face can be resolved using the four steps discussed above. Other situations will require a more structured approach using negotiation because they involve issues that are not easily resolved through a four-step method. It is extremely useful to understand how negotiating interacts with conflict resolution because the two are not at all separate. Conflict resolution—not negotiating—is one of your leadership goals. Negotiating is simply a highly effective process and skill that you can use to resolve certain types of conflict.

Knowing how to apply negotiating skills to your everyday leadership responsibilities is invaluable in resolving routine conflicts such as interpersonal friction or performance problems.

Knowledge of how to apply negotiating skills to your everyday leadership responsibilities is invaluable in resolving routine conflicts such as interpersonal friction or performance problems. Sometimes a negotiation will be a five-minute encounter with subordinates; at other times it may be a three-week session with international clients. Negotiating skills, therefore, will assist you as you increasingly confront greater responsibilities, such as resolving contract disputes, organizational change issues, or strategic alliance questions. As you think of negotiation, try not to limit it to its more glamorous or well-known areas such as corporate mergers or large contracts. Instead, relate it broadly to all the routine situations that you encounter everyday at work, home, and in the community, with your subordinates, peers, supervisors, customers, and family members.

Much of the discussion so far in this chapter concerning conflict resolution has implicitly contained some elements of negotiation. The topics of attitude, interests, positions, and win-win solutions, for example, are fundamental negotiation concepts that are invariably mentioned whenever negotiation is taught. The remainder of the chapter will build upon what you have learned so far and show you how to use the essential skill of negotiating to resolve conflicts the best way that you can.

A Leader's Approach to Win-Win Negotiations

As you practice the skills necessary to be an effective leader, you are simultaneously practicing the skills necessary to master a win-win style of negotiating.

It will be quite simple for you to develop your negotiation skills because there are so many resources available to increase your knowledge. There are scores of excellent, informative books, tapes, and seminars with detailed techniques that can be tailored to your particular needs. You can learn numerous tactics involving everything from room layout to preventing stonewalling. You also can explore all that is discussed in this chapter in much more detail. Any specific challenge you may have is probably addressed in one or more of these resources. Until you choose to invest your time in additional study, you can adapt the basics in this chapter for use in any of your negotiation situations.

A leader's approach to win-win negotiations consists of seven steps.

- ▶ Explore your objectives.
- ▶ Prioritize your interests.

Win-Win Negotiating

You believe in not only getting the job done correctly but doing it by focusing on objectives that you and your subordinates have in common and by maximizing the outcomes for both of you. This involves using your many technical, analytical, and relationship skills to accomplish with others what might not have been possible. As a result, everyone benefits and no one loses. Since you believe that the feelings, opinions, and knowledge of other people must be considered during negotiations, you are willing to completely involve them in the process, to listen objectively, and to compromise when necessary. You are interested in solving the problems that are identified during the negotiation by developing alternatives that can satisfy all of the parties involved.

▶ Improve your negotiating position.
▶ Finalize your negotiating strategy.
▶ Recognize the distributive negotiator.
▶ Respond to the distributive negotiator.
▶ Create a win-win solution.

Explore Your Objectives

Clearly identify the primary objectives that you want to achieve from the negotiation. Objectives are similar in concept to the positions that were earlier described. Clear, precise, realistic, tangible, and intangible objectives are crucial to later developing the planning aspects of your negotiation, such as your shorter-term negotiating tactics. The objectives also will guide and focus your efforts when you are in the middle of a quickly moving or complex negotiation. As with any other challenge that you have as a leader, if you spend a little time at the beginning of the process thinking about your objectives, you will later achieve them more easily.

Once you have identified your objectives, decide how you would most and least like to achieve them, by determining alternatives that represent

Focusing on Objectives

Develop a range of primary and secondary objectives so you will have flexibility in negotiating. Primary objectives are the most important to you; they usually include such areas as price, salary, job description, deadlines, and terms of purchase. Secondary objectives could include anything else that is related to the negotiation, such as options for additional purchases, discounts for bulk purchases, salary incentives, or public relations issues.

best- and worst-case scenarios of what could happen during negotiations. Doing this will give you the courage and confidence to approach the negotiations with the right attitude. If you do not reach an agreement in which you achieve an objective, you will know that all is not lost because you have identified a range of acceptable alternatives. These alternatives will also increase your negotiating power and the likelihood of a successful agreement because you will not be forced into accepting an unfavorable deal.

For example, if you were about to negotiate with a subordinate concerning a pay raise, you would identify in advance several objectives and most- and least-preferred alternatives for each of them. These could be a pay raise ranging from $2,000 to $5,000, a bonus potential ranging from one to three percent, a workload increase ranging from a major increase in responsibilities to a minor increase, or an expense account increase ranging from $500 to $3,000 per year. Naturally, you would prefer an agreement that is closer to each objective's most-preferred alternative than to its least-preferred, but this is not realistic nor is it mutually advantageous to you both, as you will soon see. Adding mystery to this process is not knowing the most- and least-preferred alternatives of the other person.

Here is an example of a simple negotiation involving only one objective. You are negotiating a deadline extension that a team member has requested. You may ideally want to approve a one-week extension, but would settle for up to a two-week extension. The other person has requested a four-week extension, but would settle for a two-week extension. The negotiating process allows you to close this gap and reach an agreement within the range that benefits both parties. Most likely, the agreement will be about or exactly a two-week extension. However, if the person's least-preferred alternative is three weeks instead of two weeks, there is a gap of one week that you must address. With only one objective to negotiate, the extension, you both must change your expectations to resolve the gap or there could be ill will between you or, even worse, the deadline extension might not be approved even though it is probably needed.

Reliance on a single objective and an alternative that could be synonymous with a bottom line protects negotiators, somewhat, from yielding to

Your Range of Acceptable Agreement

These alternatives are placed in what is called a *range of acceptable agreement*. This range goes from your most-preferred alternative to your least-preferred alternative for each of your objectives.

Knowing Your Least-Preferred Alternatives

In more involved negotiations, the stakes may be higher for you or your organization and you may not be as willing to change your expectations as you would in a simple deadline extension. That is the reason to know your least-preferred alternatives, because if you absolutely cannot achieve them, individually or in combination with other alternatives, you might be just as well off not reaching an agreement and continuing to operate as usual or pursuing further options. Otherwise, you could end up worse off than in your current situation.

intense pressure during the heat of a negotiation. At the same time, however, it also constrains you into falsely thinking there is only one way of reaching an agreement: by achieving or doing better than your bottom line. Having additional objectives, each with a set of alternatives, or at least having a single objective along with a broad mix of alternatives that you are willing to accept increases the opportunity for agreement. You can then negotiate combinations of solutions, some variation of which may be acceptable. For these reasons, always attempt to negotiate with more than one objective.

It is always good, therefore, to know your alternatives if you choose not to negotiate an agreement. By explicitly identifying these no-agreement alternatives to choose from if you fail to reach an agreement, you will be able to analyze the final offers in terms of how they compare with the certainty of these no-agreement alternatives, not just how the final offers compare with your least-preferred alternatives. In addition, establishing your no-agreement alternatives before negotiation begins will reassure you that you do not have to accept an agreement if it is not in your best interests.

When you have viable and realistic no-agreement alternatives to choose from if you cannot reach a negotiated agreement, you will add to your negotiating power. For example, despite your best attempts at negotiating and reaching a win-win solution, a key supplier of resources may give you a final offer—which actually may not be his or her true final offer—of a 20-percent price increase. Your least preferred alternative is 15 percent. Examine a 20-percent increase in relation to your no-agreement alternatives. If you find that there are no other companies to supply you, a 20-percent price increase is more acceptable than enduring lost sales or bankruptcy. On the other hand, if you have many suppliers from which to choose or if you have an enormous inventory of these supplies that will last several months, it may be more advantageous for you to reject the final offer or to attempt again, forcefully and confidently, to negotiate a better settlement than 20 percent.

Always attempt to negotiate with more than one objective and recognize the difference between least-preferred alternatives and no-agreement alternatives.

*I*nterests are
those individual
matters that are
of underlying con-
cern to you and
to the other party,
and they are a
matter of
perception.

Prioritize Your Interests

Interests are those individual matters that are of underlying concern to you and to the other party. Using the assistance of someone on your negotiating team or someone else you trust, analyze in detail why you want to achieve the objectives you have identified.

Once you have identified your interests, prioritize them according to the value of each to you and relative to the other interests. For example, your objective may be to lease a particular office suite for under $1,000 a month. You analyze why you want this objective: you have a limited budget, you value the suite's proximity to your house, there is an abundance of nearby restaurants for client lunches, you will need an office within six months, and the office building is well maintained. These are your interests. After priori-tizing these interests, you find that their order of importance is rental price, location, condition, and availability. Furthermore, price may be only a little more important than location, but it may be much more important than the condition and it may be extremely more important than availability. You can develop any type of ranking system as long as it makes sense to you.

During the negotiation for the lease, take specific action to identify the interests of the other party, the leasing company. Now that you know your interests, you can negotiate based upon your four interests and their inter-ests. This is far preferable to negotiating on your overall position, which in this example has only one objective. You may discover that the leasing com-pany is willing to reduce your monthly rent to under $1,000, which is your primary interest but not its big concern, if you can move in quickly and gen-erate immediate revenues, which is the company's primary interest but not a big concern for you.

As you can see, a thorough knowledge of your interests is extremely valuable in comparing the cost of giving up one interest and the value of gaining agreement on another interest. It is also helpful in predicting how

Interests Depend on the Person

It is important to emphasize that interests are a matter of perception, as are people's needs, values, or preferences for rewards. What may matter most to you could matter least to others while something they value could be of no practical concern to you. This is why you always want to identify your interests and continually seek to determine the interests of the other party. It is the two-way, progressive, and mutually beneficial discussion of all these differently val-ued interests that will be the heart and substance of your negotiation.

The Combination Approach

During the negotiations, you will negotiate each interest either separately or in combination with your other interests and the other party's interests. More often than not, the combination approach will be your best method, simply because it gives you more flexibility and will more likely lead to a win-win situation. To make this approach work well for you, develop values for different combinations of interests so that you can forecast the results if you agree to a particular combination. Knowing the values will later enable you to quickly make objective decisions based on the other party's offers and counteroffers.

interests interrelate and how each interest is affected when the other interests are negotiated. Before the negotiations begin, approach your negotiating team members or other responsible co-workers and discuss what you have determined about your interests to this point. They will give you valuable input or verify how you prioritized your interests.

For example, your perception of the value of Combination A, which specifies $1,100 rent, no availability for eight months, and free janitorial services for one year, may differ from how you value Combination B, which specifies $1,000 rent, immediate availability, and six months of free janitorial services.

Improve Your Negotiating Position

The best way to improve your negotiating position is to thoroughly analyze those elements that most affect your situation. Three such elements are information, time, and power.

The old saying that knowledge is power is especially pertinent during a negotiation. This means knowing everything you can about what you are negotiating well in advance of the negotiations so you can develop your objectives, interests, and strategy. A well-informed negotiator will know all the minor and major details about such things as values, costs, and previous negotiations on the subject. You certainly will want to spend more effort researching those negotiations that are more important or risky to you. It is always wise, though, to prepare just as thoroughly for routine negotiations, because the more knowledge you have, the better you will do during the negotiation. Because information is exchanged during a negotiation session, the quality, quantity, and indisputability of your information will give you enormous negotiating power in promoting your interests, countering arguments, and making as few concessions as possible.

Gathering Information

Gathering information is an ongoing habit, something that you do daily through conversing with everyone you meet, including subordinates, clients, supervisors, and peers. The best time to gather information about upcoming negotiations is before the negotiations are scheduled or even conceptualized because people are much less guarded then and will more likely give you the information you need. People are used to leaders inquiring about all sorts of topics, so you probably will be able to methodically and inconspicuously approach anyone who could possibly give you information. Remember that astute people will not continually give you information unless you give them some information in return; therefore, be prepared to reciprocate by sharing some knowledge with them.

Of particular interest to you are the people with whom you are negotiating. If these are people you already know, such as colleagues, subordinates, family members, or clients, you are at an advantage because you understand how they think and behave. If you have little knowledge of them, find out what others think about them, their reputation, negotiating tactics, needs or problems, and authority to make decisions. Information about their organization's financial condition, strategic intentions, or competitive pressures is beneficial. Any information is good because it gives you insights that may be of value during the negotiations.

At this stage of the negotiating process, brainstorm and then analyze the other party's potential objectives, interests, and arguments using the same process as you used earlier for yourself. This will help you in case you need to adjust your objectives, the value of your interests, and your negotiating arguments.

Time is a resource that affects your negotiation in two significant ways. First, it tells you how many days or hours you have until the negotiation begins. If more time is available, you can better prepare for the negotiation. Conversely, less available time means that you have to work quickly and prioritize your negotiation plan. Second, it is vital to know the approximate duration of the negotiation because the process of negotiation works in stages. Adjust your expectations and strategy to account for these stages.

For example, as the negotiations begin, very few concessions will occur because both of you are staking out your positions and attempting to uncover each other's interests. Most significant concessions occur at the very end of the process, near or after the deadline. If both parties have the same deadline, negotiations will move forward with the goal of closure at a defined moment and concessions likely will be made bilaterally. If, however, one of the parties has a more flexible deadline or does not reveal it, then he or she can proceed at a slower pace and delay making concessions. This will increase the pressure on the other party, who will more likely make final concessions earlier.

Power, in the context of leadership, is the ability to influence or exercise control over some aspect of your duties. You have seen throughout this book the power you have as a leader in making things happen and in convincing others that you can help or harm them. Confidence in your power is not something you should abuse, but you can generally use it as a leader and specifically as a negotiator. Knowing how the other person perceives your position of power will help you craft effective negotiation strategies and respond better during the negotiations.

Knowing how the other person perceives your position of power will help you craft effective negotiation strategies and respond better during the negotiations.

You can emphasize any of these sources of power, depending upon the situation in which you are involved. Every party in a negotiation has some type of power, but the key here is to identify the relative positions of power before the negotiations begin and to develop your strategy with these conclusions in your mind. You may want to emphasize one source of power over another because you believe it will be more effective in changing the negotiating behavior of the other person and be less likely to damage your relationship.

For example, if you are negotiating with a subordinate for a one-week deadline extension, you have several sources of power that you could draw upon, either overtly or covertly, during the discussions: reward power, punishment power, positional power, and coercive power. It is unlikely that you would want to use all the sources during the discussions and it may not be necessary. Subordinates instinctively know the power that you, the leader, have over them and they are unlikely to challenge it because they recognize their obligation to comply with your directives. From a negotiating perspective, this is good for you and bad for them. However, subordinates can draw upon their sources of power in the negotiations. This person may be the only

Sources of Negotiating Power

If you understand how you are perceived, you can likewise use this information to reinforce or dispel those perceptions. The sources of your negotiating power are numerous, including the power to help or harm; to convince or compel; to garner more resources, such as time, information, or money; to exercise leadership or supervisory authority; or to inspire complete respect and trust in you.

one in your department who can expertly complete the assignment or the project may not be needed for several more weeks. The negotiation for the deadline extension will involve these power considerations but will not ultimately depend upon them. More important are your interests and your subordinate's interests and how you can best satisfy as many as possible. Since your only interests are that the project be finished reasonably soon and without error, you may have no objection to the subordinate's request as long as he or she can satisfy your concerns.

Finalize Your Negotiating Strategy

Before the negotiations begin, look over all your information and finalize your strategy. If someone else is on your negotiating team, it is helpful to meet at least once and discuss the details of your strategy. Go over everything you have determined so far about your interests and objectives, the facts, the other party, and your negotiating situation. Talk over the tactics that you will use during the negotiations, including opening statements, your opening offer, who will speak for the team, and any other procedural rules. Once you map out your strategy, spend some time rehearsing it alone, with your team, or with someone whom you can trust.

Before you begin the negotiations, verify that the other party has the authority to make the decisions that will lead to a negotiated agreement.

The opening hours of the negotiation can be fruitful because this is the time when you discover the tactics and interests of the other party. You can use the following three guidelines to make certain that you take full advantage of this period.

First, before you begin the negotiations, verify that the other party has the authority to make the decisions that will lead to a negotiated agreement. If not, you will waste your time because you will end up making most of the concessions and offers and probably have to negotiate again with someone else.

Second, it is usually best if you let the other party make the initial offer because it is preferable to first know what he or she is thinking before you reveal what you are thinking. A key tactic during a negotiation is to make ample use of questions whenever you see the opportunity, since they often bring you the answers you need. In addition, the other person may feel less threatened by probing and thoughtful inquiries than he or she would have felt had you simply made counteroffers or forceful declarations. Any time that you can get information, rather than give it, it is usually good.

Finally, it is common in negotiations for opposing sides to begin with distant stances and then make gradual concessions to arrive at a more realistic and mutually acceptable agreement. Win-win negotiating does not preclude these wide differences in offers. For this reason, your initial offers on the issues should be high, relative to the other person's offers, to give you both plenty of room to negotiate toward each other for the final agreements. This approach will also allow you both to feel that you are indeed accomplishing something. It also will help minimize deadlocked negotiations, which often occur when one or both sides are unwilling or unable to make more concessions. A high offer, as long as you can justify it, is an acceptable tactic during a negotiation and is somewhat expected; a low offer could be perceived as a sign of weakness or as a sign that you have inadequate negotiating information.

Recognize the Distributive Negotiator

As previously suggested, it is best for a leader to use a win-win approach to resolving conflicts. Not only will a win-win attitude and an interests-oriented approach consistently yield you better overall solutions but you will also gain esteem in the eyes of the other party. This will lead to later successes, both in negotiating and in your other duties. Despite the increasing acceptance and use of win-win negotiating over the years, there are many people who will use *distributive negotiating*, which is the accepted name for a highly competitive win-lose style.

A win-lose style of distributive negotiating, whether done informally with a co-worker or formally in high-stakes discussions, is not the optimal way to solve a conflict.

A win-lose style of distributive negotiating, whether done informally with a co-worker or formally in high-stakes discussions, is not the optimal way to solve a conflict. It often is used in traditional positional bargaining situations, such as purchasing a home or buying items at a flea market. More importantly to you as a leader, it is used in the workplace, in the family, and in other organizations with which you affiliate. It may appear to be the best style to use when resources are limited or the positions of the negotiating parties are in direct and obvious conflict. Because most people in

Effects of Distributive Negotiating

Distributive negotiating frequently breeds mistrust, injures relationships, and can easily, although not always, descend into misleading statements or outright lying. This type of negotiating is more successful when any relationship between the parties is limited and when they have little regard for ethics or fair play. It is, therefore, not a style typically used by leaders who have high regard for their team members and others. However, you should be able to recognize immediately when someone else uses this style so that you can develop actions and strategies to effectively conduct your negotiations to everyone's benefit.

An important conclusion to make about distributive negotiators is that their tactics work, sometimes well and sometimes not so well.

these situations naturally believe they should get as much of those limited resources as possible, they will negotiate in a manner that they believe helps them achieve that objective—a distributive approach.

Distributive negotiators are not all alike in the intensity of their style and certainly do not all conform to a stereotypical description. Most, however, are usually fixated on winning at all costs on their own terms. They are not concerned with how you feel, whether your needs are satisfied, or whether you are treated fairly. Their objective is to defeat you. Although you may not initially notice that you are dealing with this type of negotiator, certain tactics will eventually tip you off.

For example, note whether the person:

▶ Has unreasonable and extreme initial positions

▶ Uses intimidating emotional and psychological actions, such as guilt projection, outbursts, threats, insulting laughter, or periods of silence

▶ Does not believe in making reciprocal concessions

▶ Claims not to have the authority to negotiate an agreement

▶ Refuses to establish rules or later disregards rules that organize the negotiations, such as those pertaining to etiquette, deadlines, and good-faith bargaining

An important conclusion to make about distributive negotiators is that their tactics work, sometimes well and sometimes not so well. Since all participants in a negotiation are human and have their own feelings and comfort levels when confronted with such tactics, each person responds differently. So this type of negotiator is sometimes successful when confronting the meek and uninformed, but not as successful with others. The fact remains, though, that these want-to-win individuals use these tactics because they like them and, for the most part, they are successful with them. Despite the obvious disadvantages of dealing with a distributive negotiator, remember you have the choice not to play that game.

Respond to the Distributive Negotiator

The best way to respond to a distributive negotiator is to persistently continue to negotiate based upon the principles of win-win negotiating. Even in the face of attacks, positional bargaining, and other distributive techniques, you can still make progress by attempting to turn positional statements into expressions of interests and needs, which are the basis for win-win negotiating. When faced with unreasonable, illogical demands, do not fight or dis-

Stopping the Distributive Negotiator

When you treat people as though they are interested in problem solving, even though their actions clearly suggest otherwise, they may begin to negotiate constructively. Probe by questioning about their positions; in doing so, you can uncover a wealth of information about their interests. Let them think you are considering the unreasonable demand as a possible option as you question and try to understand their reasoning for proposing it. There is nothing wrong with ignoring and sidestepping callous or ridiculous remarks and then continuing with your negotiating strategy.

miss them as impossible but acknowledge the point and continue to use calm, rational persuasion and other win-win techniques. The reactions and other information you uncover through effective, nonthreatening questioning will help you explore ways to use the proposed alternatives as a starting point for more mutually acceptable alternatives. Ask the person for advice on anything related to the alternatives, such as what he or she thinks about certain solutions or how business has been done previously. Ask exploratory, open-ended questions, such as how this alternative would work, why not use another particular method, or why this has not worked in the past. Use this information to present improved alternatives. The person may criticize your alternatives. Do not take the attacks personally; instead, use them to continually improve upon the alternatives. Even when faced with the most determined and hard-bargaining negotiators, eventually you will progress toward an agreement.

If you find you are making absolutely no progress, resort to other methods. Although you can certainly attempt to negotiate distributively, avoid this because it is inefficient and does not produce optimal agreements. One good alternative is to expose the tactics by directly or indirectly letting the person know that you will not negotiate in this manner. Simply questioning the tactics may cause the person to cease. If he or she issues ultimatums, ignore them as if they did not occur. You may even patiently and selectively employ some of the person's tactics—not the mean-spirited ones, though—such as laughing at the person's comments, allowing several moments of silence, saying you do not have the authority to approve such requests, or taking your time in negotiating.

You can always deflect frequent attempts to confuse you by saying that these concerns the person is introducing are separate issues from what you were discussing. Once the person realizes you are wise to those tactics and are willing to call his or her bluff, he or she may start to negotiate more sensibly. If not, halt the negotiations, make an issue of the tactics, and firmly negotiate over what processes and procedures will be used during the negotiations. After you both have agreed on how best to conduct the negotiations, you then can return to substantive and problem-solving negotiating.

If the other party is unwilling to make any concessions or his or her hard-headedness is blocking all progress, you can try to break the impasse through one effective method: the use of objective standards and procedures that are fair, reasonable, readily obtained, and acceptable to all parties in the negotiation. This technique provides the parties with a shared goal—that of determining the standards or procedures—and lays the groundwork for increased trust, persuasion by facts, face-saving if necessary, and unselfish, long-lasting solutions.

Most people successfully use objective standards and procedures in many aspects of their daily lives. Tax assessors, for example, do not bargain with car owners individually over the tax they owe for a tag; they simply compute the tax based upon predetermined and preannounced factors such as the location of the vehicle, its age, and its model type. Some retail stores promise that if you can produce evidence that one of their items can be purchased elsewhere for less, then they will sell it to you for that price; otherwise, they will not negotiate the price with you.

You can use the same technique in your negotiations every day and arrive at mutually acceptable agreements. Here are some examples.

▶ Resolve disagreements over annual price increases by basing them on the government's inflation calculations.

▶ Create procedures to follow if one party later breaks an agreement by agreeing in advance on mediation by a neutral party.

▶ Set merit pay increases based on a standard of productivity measurement.

▶ Arrive at the cost of several items of used equipment by calculating purchase price minus depreciation.

Make sure you frame your offer around an objective standard with which you are willing to agree. Your task then is get the other party to also agree to it. Be open-minded yet firm in your conviction not to yield to threats, intimidation, or any other pressure that the distributive negotiator may try. You are offering a fair and objective way to help both of you reach a mutually satisfying agreement—which is a great alternative to endless arguing.

You can always deflect frequent attempts at confusing you by saying that concerns the person is introducing are separate issues from what you were discussing.

190

Create a Win-Win Solution

The conflict resolution process discussed throughout this chapter is the foundation for the win-win approach to negotiating. More than anything else, it is a mind-set in which both or all parties can achieve more of what they want if they establish an environment conducive to conflict resolution, if they focus on interests and not positions, and if they truly want a mutually satisfying agreement. Some final suggestions will help you reach your negotiating objective of a win-win solution.

Rely upon your interpersonal skills. Negotiating involves interpersonal skills that are identical to those that you use as a leader. Just because your subordinate, client, or supervisor is now in an opposing position does not mean that you should become uncivil, insensitive, or inconsiderate. Assertiveness, clarity, and resolve are the traits for you to show in a negotiation. If the other person perceives you as being timid, apologetic, or lost in thought, he or she may view you as weak and attempt to steal your power.

A negotiation is an excellent opportunity to show your self-confidence as a negotiator by treating the other party with respect, trust, and courtesy throughout the negotiation. One of your objectives is to get the other person to identify with you so that he or she will easily understand your negotiating arguments, empathize with your concerns, respect you as a person, and maintain a positive long-term relationship with you.

Keep your ego in check. Avoid pretending that you are more knowledgeable about the negotiation facts or anything else. When negotiating, do not assume that your version of facts is correct, but rather ask for the other party to concur when he or she believes the facts are true. Attempt to genuinely understand the other person on a personal level, but do not bother with obviously insincere or contrived conversations that will simply offend. Disregard anything you may have heard about negotiation tactics that emphasize rudeness, foul language, unreasonable demands, shouting, or

> *Rely upon your interpersonal skills and remember that a negotiation is an opportunity to treat the other person with respect, trust, and courtesy.*

Mutually Beneficial Solutions

Create solutions that will satisfy everyone's interests, not just yours. The solutions that you both generate, besides being innovative, numerous, and effective, must be mutually beneficial. Be open to any solutions that will satisfy the interests of both parties. Develop possible solutions before the negotiations begin by brainstorming with your team. As the negotiations progress and you learn more about the other party's interests, you will be able to generate more ideas.

threats, because these actions do not portray you as a leader; they damage your reputation and are ineffective as well.

You also can brainstorm with the other party, even though the thought of doing so may upset you. Remember that both of you are sitting down together to agree to solutions that will benefit you both. Since everyone has invested significant time in negotiating, there is a good chance the other party will be willing to generate new alternatives. Brainstorming can help you collaborate on solutions as long as you are careful not to reveal any of your confidential information. As discussed earlier in this book, do not evaluate the worthiness of the suggestions until after the brainstorming is finished; otherwise, you may eliminate some alternatives prematurely. The more solutions you develop, the more chance you will have of finding mutually acceptable solutions.

Of utmost interest to you is the other party's needs and interests; never lose track of these.

Look closely at the commonalties and differences you share. They could actually generate ideas for solutions. For example, if you and a subordinate share an interest in getting a project finished quickly, talk about it and attempt to develop mutually acceptable solutions that will accomplish just that. If you and a key supplier are in disagreement over price, talk about your shared interest in preserving your long-term relationship. You each might fervently differ over how you expect future events to unfold or how risky one course of action is; a discussion might create solutions.

The key is to structure a solution based upon these differences, in which a low-cost concession by you could be a highly advantageous solution for the other party and vice versa. If the disagreement is over price and future events, for instance, you could develop price schedules based upon different economic or political scenarios, thus minimizing the risk for both of you.

Stay alert and reassess your negotiating situation. As the negotiation continues, evaluate everything that occurs: the words that are spoken and not spoken, nonverbal communication, attitude, interests, and needs. You may not have much time to do an extensive evaluation, so be prepared to think clearly and rapidly.

Remind yourself during the negotiations that you have something that the other party does not have and wants; otherwise, he or she would not be sitting there negotiating with you. Of utmost interest, therefore, are the other party's needs and interests; never lose track of these. It is important to note the reasons why he or she needs an agreement with you. These are leverage points that indicate how badly the person wants an agreement, how much of a concession he or she may make, or how highly he or she values the items that are being negotiated. In particular, determine what alternatives you both have if you do not reach an agreement. You both will rely upon these alternatives as leverage in the negotiation. By using your leverage points to your advantage, you will better hold onto your convictions and retain the courage to negotiate with strength and confidence.

Remember that the negotiating picture is constantly changing because both sides are yielding points, making concessions, gaining concessions, and divulging new information. Every tactic you use is probably also being used by the other party. You must, therefore, constantly reassess your negotiating situation or you may become too overconfident.

Take your time and do not rush through the negotiations. A step-by-step, deliberate approach will allow both sides to follow the negotiations and achieve incremental successes. These constant successes, in turn, will give both of you the confidence that a final agreement can be reached through a win-win attitude. Once you determine that you have achieved a mutually satisfying agreement, conclude the negotiations and commit to honoring it.

Chapter 15

Coaching

Valerie, a departmental manager, is required to evaluate each of her team members once a year. She is looking for a less formal but more effective process that would let her guide her team throughout the year—not just at year-end. She is a good leader and has great skills. How can she incorporate coaching into her daily routine?

COACHING IS THE PROCESS OF GUIDING AND ENCOURAGING YOUR subordinates to achieve superior performance results. It is an active and participatory skill that allows you to become involved in the goals and work activities of others and to encourage them to succeed at what is best for them and the organization. In practical terms, coaching gives you a method to change behaviors so that subordinates or co-workers start or continue doing what they should do, cease doing what they should not do, and perform progressively better over time.

Coaching is normally associated with superior-subordinate relationships. In today's work environment, coaching techniques can be used with peers, co-workers, your manager, and others. This chapter will focus on the superior-subordinate aspects of coaching.

Coaching is not a skill that stands alone; it integrates all the leadership skills you have learned so far in this book. It is the pinnacle of the six relationship skills. Having just studied 11 leadership skills, you now can consolidate these skills into an inclusive process that you can use every day to inspire great performances from each of your subordinates.

You might wonder why you need a coaching process, particularly if coaching represents skills you have just studied and learned. There are two primary reasons.

First, your job is to lead. Of all your leadership skills, coaching comes closest to defining what leadership is all about: getting the rights things accomplished at the right time with the assistance of other people. Coaching provides a workable and easy-to-use process of immediate value that will enable you to use all your leadership skills to focus on getting the right results. Individual leadership skills by themselves will not ensure great leadership. It is the coordinated and correct application of all these skills that results in great leadership. Coaching, when you the leader do it consistently and enthusiastically, will result in immediate and tangible results for you, your subordinates, and your organization.

Second, your subordinates need someone to routinely encourage them to take advantage of opportunities to achieve the most they can, to set high yet realistic expectations, to steer them in the right directions and give them the power and authority to move forward, to listen to them and support them as they encounter difficulties and challenges along the way to achieving their goals, and to advise them based upon knowledge, skills, and experience. Leaders are in an excellent position to coach subordinates because leaders interact so closely with them and are ultimately responsible for their performance successes and failures. What better person is there to be the coach than the one who is most responsible?

> *Coaching is the process of guiding and encouraging your subordinates to achieve superior performance results.*

A Coach's Attitude

A coach is a leader. A coach's attitude is a leader's attitude; a coach's skills are a leader's skills. If you acquire the knowledge and practice the leadership skills throughout this book, you will lay the foundation to become a great coach and a great leader. The purpose of this section is to emphasize three key characteristics of a great coaching attitude.

A great coach commits to and gains commitment from subordinates. As a coach, you understand and accept the pivotal responsibility for preparing, teaching, and guiding subordinates to success through the coaching process.

A great coach commits to and gains commitment from subordinates, is willing to check progress, and feels comfortable communicating face to face.

You believe so strongly in the positive benefits of coaching that you are committed to investing whatever time and patience it takes to coach each subordinate personally. You expect the best from subordinates but are not upset, discouraged, or punishing when they try and fail. In return for these strong convictions, you gain the commitment of subordinates to cooperate with the coaching process, to take responsibility for their work, to increase skills and improve performance, and to focus on the best ways to achieve goals.

A great coach is willing to co-develop performance plans and check progress. The coaching process heavily relies upon your comparing a subordinate's performance with the job standards and goals. It is incumbent upon you as the coach to meticulously develop and monitor performance plans with each subordinate. These plans become the official yardstick against which you analyze performance problems, discuss concerns with the subordinate, suggest areas for improvement, and decide together with the subordinate on what positive actions to take.

A great coach feels comfortable communicating face to face. Since coaching is foremost a communications process, it is vital for you to understand and be comfortable with all aspects of face-to-face communication. You must be able to question, listen, and give performance feedback without creating resentment. For the coaching process to work best, you and the subordinate must be capable of communicating with each other easily, openly, and honestly.

The Coaching Process

The coaching process in this section is based on an important assumption: that you and your subordinate have previously developed and agreed upon job standards and goals. It is after this point in the performance management process that you use coaching to achieve these goals. Since coaching should become one of your most natural and frequently used leadership activities, it is helpful to use the mnemonic COACH for the process so you can easily remember each step.

The coaching process (COACH) can be separated into five steps.

Compare performance with standards and goals.

Offer feedback.

Ask for comments and analyze the performance.

Collaborate on a solution.

Honor your subordinate.

Compare Performance with Standards and Goals

Two reliable tests of whether your subordinate has a performance problem are to see if he or she is deviating from a standard of performance or not making progress toward his or her goals. If there is no problem in these areas, you still should use the coaching process to review the performance with the subordinate because people need to hear the positive as well as the negative. In addition, this will lead to opportunities for you to coach your subordinate to higher levels of performance by increasing his or her expertise and job knowledge. Coaching helps you prevent problems by identifying weak areas before they become problematic. If the subordinate is not on track to achieve standards or goals, for example, you can use the coaching process to discuss performance behavior, develop solutions, and agree on a corrective plan of action. Due to your time limitations and the importance of correctly coaching for improved performance, do not spend time on your subordinate's insignificant or irrelevant behavior issues; focus instead on critical performance-related issues.

> *Two reliable tests of whether your subordinate has a performance problem are to see if he or she is deviating from a standard of performance or not making progress toward his or her goals.*

Causes of Performance Problems

You learned in Chapter 5's problem-solving section that it is a straightforward process to observe and then recognize that a subordinate has a performance problem. What is less easy is determining the cause of the performance problem. At this stage of the coaching process, you can only speculate on possible causes. Despite your gut feelings or leadership wisdom, avoid concluding what the causes are until you investigate further; otherwise, you could make seriously erroneous assumptions. Your face-to-face coaching session with your subordinate is the time to delve into these potential causes.

After exploring possible causes, if you determine that the subordinate is not primarily the cause of the performance problem, seek to eliminate the more important cause of the problem and not take the coaching process any further. Why should you coach a subordinate on improving his or her behavior when the behavior is not the cause? For example, you may find out from another subordinate that none of the team members has been officially trained in the skill that is related to the performance problem. Your solution, therefore, is to schedule the training so that performance levels can improve. In another example, you might determine that organizational barriers, such as a shortage of resources, prevent the subordinate from accomplishing the tasks. Again, the leadership solution is to spend your time finding the necessary resources, not coaching the subordinate.

Offer Feedback

The next step is to immediately begin the face-to-face portion of the coaching process by offering feedback. Schedule some uninterrupted time alone to speak candidly with the individual about his or her performance. The best places are in your office, since you can block out potential interruptions such as the telephone or visitors, or at the employee's location, if it is completely private. To prevent misunderstandings, focus quickly on the problem and describe specifically what you think the problem is. Use good communication techniques to minimize apprehension and defensiveness and explain your observations specifically, such as "You missed your sales goal by $500," not "Your sales are off this month." If a subordinate is not following an office rule, for example, say, "The policy is for everyone to have four ten-minute breaks per day, and I noticed that you have been away from your desk for over 20 minutes each time." Support your comments with objective facts, such as reports, performance observations, and measurable job standards.

Ask for Comments and Analyze the Performance

The objectives of this step are for you and your subordinate to recognize and acknowledge that there is a problem with performance, to jointly identify the problem, and to determine its cause. The easiest way to see if your subordinate is aware of a performance problem is to ask about it. You could do this separately after you finish offering your feedback in step two or in conjunction with step two. For example, you could ask, "Did you know that you have been taking 20-minute breaks this week when the allotted time is ten minutes?" It may be that the person is aware of the behavior but assumes that the ten-minute rule is only a guideline.

When the subordinate acknowledges a performance behavior problem, determine why he or she is not performing to standard. As with any problem, there could be numerous causes, so avoid prejudging or losing your composure; focus on completely identifying the true cause or causes.

Effects of Subpar Performance

More often than not, if you just state that this behavior is undesirable and explain how it affects the team's operations, the person will correct it. Explain the consequences on others, such as when team members must cover the work or when delays keep meetings from starting on time. It is important to get your subordinate to verbally acknowledge a performance problem. This is a crucial part of the coaching process that must be done before you continue any further.

Question the person to find out whether he or she understands the details of what must be done and how it must be done. You will soon determine the cause of the behavior problem, such as a miscommunication of the scope of the task, a misunderstanding of what you needed, personal challenges that affect performance of the duties, or motivational issues.

Collaborate on a Solution

Your objective in this step is for both of you to find a solution that eliminates the unsatisfactory performance. This means linking the behavior that must be changed to specific actions that will result in your subordinate doing things correctly. As in all problem-solving sessions where you are open to various suggestions, jointly identify as many possible alternative actions as you can. Discuss each in detail and agree on the best course of action that will solve the performance problem by a specific date.

After the coaching session, both you and your subordinate should clearly know how you define satisfactory and unsatisfactory performance.

After the coaching session, both you and your subordinate should clearly know how you define satisfactory and unsatisfactory performance. Not only will this help you later as you monitor your subordinate's performance but it will also be one last reminder of what kind of behavior you expect. Make your final statement one that expresses your complete confidence in the person's ability to implement the solution.

Honor Your Subordinate

Throughout the coaching process, treat your subordinate with respect, show your desire to resolve the problem, and express much optimism about the future. By honoring the person as a human being and as a contributing team member, you will reinforce his or her efforts to succeed. Part of this honoring process is your continued commitment to guide the person toward achieving his or her goals.

Throughout the coaching process, treat your subordinate with respect, show your desire to resolve the problem, and express much optimism about the future.

Respect is an aspect of honor. The coaching process may initially intimidate your subordinates. Reassure them that coaching is a productive process that furthers the goals of both the individual and the organization. Assure them that coaching focuses on improving performance, not on demeaning people or changing their personalities.

Following up is also an aspect of honor. As you learned in Chapter 8, monitoring ensures that your leadership efforts are effective. This is particularly crucial in coaching, because if you do not check to see if your subordinate does as agreed, he or she may not perform acceptably over the long run. Within hours or days after the coaching session, let your subordinate

Progress Is Good

Even if the person is only making progress and has not yet passed the threshold to acceptable performance, encourage the behavior by acknowledging you are pleased with his or her progress. Occasionally examine whether the performance continues to be acceptable, because some people will revert to earlier behaviors if they are not periodically checked. Remember: we all learn from our mistakes, so there is no need to constantly remind a subordinate of his or her past mistakes. Honor subordinates for their commitment to improve their behavior.

know how you perceive his or her progress. If the behavior is acceptable, say so—he or she has earned positive recognition. As discussed in Chapter 12, the sooner you recognize positive behavior, the better are the chances at sustaining it, which is your objective.

During follow-up, if you discover your subordinate has not responded well to the coaching process, repeat the process and explore the reasons why the person has not changed as agreed. You are not again trying to solve the original problem; now you are trying to solve the new problem of the subordinate not taking action.

If subordinates do not comply with agreed-upon solutions in the first couple of sessions of coaching, they probably have ignored the consequences of their actions on team members or on themselves. It may take repeated coaching sessions for your subordinate to completely understand the effects of underperformance. You may need to eventually resort to punishment, such as docking pay, reprimanding, transferring, or replacing the person.

You have a responsibility as a leader to ensure that you do everything possible to improve a subordinate's unsatisfactory performance. This means that you do not give up when the first session of coaching does not result in perfect behavior. Each person will respond differently to coaching, but because coaching works, almost everyone will eventually respond favorably to your coaching efforts.

Honor your subordinates by consistently coaching all of them. Coaching is not something to start doing and soon forget—it is too important and effective as a leadership skill. Your leadership obligation to your subordinates demands that you offer the best leadership you can, honestly, courageously, and consistently.

The Results of Coaching

Coaching is at the heart of leadership, because when two people can come together to discuss performance behavior and develop positive solutions, they can improve their organization. All your subordinates routinely need your involved attention, whether the job they are doing is mediocre, average, or outstanding.

Although the discussion in this chapter has focused primarily on coaching a subordinate who is performing poorly, it is important that you coach all employees at all levels of performance. A subordinate who performs adequately can be coached to perform outstandingly; a superb performer can be coached to perform better in some areas or to assume responsibilities in new and challenging areas. Few things motivate people more than praise from their leader when they deserve it. As a leader, you can always show your subordinates how they can help themselves and their organization do better.

Part Four

Strategic Skills
(Upper-Level Leadership Skills)

Chapter 16

Vision

Rob is a departmental manager who wants to better align his team with the organization's new vision, which was announced recently. He never has had to develop a vision, though he believes he is quite a visionary person. What can he do to create a realistic vision?

VISION IS THE ABILITY TO PERCEIVE THE MANY POSSIBILITIES THAT are open to you and your organization and to create an ideal picture of where you and your organization will be at a future point. Vision is much more than setting a goal, writing a statement of purpose, or planning for the long term. Vision is setting a clear, focused, desirable direction that will take your organization to some specific destination.

This direction is the culmination of your efforts at observing, analyzing, and consulting with others. It entails a clear understanding of your current situation and where your organization is headed, a continual assessment of the possibilities that could move you forward in the same or a different direction, and the courage to act upon the best of these possibilities to produce change.

The exciting direction that you envision places an emphasis on what can go right, not on what may go wrong. As a visionary leader, you often think about the future and attempt to influence in advance your organization's place in it, not simply to react as the future unfolds. The vision you create is bold, energizing, and exactly where everyone wants to be one day; therefore, your followers will do their best to help get there.

As a leader, you need vision because it is imperative for your organization to frequently reassess the present and the future, particularly since change is constant. You must periodically adjust the direction in which you are leading your team and others. Be open-minded, curious, committed to the organization, and capable of articulating the vision to people whose support you need. You can be a visionary leader at any organizational level—not just at the top. Your vision does not have to be original or brilliant; however, it must be a well-developed, sound, and realistic conception that rallies and focuses members of the organization toward specific objectives each day.

As a visionary leader, you often think about the future and attempt to influence in advance your organization's place in it, not simply to react as the future unfolds.

The Visioning Process

You can become highly skilled at the visioning process by developing some simple habits and by practicing proven techniques, many of which have been discussed in this book. Following this five-step process will help you create and achieve the right vision for your organization.

- ▶ Acquire a visionary attitude.
- ▶ Understand your organization.
- ▶ Develop your vision.
- ▶ Communicate your vision and obtain commitments.
- ▶ Support your vision.

Acquire a Visionary Attitude

To acquire a visionary attitude, you must begin to think like a visionary and then practice that attitude as often as possible. Here are some examples of visionary thinking.

Visionary leaders think about the possibilities in almost everything they do. They know the power of an idea and how the right ideas can lead to enormous success for them and their organization. Even though they focus on the future, they are not unhappy with the daily responsibilities of implementing ideas or fulfilling other, more routine functions; however, they believe in giving their team the autonomy to assume more and more of the important daily responsibilities. This frees their time for imagining and shaping the direction of their organization.

Visionary leaders know that the future is not preordained but is influenced daily by people like themselves. Since they believe in the power of innovation, they regularly improve their creative thinking skills and encourage others to unleash their creativity. They realize the right vision will develop more quickly if they are completely involved with the ideas, concerns, and needs of everyone with whom they operate—subordinates, customers, peers, and competitors. They openly encourage team members to come forward with their ideas, thus inspiring their confidence. They constantly inform everyone as to where they and the organization are going.

Understand Your Organization

You must thoroughly understand the nature and challenges of your organization at your own level and at other levels. This understanding includes a knowledge of culture, values, financial condition, competitive situation, customers, and strategy.

Questions to Ask

As a visionary leader, develop a habit of routinely questioning all significant departmental and organizational areas by considering general questions, the answers to which will lead you to profound conclusions.

Examples of inward-oriented questions might include:

- What does our organization do best?
- What systems, strengths, and factors cause us to perform so well in these areas?
- Which business units or departments are doing well? Which are not? Why?
- What are our organizational values and how can we sustain them over the next decade?
- What would be an ideal type of organization?
- If I had the power to influence the future, what would it look like and what type of organization would we become?

More outward-oriented questions, which are also important in understanding your organization and its environment, include:

- What is our competition doing in response to market changes?
- How is our industry changing?
- What markets should we be in?
- What are our customers telling us about their needs?

You must thoroughly understand the nature and challenges of your organization at your own level and at other levels.

These are just some of the questions that you can develop and pose to yourself and your team. The questions will give everyone the opportunity to think creatively and freely; questioning also will stimulate hopes and aspirations that will start you on the path toward shaping a vision. You cannot determine the answers overnight because the answers have to be experienced and developed over time. But once you are in touch with the right answers, you will reap much benefit from them.

Take the time to routinely and thoroughly examine everything that affects your organization because it is these discoveries that will lead you to visionary conclusions. If you neglect to do so, you will make erroneous assumptions about the status of your organization, which will cause you to miss opportunities or take a wrong path. Armed with this knowledge and a complete understanding of your personal values, you can proactively think about the best ways to help your organization and to lead your team to do the same. If you know where your organization is going, you will more easily spot opportunities each day. Only by truly understanding your organization will you create a vision that is aligned with your organization's core values, culture, and potential.

Develop Your Vision

With a deep understanding of your organization and your personal commitment to maintaining a visionary's attitude, begin the process of developing your vision for the organization. Imagine the ideal futuristic state for your organization, including what it will look like, what environment you will operate within, and how you can take advantage of the opportunities.

Imagine the ideal futuristic state for your organization, including what it will look like, what environment you will operate within, and how you can take advantage of the opportunities.

Develop a specific, clear, and simple-to-understand vision for your areas of responsibility. The vision should evolve from what you believe is possible, right, and needed for your organization; what will support your organization's strategic direction; and what will inspire your team members to succeed despite the inevitable obstacles that they will encounter.

As is always true when solving problems, managing projects, or making decisions, you will greatly benefit from consulting with members of your organization as you develop your vision and its details. Few leaders have the responsibility or capability of designing a vision alone. You will not achieve your vision alone, without the committed efforts of your team. If they are to achieve it, your people must believe in the vision. If they are to believe in it, they must participate in its development. Assistance from others also will reveal any erroneous assumptions you may have and will help you develop the specific details of the vision. For the vision to be realized, your subordinates must voluntarily assume responsibility to own it and to achieve it—you cannot force this to happen.

Part of your visioning skill is the ability to elicit from others their visions for the organization. If you desire a high level of team involvement in the process, you could even formally ask the members to jointly develop and approve the vision. This will give them all the opportunity to incorporate their personal visions and dreams for the organization, describe the work environment necessary to achieve the vision, and increase their long-term commitment to it. They will realize that they have control over their own future and that the vision can help them meet their own needs. After your team members develop a common vision and realize how they can reach it through cooperation and collaboration, they will become a stronger, more unified group.

Vision statements are a means of communicating your vision. They are useful if you truly intend to do what is necessary to realize your vision; otherwise, they are useless and could cause more harm than good if people perceive them as another "catchy gimmick of the month." Vision statements can be of any length, ranging from one paragraph to several pages, and can address solely the overall vision or explain in detail the areas that relate to it. Statements that are precise and succinct, however, are usually best.

Vision Statements

Here are examples of simple but powerful vision statements for two organizations.

- ▶ We resolve to be the service leader in the computer industry and always do what is right for our customers, employees, and shareholders.
- ▶ Our organization will pursue excellence and will be recognized as the best chain of grocery stores in North America.

Since vision involves a future reality, not all details can be set forth. With a clear statement of the direction that you want to set for the organization, however, you and your subordinates later can concern yourselves with the details and inevitable uncertainties involved in pursuing the vision.

Communicate Your Vision and Obtain Commitments

If your team members are to achieve your vision, they must clearly understand it, believe it is an important and worthwhile cause, see exactly how it will benefit them and the organization, and fully commit to achieving it. As you might expect, aligning your team in such a manner is more complex than simply telling them about the vision or writing them a memo.

If your team members are to achieve your vision, they must clearly understand it and fully commit to achieving it.

You have to treat vision in a special way, out of the routine, because vision causes more fundamental change to your organization and its employees than do routine events. If you communicate your vision properly, people must line up to support it and to achieve it. That is why it is almost always better to involve your team early in developing the vision. When you and others understand the vision in its entirety, you will minimize any uncertainty and resistance.

As your subordinates come to believe that they have the responsibility and authority to step outside of traditional boundaries to move the organization toward its vision, then they will continually take those actions and risks that you need to achieve your vision. Explicitly ask for and obtain commitment from all your subordinates to work toward achieving the vision. Determine which other members within the organization are crucial to realization of the vision, including other staff members and your supervisor. Since these people are integral to creating and sustaining the alliances you need, they also must commit to your vision.

Support Your Vision

After you properly communicate your vision, your actions now become the proof that you are intent upon following it through. Your subordinates will watch you closely for evidence that you are personally committed to the vision and will not suddenly change your views or back away from it. They want you to set the example by leading them through the unknown and by showing them that you are willing to share the hazards and the rewards of charting these new paths. If they know that you are courageously in front of them, they will loyally and enthusiastically support you.

You will need to continually repeat your vision in casual conversations, meetings, speeches, and most organizational communication. Whenever you interview new team members, remember to speak about your vision and the opportunities that lie ahead. Because your actions will prove to your team that you are intent on achieving your vision, remember to view everything you do as being either supportive of or detrimental to achieving that goal. In particular, watch closely your comments, reactions to everyday occurrences, and your attitude.

Update Your Vision

The visioning process is an evolutionary one that never ends because of the constant change that you face; therefore, do not hesitate to review and adapt your vision. Look for opportunities to broaden its scope throughout your organization so the vision becomes not just a concept but an achievable, credible, and accepted reality that permeates all your operations and all facets in the daily lives of your team members.

If your organization is to survive and thrive, you and other leaders must be catalysts to initiate vision, seek input from others, and align your teams behind it. You then can move on to develop an innovative framework or strategy—the means for implementing that vision.

Chapter 17

Strategy

Samantha's department has just developed some exciting goals for the upcoming year. Though she has been on the team only three years, she has seen that her department never seems to arrive at great ways to achieve its vision. Usually people just each figure out their parts of the plan and do it. The department usually does not reach the lofty goals it sets. What can she do to inspire others and herself to become more strategic and develop plans that work?

STRATEGY IS BOTH A SKILL AND A DEFINITIVE HIGH-LEVEL PLAN THAT results from extensive, integrated, and long-term thinking and decision making; it is the way by which you achieve the vision of your organization. By establishing a vision, you are thinking strategically. To lead your organization strategically, you must take this thinking process further and apply it to all aspects of your organization. When using your strategy skills, you are considering the broad issues and factors that affect your organization's future in all areas, including long-term competition and growth, marketing, manufacturing, finance, operations, customer service, and responsibilities to your employees and shareholders.

Planning and Strategy

Planning is a necessary and important part of any leader's daily responsibilities, whether done informally throughout the day or formally with a staff or other assistance. It permeates all your leadership skills because it is an essential activity that provides the structure needed to accomplish daily organizational activities. Planning, however, is usually associated primarily with the managerial aspects of a leader's responsibilities because its objective is to keep the organization functioning well without major disruptions or problems. If an organization is to achieve what it sets out to do, it must plan.

Leaders agree with this philosophy but also approach planning from a different angle, believing that it is strategies, not plans, that provide the framework and guidance that make organizations successful. While recognizing that most activities require planning, leaders do not rely on planning at the expense of developing strategies. Leaders realize that in a fast-paced and constantly changing world, plans are not the definitive answer to the challenges of an organization because plans are time-consuming to prepare, quickly become obsolete, and cannot possibly prevent all challenges or problems. Leaders invest an appropriate—not excessive—amount of time in planning, yet they also take calculated risks that could result in achievement of the vision. They keep an anticipatory eye on the changing big picture and respond to events as they unfold.

In other words, leaders at all levels develop a series of nimble strategies—not detailed and rigid long-term plans—that allow them to achieve their vision. Planning will naturally follow the development of strategies, but the best plans will be short to medium term, well guided by clear and focused strategies, developed with the assistance of knowledgeable co-workers, and inherently adaptable to changing conditions.

While recognizing that most activities require planning, leaders do not rely on planning at the expense of developing strategies.

The Strategy Process

When selecting ways to create and implement strategies, you have many methods from which to choose. Several excellent commercial books and programs exist that can guide you through the strategy formulation process for either specific functional or broad organizational areas. If your budget can handle it, it is useful to employ strategy consultants to help guide you and other top leaders to the right decisions for your organization. Besides outside sources, your organization may have its own systems or departments

Strategic Thinking

Regardless of what strategic systems you may have available, the best initial approach is to concentrate thoroughly on strategic thinking before you begin strategic planning and implementation. Thinking strategically involves seeing the connections in apparently unrelated happenings and understanding how myriad trends and occurrences interrelate to affect your organization. You should think strategically every day and encourage leaders and co-workers throughout your organization to do the same.

that use some of the proven techniques of strategic planning or strategic management. Even with all these resources available to you, there is no consensus as to which techniques or planning systems are best. You decide what is best based upon what works well for your particular department or organization. As you get more experience in this area or if you later use strategy experts, you will become increasingly effective as a strategist.

As you learn and use the strategy process that follows, strategic thinking will be the underlying skill that you develop.

▶ Know your environment and its relationship to your vision.

▶ Involve co-workers and others in strategy building.

▶ Develop and implement strategies.

▶ Align your day-to-day mission with your vision and strategy.

Know Your Environment and Its Relationship to Your Vision

In the visioning process, understanding your organization was a key step to recognizing its potential. Now that you have pinpointed some exciting possibilities for your organization, you must understand as much as you can about those internal and external factors that will either help you achieve your vision or get in your way.

Knowing your environment involves understanding four key areas: assumptions, resources, market, and external conditions.

You have a duty to recognize and promote your organization's strengths and other advantages because these assets will increase opportunities for developing and implementing winning strategies. Likewise, it is essential to anticipate and react to factors that could threaten your organization and prevent it from achieving its vision. Knowing your environment involves understanding four key areas: assumptions, resources, market, and external conditions.

Identifying assumptions that you and others make about your organization will help you corroborate facts and avoid wasting time and effort. Few things are more discouraging to people than to discover, after investing large amounts of time, that their ideas and recommendations are useless because they were founded on unrealistic or false assumptions. Imagine the wrong directions strategy development could take if people were not aware that the organization was eliminating a major product line, planning to reorganize sales districts, or about to become a public corporation. This is why it is always wise to discuss assumptions before developing strategy.

Assess the resources that you have available currently or could acquire for use to achieve your vision during the strategic timeframe. Compare these with the resources that you require to achieve your vision. In addition to examining typical resources, such as equipment, employees, and skill capabilities, look at others, such as the time you need for major projects and the quality of your relationships with suppliers and customers.

Staying in touch with your market will help you identify threats to your organization and opportunities to pursue. A thorough understanding of your market means knowing:

▶ Your customers, such as what they think about your organization, who they are by category, and what services and products they want now and in the future

▶ Your competitors, including what they offer or do not offer in the market, their competitive strategies, how might they react to your competitive actions, and their strengths and weaknesses compared with your organization

▶ Your competitive position within the market, such as how your organization presents or differentiates itself, what value it offers, and what features distinguish you from the competition

Anything external to your organization has the potential to affect it positively or negatively Avoid tunnel vision by staying aware of political, economic, sociological, cultural, technological, and industrial events and trends. This up-to-date knowledge will permit you to evaluate the impact of an external issue upon your organization and then allow you to develop the right responses.

Involve Co-Workers and Others in Strategy Building

As was true in developing your vision, it is wise to involve your co-workers and others in developing the strategy to achieve that vision. Your strategy will be more viable and innovative if you use a variety of available expertise and if you truly listen to what everyone tells you. There was a time when organizational strategy building was often controlled and developed centrally; in many instances, that's still the case. But if you develop strategy only at the highest levels of your organization or if you fail to adequately consult with those people who have the knowledge and experience to help, you will probably end up with an inadequate or failed strategy. That assuredly will later jeopardize your organization's survival. Avoid this mistake by involving various people in formulating strategy, such as customers, resource providers, outside experts, and people from multiple organizational levels.

Develop and Implement Strategies

A strategy addresses the issues of breadth, depth, objectives, and implementation.

To achieve your vision, you must translate it into specific strategies. These consist of understandable, achievable objectives and plans that are long, medium, and short range. The strategies will apply to multiple organizational levels and functional areas, each with its own details of implementation, and will be developed with the assistance of members of your organization. A strategy addresses the issues of breadth, depth, objectives, and implementation.

"Breadth" refers to the organization's top-level intentions across a wide operational range that will enable it to succeed in a variety of areas or businesses. These broad aims usually are referred to as a *corporate or organizational strategy*. It seeks to address which specific products and services will be offered, where the organization will function or compete, what the growth plans are, and what resources will be allocated to subordinate organizations.

The typical organization does not rely upon one overall corporate strategy to achieve its vision; it implements several strategies in depth so that multiple objectives can be met. These strategies belong to specific organizational levels, business units, or autonomous units. The strategies at major business levels are usually referred to as *business strategies*. Strategies at this level are in alignment with the organizational or corporate strategies, but they also address more specific actions that the major business unit must take to achieve its mission. As is similar with the operations of a team and its members, it is the collective efforts of many business strategies that help the organization succeed at its strategy. If you and other top leaders effectively integrate the diverse business units within the organization and take advantage of complementary resources and synergistic capabilities, your organization will function much more effectively at each level.

Functional strategies support specific business strategies through such functional areas as human resources, marketing, finance, research, production, or operations. Each of these functional strategies has its own set of tac-

Consistent Strategies All Around

One of your major strategy challenges as a leader is to ensure that all your organizational strategies are consistent with each other in breadth and in depth. It is not enough to develop a hierarchy of strategies; they must all support the overall corporate strategy. No matter what level of organization you lead, you must be unrelenting in keeping your organization on track. When you notice inconsistent strategies, bad judgment, or a need to revise a previously approved strategy, speak up.

tics, or implementation plans and procedures, that detail the daily work that must be done to promote the functional strategy.

You can develop winning business and functional strategies by using your experience, research, and consultation with experts. Since every organization faces unique competitive challenges, explore wisely all available resources so that you and your organization can examine a range of alternatives before making final strategic decisions. Fortunately, there are numerous resources (including books, software, and strategy consultants) to help you think through this process and guide you to the best decision.

For example, if part of the overall organizational strategy is to increase revenues ten percent a year, then the business and functional strategies should support and reinforce this growth objective, not contradict it. In this example, individual business strategies should focus on competitive markets that can produce sales growth or they could focus on regular introduction of new products and services. In turn, the functional strategy of marketing would similarly reinforce these strategies, the sales strategy should encourage and reward high performance, the advertising and promotion strategy should bolster high-potential markets, and the quality and customer service strategies should focus on product excellence and customer loyalty and retention.

As with any leadership undertaking, you must clearly establish prioritized objectives that will unequivocally show what you and your team members must accomplish to achieve the vision. This is particularly important at the strategic level, because if the objectives are missing or unclear, all related activities downstream will be similarly flawed. Your organizational objectives address the many areas of strategic concern to your organization: profitability, growth, competitive performance, innovation, quality, concern for customers, employees, shareholders, or society. Regardless of the objectives that you choose, each should have specific targets that can be periodically evaluated by measures of performance, such as return on

One of your major strategy challenges as a leader is to ensure that all your organizational strategies are consistent with each other in breadth and in depth.

Strategy Implementation

It would be naive to think that implementation of a strategy can be effectively summed up in a few paragraphs. The process leading up to strategy formulation involves meticulous thinking, planning, rethinking, and decision making. This also is true as you implement the strategy, because internal and external organizational changes occur, causing you to periodically adjust your plans. All this happens in an environment of economic ups and downs, global uncertainty, competitive pressures, and change. Fortunately, your leadership efforts at a strategic level succeed with the same skills that you use daily at team levels. The main differences with strategic issues tend to be their broadened scope, lengthier time frames, increased complexity, and higher levels of uncertainty. You are still dealing, however, with human beings who want to be led properly, who must be given the support they need to achieve your vision, and who want to make meaningful contributions.

The keys to implementing your well-developed strategy are based on the main points you have learned throughout this book.

investment, sales increase, market share, cost savings, product defect rate, or customer satisfaction.

Develop enough objectives within realistic time frames for each of your strategic intentions. Start with your long-term organizational objectives of two to ten years; then develop them into medium-range objectives of one to two years and short-term objectives of one month to one year. Each operating unit within a business division, major group, product line, functional department, or international operation will in turn develop its own long-, medium-, and short-term objectives that are compatible and consistent with the higher levels of the organization.

The keys to implementing your well-developed strategy are based on the main points you have learned throughout this book.

- ▶ Develop viable but flexible plans using the assistance and wisdom of your team members.
- ▶ Communicate your strategy to your team members, gain their commitment to the strategy, and give them the responsibility and authority to achieve it.
- ▶ Provide your teams and organizational units the resources they need to achieve strategic objectives.
- ▶ Ensure that organizational processes, policies, and reward systems encourage everyone to assume the long-term focus necessary to implement strategies successfully.

218

▶ Monitor both your organizational environment and the market; then reassess and adjust elements of your strategy as needed.

Continual monitoring is particularly crucial to strategy implementation, because your swift reaction to the short-term and incremental changes will help you successfully adjust your strategy. During the implementation phase, many things can cause your strategy to falter or deviate from your initial expectations. These could be changes in assumptions, lack of progress in the tactical plans, an increase in barriers, a change in environmental factors, or a need for organizational redesign. If you assess organizational performance, environmental conditions, or progress on strategy implementation only twice a year, for example, you may not be able to react quickly enough to adjust a failing strategy, react to impending problems, or make any needed tactical changes.

Align Your Day-to-Day Mission with Your Vision and Strategy

A mission statement expresses why your organization exists by specifying the organization's purpose, what it does best, and what it does daily to serve its customers, employees, and shareholders. Unlike the future orientation of the vision statement described in Chapter 16, a mission statement is a detailed guide of one paragraph to several pages that focuses on the present. You develop it after realistically examining the strengths and competencies of your organization and deciding what you have to do each day to continue to survive, progress, and exceed performance objectives.

Your organizational mission probably has had months or years to be tested and refined to a logical, accurate reflection of what your organization chooses to do and what it does best. Your mission statement may even seem to be working well. Having just recently identified the right vision for your organization, however, you should now review your mission statement to ensure that it is in alignment with your vision.

It is your responsibility to align the daily focus of your team members with your vision.

Although your mission statement is oriented toward daily challenges, it is a pivotal link to your efforts at implementing your strategy and achieving your vision. It is not sufficient for you to loudly and periodically proclaim what your organization intends to accomplish; you must wisely ensure that everyone is marching in the same direction every day. It is your responsibility, therefore, to align the daily focus of your team members with your vision.

This is where the detailed and unambiguous guidance of a mission statement is particularly helpful. Because most of your team members naturally tend to concentrate on the daily aspects of their jobs, it will not be difficult for you to instill a focus on the mission. Current daily operations are quite important to you, so your mission statement must accurately reflect the detailed level of excellence that you expect from your teams and your organization as a whole. Not only will an emphasis on the mission help everyone accomplish the right things every day, but the resulting incremental successes from committed workers will collectively lead to the long-term achievement of your vision.

Winning Strategies

Your purpose for developing strategy skills is ultimately to produce or improve winning strategies for your organization. As a leader, you implicitly recognize your full accountability to the core constituencies of employees, shareholders, and customers. This is why you take seriously your responsibility to know what is happening strategically with your organization. If you and your fellow leaders are not involved in strategy development, the organization will not thrive in the long run. It is up to you as a leader, therefore, to develop and practice your strategy skills so that you can have a positive and long-lasting impact upon your organization.

Chapter 18

Change

Frank's company is restructuring and this massive effort requires the coordination of all business units. He and his team, who are led by a new manager, are a small part of the company, but they will need to make major changes in the way they do their day-to-day work. What advice can you give Frank as he helps in this restructuring project? What challenges and opportunities lie ahead for him and his organization?

REMEMBER THE DEFINITION OF A LEADER AS ONE WHO USES ALL OF his or her skills to get the right things accomplished at the right time with the assistance of other people. This implies that leaders guide others from where they are to where the leaders want them to be. This process of leadership, therefore, is fundamentally one of change. Your objectives for change are to perceive the need to leave the status quo, to recognize the opportunities involved with change, and to muster the confidence to calmly lead your subordinates and others along the uncharted path of change. You achieve these objectives by integrating your leadership skills with the specific change skills discussed in this chapter, which are to prepare for, initiate, and implement change.

Prepare for Change

Leaders guide others from where they are to where the leaders want them to be; this process of leadership is one of change.

If you know that something is certain to change at a future point, doesn't it make sense to proactively use your time now to prepare your subordinates and your organization for the change? The change process involves all of the skills you have learned in this book. In addition, you should grasp the following four key steps involved in preparing for change.

- ▶ Understand the different perspectives of change.
- ▶ Maintain a positive attitude toward change.
- ▶ Promote continuous learning.
- ▶ Be aware of your environment.

Understand the Different Perspectives of Change

Change can be seen from the differing perspectives of the environment, the organization, its members, and its leaders.

Change can be seen from the differing perspectives of the environment, the organization, its members, and its leaders.

Anything in the environment external to the organization can be a catalyst for change, so prepare to anticipate and respond to these known and unknown events. Notable examples of external changes include changing customer needs, technological innovation, domestic and global competition, market maturation, and regulatory requirements. Many of these external changes are out of your control and may challenge your organization's very survival; however, you and your organization can handle most of them well through thoughtful anticipation and the right responses, such as being willing to improve your performance and increase innovation.

Organizational change is a pervasive and long-term process that results in significant widespread changes in the behaviors of its members and the organization as a whole. Examples of these changes include environmental changes, strategy implementation, and the integration of technology. Ideally, any needed changes should support attainment of the organizational vision within the context and constraints of the environment. It is usually a challenge to change ingrained attitudes, beliefs, and culture within an organization, but you can most assuredly change them over time.

As for the members of an organization, it is natural for most people to prefer little or no change because change typically upsets order and stability, threatens self-interests, increases stress, and involves risk. Whenever personal or organizational change occurs—whether through a reorganization, a bold new strategy, a change in leaders, a revised benefits policy, or a

> ## The Uncertainty of Change
>
> Frequently, it is not the final changes that scare people but rather the confusion and upsetting consequences that the changes produce along the way. Since each stage of the response pattern cycle is important but varies in significance for each person, you must encourage the free flow of information related to the changes, promote specific change assistance programs, and allocate sufficient resources. For example, to help ease and hasten the release of the old ways, your subordinates might appreciate unstructured informational meetings, question-and-answer sessions with experts, access to counselors, or specific customs such as kickoff or farewell ceremonies. To help your subordinates cope with the uncertainty throughout the change cycle, intensify your leadership presence by being unambiguous, reassuring, and positive about what they must do to implement the changes.

tragedy—people tend to respond in a certain way. This response to change follows a four-part pattern:

- ▶ It begins with fear and denial.
- ▶ It continues with feelings of loss and grief about the old ways.
- ▶ It improves with acceptance of the change and release of the old ways.
- ▶ It ends with implementation of the change.

By recognizing that this change process is perfectly normal and healthy, people should strive to limit, but not eliminate, the time they spend in the first two stages and focus on the last two stages. By using the leadership skills that you have developed and by creating the organizational structures and systems to support change, you can lead your subordinates and others deliberately through this process. They are depending on you for decisive leadership to reduce the personal and organizational upheaval that is expected.

Leaders are aware of the reactions that change causes in others, but, as you would expect, effective leaders choose not to let change provoke a similar response in themselves. See change as an opportunity to help everyone achieve greater success in new, exciting ways. Since change is a fundamental part of your leadership responsibilities, whether you are envisioning and initiating the changes, implementing the changes, or reacting to unexpected changes, make sure that the change process works well.

Maintain a Positive Attitude Toward Change

You learned in Chapter 3 how important the right attitude is for a leader. Since change is such frightening for many people, it is essential for you to maintain

Change Is Good

Change is often feared because of the effect it has on some people—the naturally upsetting and stressful feelings of uncertainty, failure, loss of control, or conflict. The healthy attitude to have about change is that it is good because, if it is properly handled, it helps promote personal and professional growth, new opportunities, and increased fun and satisfaction on the road to achieving your organization's vision.

Change is inevitable and, like the challenges you face in your personal and professional lives, change will occur whether you want it to or not.

a great attitude and then promote this positive attitude with your subordinates so that they can better understand change and see it as an opportunity.

Change is inevitable. Like the challenges you face in your personal and professional lives, change will occur whether you want it to or not. Although you may have felt more comfortable and safe when changes were infrequent or more manageable, you cannot live and work by yesterday's reality. It is more realistic and less stressful to adapt to today's realities. Even though change requires that you lose something, such as the old way of doing things or a feeling of security, it replaces what it takes with new ways of doing things or a different type of security. Instead of blaming someone or something for causing a change or instead of completely ignoring or avoiding the changes, accept your professional responsibility to embrace change and respond to it by maintaining an optimistic, solution-oriented attitude and behavior.

Change is conquerable. Despite the inevitability of change and the destabilization that it brings, you can control how you react to it and thus, in essence, control the change. The right reactions are curiosity, enthusiasm, flexibility, confidence, and a willingness to take action and possibly make mistakes. Such responses allow you to overcome the challenges of change and use them to your advantage. Wrong reactions—such as ambivalence, skepticism, negativism, second-guessing, blaming, retreating, risk aversion, and a desire to maintain the status quo—almost always guarantee failure.

Part of the solution is keeping a positive attitude, believing there is no change that you or your team cannot overcome. This is the belief component of the solution. The other part is seeing the superb results that change brings, which is the proof component of the solution. As a leader, it is essential for you to keep the belief and proof levels high among your team members.

Continuous learning—itself an exercise in change—will help your subordinates better anticipate and react to changes.

Promote Continuous Learning

Continuous learning—itself an exercise in change—will help your subordinates better anticipate and react to changes. As discussed in Chapter 9, if your subordinates constantly seek new and better ways to carry out their responsibilities, they will continually expose themselves to new ideas and methods. This intellectual stimulation will lay the foundation for them to acquire the skills and knowledge to successfully anticipate changes, recommend solutions, and implement changes. Everyone must realize that he or she alone is responsible for preparing for the certainty of change. You as the leader, on the other hand, have an ongoing responsibility to identify and support any special training needs that develop as conditions change.

Be Aware of Your Environment

You have learned throughout this book the importance of knowing your internal and external organizational environments. If you commit to regularly updating this knowledge and applying what you learn, you will anticipate changes better. You also will lessen your own and others' anxiety about the future by constantly gathering more information about trends and upcoming changes. For example, if you regularly quiz your customers or study their purchasing habits, you will know their preferences, opinions, complaints, and suggestions. You then will have more time to respond correctly as their needs change. Likewise, if your organization relies heavily upon catalog orders, you should notice and react when you hear that postal rates will increase next year or that your competition's sales over the internet are increasing dramatically.

This principle of knowing what is going on around you applies to everything in your internal and external environments—customers, members of your organization, the competition, technology, the economy, and politics. You are not expected to be clairvoyant, but it is helpful to have dependable sources of information, such as technology experts, trusted and frank advisors, and news publications on business, industry, and the world in general. There is no point, however, in being a newshound who collects information indiscriminately. The key is to stay alert and in touch with those areas that influence your organization and to use relevant information to help make better and timelier leadership decisions.

Initiate and Implement Change

When a leader believes that change is needed for any reason, it is usually better to initiate the change if possible, instead of waiting for someone else to discover the need and start the process. Because leaders accept the inevitabil-

When a leader believes that change is needed for any reason, it is usually better to initiate the change if possible, instead of waiting for someone else to discover the need and start the process.

ity of change, they do not delay in initiating needed changes or wait until the last moment to react to impending changes. They confidently take action to incorporate the changes and benefit their constituencies of subordinates, shareholders, customers, and others. They also create opportunities for change when no one else can or will.

Change is not something you can separate from your other responsibilities; it is a pervasive aspect of everything you do. It may be so pervasive you overlook the fact that you have some power over the process of change. Approach change proactively by following these four guidelines.

- ▶ Realize that many roads lead to your destination.
- ▶ Eliminate barriers to change.
- ▶ Monitor your change efforts.
- ▶ Preempt change with innovation.

Realize That Many Roads Lead to Your Destination

Since you have already developed your vision, strategy, and implementation plans, your responsibility now is to move forward. If you keep a steady focus on your vision, you will realize that there are many ways to achieve it, some that you anticipated and some that you did not. Be adaptable to adjustments in your implementation plans based upon changing environmental conditions, unexpected resource surpluses or constraints, and new developments that you had not anticipated. As with your other duties, know exactly what changes you want to make and how you will measure your success in making them, while leaving open for modification the various paths along the way.

Long before any changes begin, seek the input of your team and others so that you can develop consensus on the need for change, demonstrate the rewards of change, collaborate on the best overall change decisions, and obtain the commitments to support and not resist the changes. One of the common reasons that change implementation fails is from a lack of a commitment for change throughout the organization. Everyone—subordinates, top leaders, and staff—must unequivocally accept and support the changes. While not everyone will completely agree on the details or be equally enthusiastic, it is imperative that you and your team collectively support the change efforts.

Eliminate Barriers to Change

Expect to encounter resistance and obstacles to change because it is natural for this to occur. But as a leader, you must persistently work to remove any barriers that will prevent you and your organization from handling change and achieving your vision. Anything can be a potential barrier, such as a subordinate's attitude, a top leader's lack of commitment, political infighting, resource constraints, or economic conditions. Continually reevaluate conditions so that you are always alert to any potential barriers.

To turn a change barrier into a change booster, use your array of leadership skills to do the following:

▶ Communicate the consequences of failing to change.

▶ Overcome people's doubts.

▶ Gather input from all those affected.

▶ Gain everyone's commitment to support the changes.

▶ Form energized, winning teams of change stakeholders.

▶ Hold people accountable for their change responsibilities and results.

▶ Solve unexpected problems and conflicts quickly.

▶ Collaborate to create win-win solutions.

Communicate the need for change throughout your organization by clearly explaining why change is necessary and achievable and by expressing your confidence that everyone is capable enough to tackle the upcoming changes. You will rarely be able to convince everyone all the time about your change ideas, so avoid setting yourself up for disappointment. A more realistic objective would be to ensure that, by using all your leadership skills, your team and others will understand three things: where they are now, why change is needed, and how change will occur. It might take several attempts for everyone to understand these three things, but persistence will pay off.

During periods of change, particularly those intense changes with a high degree of long-term uncertainty, such as a reorganization, it is helpful to keep your subordinates focused and busy working on those things that you are certain of, including their short-term objectives, excellence in performing their day-to-day duties, and priority customer service.

Monitor Your Change Efforts

Monitoring is particularly crucial during the change process, primarily because of the many forces that will challenge, resist, or disrupt your efforts, despite the change momentum that you create. Additionally, as your organization undergoes change, there is still the need to effectively maintain day-to-day functions, which adds to the complexity of change implementation.

You must persistently work to remove any barriers that will prevent you and your organization from handling change and achieving your vision.

Monitoring is particularly crucial during the change process, primarily because of the many forces that will challenge, resist, or disrupt your efforts.

However, the long-term implications of not monitoring your change efforts are enormous for you and your organization. If, for example, your team members perceive that you or other top leaders are more interested in starting new programs than in the necessary follow-through that monitoring requires, they will be less willing to commit their efforts. They will lose confidence in your ability to lead them and will be tempted to ignore your future change ideas.

While monitoring your changes, remember to do these four things:

- ▶ Give your subordinates the authority to implement changes.
- ▶ Continually inform subordinates on the progress of changes.
- ▶ Listen to their needs and concerns.
- ▶ Reward them as they support the change efforts and achieve milestones.

Preempt Change with Innovation

You can use innovation to get the jump on change. An organization-wide focus on innovation means that there is widespread acceptance of creating and applying new ideas that relate to your vision and strategy. Your organization must constantly update itself by searching for new ways of operating, such as with new products and services, customer service improvements, and new technologies. The competitive importance of change requires your organization to be as proactive and anticipatory as possible in developing the right responses to upcoming or possible changes or else other organizations will jump in ahead of you to do the job. Innovation is not a simple and

Stay Involved

You must stay attuned to everything that is happening in your organization so that you can make adjustments quickly when needed. There is no magic formula to help you monitor change in your organization. However, it may help you to review the discussion of monitoring in Chapter 8, with an eye toward how it can help lead you through change. The key is to stay closely involved with what is happening with your subordinates by communicating well, demonstrating your concern for their welfare and goal achievement, and committing to do whatever is necessary to make the change successfully. If you do these things while continuing to practice great leadership skills, you will attune yourself to how well the changes are progressing and will react quickly with any adjustments as needed.

> ## Change Efforts Can Succeed
>
> Although people feel most comfortable when changes are slight or infrequent, no one can live and work by yesterday's reality. For an organization's top leaders to design and implement change successfully, they must, with the assistance of other members of the organization, identify the right changes to make, communicate these changes credibly throughout the organization, provide resources to support the changes, and allow enough time and flexibility for the changes to take place. With the widespread commitment of people throughout the organization, change efforts will succeed. Change, therefore, does not substantially alter the way a leader leads; change only reinforces that leaders must always use their skills to lead well every day.

quickly implemented event, but it is a deliberate, well-conceptualized strategy that lays the foundation for changes to occur naturally.

As a leader in your organization, you are responsible for creating and fostering a climate of innovation. Innovation results not only in organizational success but also in benefits to your team members that allow them to think creatively, make meaningful contributions, and feel fulfilled at the end of the day. As you enthusiastically lead your team through the challenges of change by using your leadership skills to model innovative thinking, you will increasingly become a great resource for your organization.

As a leader in your organization, you are responsible for creating and fostering a climate of innovation.

The End Result

By applying the knowledge you gain from this book, you will without doubt become a better leader. As a result, your team members will have greater trust and respect for you and your ability to successfully lead them through any unknown or changing situation. This, in turn, leads to exactly what you seek every day from your team: a strong commitment to you, your organization's vision, and all aspects of their jobs.

With this high level of commitment comes a responsibility for you to regularly deliver proof of your leadership promises. As you do, you will find yourself consistently, fairly, and caringly practicing great leadership skills, showing an unrelenting desire to achieve your vision, and demonstrating commitment to the welfare of all those who work with you. As a final benefit, you will see your own abilities develop while you tremendously improve the lives of those around you.

Index